The Port Authority of New York & New Jersey

POLICE
COMMAND
COLLEGE

John Jay College of Criminal Justice

THE POLICE MYSTIQUE

An Insider's Look at
Cops, Crime, and the
Criminal Justice System

THE POLICE MYSTIQUE

An Insider's Look at
Cops, Crime, and the
Criminal Justice System

Chief Anthony V. Bouza (Ret.)

PLENUM PRESS • NEW YORK AND LONDON

Library of Congress Cataloging-in-Publication Data

Bouza, Anthony V.
   The police mystique : an insider's look at cops, crime, and the
criminal justice system / Anthony V. Bouza.
      p.   cm.
   Includes bibliographical references.
   ISBN 0-306-43464-4
   1. Police--United States.   I. Title.
HV8138.B595   1990
363.2'0973--dc20   89-29450
                                                              CIP

© 1990 Anthony V. Bouza
Plenum Press is a Division of
Plenum Publishing Corporation
233 Spring Street, New York, N.Y. 10013

Printed in the United States of America

For
Mari and Louise

Foreword

Tony Bouza is as well known to the senior police establishment as any cop in America—which is not to say that his peers regard him with universal affection. One reason for this is that he is of independent and ranging mind, far from content with conventional practice and procedures—and worse, he says so in public and says why. And he compounds this sin by his willingness to subject his ideas to the test of critical research, and to take the results seriously and to act on them.

That is not to imply that Chief Bouza is universally rejected by the police establishment. Over the past ten or fifteen years there has gradually been emerging, in administrative positions in the city police forces of this country, a group of younger though experienced police leaders, impatient with traditional ways, willing to take seriously the important roles that police should play in social welfare, and willing to resist vigorously the long tradition of improper political meddling in their work. To them, Bouza is somewhat of a hero.

In this professional autobiography, Bouza captures the challenge and essence of policing in a vigorous and moving style. If the work of the police interests you, this is an essential book. You will not agree with its every proposition—if you did it would hardly have been worth writing—but you will both enjoy the book and be forced into further serious reflection. It is an engaging blend of an anecdotal autobiography of thirty-six years of energetic life in the police, at every level, and a spirited analysis of a series of major crime and police problems.

It is that rare book about the police: not a research monograph; not the usual sensational exaggeration of the dramas and dangers of police work; but rather a probing and sprightly account of police work and the joys and pains of police leadership.

Chief Bouza also moves out of the common mold of police chiefs in that he is vehemently and openly concerned with the miseries imposed on our citizens in the many destroyed inner-city areas—a man who recognizes that our increasingly locked-in underclass is a serious threat to social stability, who is passionately moved both by concern for those we thus maltreat and by their pervasive and maleficent influence on our lives. Consider his near-concluding sentence: "Oh for a muse of fire that would touch the public conscience . . . and awaken the nation to the danger of neglecting the fateful problems of its cities." Tony Bouza is not that muse, but the muse had better read this book.

I am tempted to relate story after story from this book: of Bouza's arresting the flag-burner and then appearing himself on television to defend the Supreme Court's 5-to-4 decision acquitting the flag-burner; of his creative experiments in relation to the policeman's duty at the scene of spousal violence, when the injured spouse does not wish to have the matter prosecuted; and many more. Instead, read the book; you will then know more about police work than all but a few.

NORVAL MORRIS
Professor of Law and Criminology
University of Chicago
Chicago, Illinois

Preface

I was born in Spain and came to America, at nine, as part of the great immigrant wave from Europe. The experience shaped my view of a country great enough to embrace the "tempest tossed" and "wretched refuse" of distant shores and raise them to prosperity and power.

I grew up in the New York City Police Department, entering it at twenty-four, on January 1, 1953, and leaving it, reluctantly, twenty-four years later, as commander of all the Bronx forces.

The intervening years were spent learning, serving, and climbing. I was lucky enough to hold almost every imaginable police job and rank, including investigations, patrol, planning, communications, intelligence, internal affairs, and everything in between. I held nine different ranks and had fourteen totally different jobs in the NYPD alone.

This lucky apprenticeship was followed by three years as deputy chief of the NYC Transit Police, who cover the subway system. I was responsible for the daily operations of the department, which I found to have a totally different culture from that of the NYPD.

Next came a nine-year stint as chief of police in Minneapolis, which gave me the chance to "run my own shop," in the parlance of the profession. I left that post when I became convinced that the agency needed fresh blood and new ideas at the top.

Those thirty-six years in policing gave me a love for the profession that has never dimmed. Just as a whaling ship proved to be Herman Melville's Harvard or Yale, the police world was mine.

As I plied its waters, though, I was struck by the reticence of my colleagues to inform the public of the horrors that were becoming a part of their daily fare and that, I felt, would never be solved until the people awakened to the dangers and acted. I broke ranks with my associates' love of silence and decided to report what I was sure we all knew to be true—that the larger society had better understand what is afoot and move speedily to shore up its inner defenses, if the nation is to survive. It was this simple if presumptuous notion that compelled me to write this book.

As I struggled with the complex issues I was immensely aided by the good counsel and unfailing support of my wife, Erica. Three selfless souls—Louise Wolfgram, Constance Caplan, and Larry Sherman—gave unstintingly of their wisdom, encouragement, and expertise. My editor, Linda Regan, acting like the sort of tough teacher we all remember, would never allow me to do anything but my best and forced me to work to the top of my ability. It will be only too obvious that the flaws are entirely my responsibility.

ANTHONY V. BOUZA

Minneapolis, Minnesota

Contents

CHAPTER 1

The Police World

Cops work in a world shrouded with mystery and power, which attracts the attention of civilians in every quarter. The public's insatiable demand for movies and television programs dealing with cops attests to the subject's allure. The chill in the heart that accompanies the sight and sound of a police cruiser pulling you over is a reminder of the sense of awe cops inspire. Yet, with all the scrutiny and disclosure of police in the incalculable number of programs depicting them, it is more than fair to say that the actual world of cops continues to elude Hollywood.

The dramatizations select highlights, true and accurate, but rare cases that, rather than typifying police work, actually distort it. Exceptions and rarities cannot lead to understanding the field of action under study. Movie and television depictions might be likened to orange juice, with the screen versions representing the concentrated form in the can. The water of boredom, routine service, and insider ritual must be added to make up the real drink. The public's fascination, however, is incessant, visceral and real, and it would surely remain so even were the full truth known. Any institution that wields as much power as the police department does is bound to be the object of interest and scrutiny. Police officers often describe their work as long stretches of tedium, punctuated by moments of sheer terror. It isn't the stretches that draw the devoted attentions of film and television producers.

The real mission of the police, as defined in their charters, is to preserve the peace; protect life and property; detect and arrest offenders; prevent crime; and most important, to accomplish the task that gives the profession its name: enforce the law.

Laws

Ours is a statutory society. If an act is not explicitly forbidden, it is not a crime. The result has been an enormous volume of laws and ordinances, covering every conceivable arena of human action. Cops are the officials ultimately responsible for enforcing the countless rules governing behavior. Given the sheer number of rules, not only have they the power to pick and choose which laws to apply but they can even prod and maneuver a target into an inadvertent breach of conduct. Experienced cops usually develop a broad, general awareness of the laws, confident that they'll find something they can, like a Procrustean bed, apply to the circumstances. A favorite ploy is to provoke an angry citizen into sufficiently loud outbursts to justify an arrest for disorderly conduct. The challenge is to push the target over an imaginary line that instinct will tell him or her constitutes a breach of something. The ability to maneuver the unwary into a trap is well known to cops but rarely realized by outsiders.

Cops

It is said that the cop on the street exercises more power over our daily lives than the President of the United States. The President can press the button and create universal incineration, but this is a final and awful holocaust, not a daily intervention. Cops tells us when to stop and when to go. They can question us or appear to ignore us. They can forbid or permit. They can snoop or overlook. Their options and scope are wider than is realized, yet, somehow, the citizen can sense the impending danger of a cop's arrival.

People instinctively recognize the power of the police in every encounter. This power has its expression in the visible gun; in the public image conveyed in countless dramatizations; in the hesitancy at approaching them; or in the tremor induced when they single any of us out. The caricature is of an impenetrable facade, made concrete by reflecting mirror glasses, behind which lurks a powerful, willful operative.

Cops have scores of encounters daily. Out of necessity, they tend to stereotype. They know much more about criminal law than most lawyers and readily develop a mastery of the handier sections. In the more subtle areas of law, they have a sound general feeling for the limits and know how to obtain the necessary help, whether from the desk officer at the station or the city's attorney later. It is important that the average person realize this, in order to avoid being stereotyped negatively. Failing the "attitude test" and being labeled "an asshole" (someone who fails to treat the cop with the proper measure of respect, or who is truculent or defiant or challenging) usually leads to problems. Cops don't take real or imagined assaults on their authority lightly. Their work is peculiar in that the greatest power and autonomy exist at the lowest rank level.

Cops also know that, as preservers of the peace and protectors of life and property, they are called on to make countless decisions and judgments daily. The system, in order to accommodate the need for action, is notably understanding of the errors that are bound to occur. Thus cops develop the sense that they can exercise power without too great a risk of being called too strictly into account for its use. Observers have commented that there is more law at the end of a cop's nightstick than in any court of law or legal tome.

Agency Policies

The most responsible police departments function on the premise that legitimate actions will be supported; that good-faith mistakes will be countenanced or supported, to the degree possible; and that bad faith actions, or wrongdoing, will be punished. This philosophy, guiding the best and most progressive police departments, affords the cop on the street additional latitude. Thus cops have not only literally thousands of laws at their disposal but the additional comfort of being able to rely on the substantial tolerance of a system that wants action and knows that it must be willing to tolerate errors in order to get it. We've all heard the arguments about how this or that reform, usually in the form of a U.S. Supreme Court decision channeling or restricting police powers, will "handcuff the police."

The debate over the uses and abuses of police power, within the ranks, has been sublimated into a discussion on police discretion—the preferred term. The police, in common with the rest of society, prefer to have their harsher truths concealed behind euphemisms. Awful-sounding bureaucratese, so prevalent in the television interviews of cops, may well have developed as a veil to mask secrets or to soften painful truths. Thus people don't die, they are "DOAs" or "stiffs." Others aren't shot, they're "blown away." Criminals aren't arrested, they're "collared," and they're not criminals at all, but "perpetrators" or "perps," who have to be "apprehended," after a suitable "pursuit." Even money gets sanitized into being "a fin" ($5), "a sawbuck" ($10), or "a yard" ($100). A corrupt act is "a score," as if one had performed an athletic feat. The realities find concealment behind the jargon.

The subject of police power, and its direction and control, is one that occupies center stage in any internal discussion relating to managing a police agency. In the final analysis, the effectiveness of a police department is determined by how responsibly the street cop's actions are directed and shaped. It is not too much to say that the average cop can expect support and understanding for even tragic blunders, even within the most reform-minded agencies. Cops are invariably, and probably mostly correctly, granted the benefit of the doubt by their superiors and by the system in which they function.

Although there is a movement afoot to enshrine good-faith mistakes into law, affording cops additional protections, the initiative does not get a lot of support from cops' unions or their allies. They don't feel the need to fight for protections they already possess.

Police Power and the Underclass

Police power assumes its most formidable aspect when cops deal with the underclass. This is the group they've been pressured, implicitly, to control. This message gets transmitted in code, as in "What are you doing about the vagrants, drunks, and bums harassing honest citizens downtown?" When cops deal with the poor (blacks, Hispanics, the homeless, and the street people), the rubber of power meets the road of abuse.

Society's problems center in the cities and their ghettos, where the underclass—the poor, ill-housed, malnourished, undereducated, unemployed, and spaced-out on drugs and alcohol—resides.

The ghetto is the volatile center of every chief's concern over long, hot summers. It is there that the excluded, disaffected, and angry reside, while getting daily messages about the lives they might be leading, from their omnipresent TV sets. It is there that a latent force lies, seemingly ready to be galvanized into furious action by a cop's mistake.

Street crime is the province of the poor, as both perpetrators and victims. The public, frightened by the specter of violence on its streets and television screens, pressures cops to erase it. The exasperation of the cops filters through, in the form of brutality, when they encounter addicts and obstreperous drunks, sociopaths, beggars, and other street types. This is the population the street cop most comes in contact with. The detectives and investigators get to handle the heavier cases and the weightier criminals. The obduracy of these criminals similarly tempts the detectives and investigators to third-degree methods or other shortcuts. Ironically, because criminals have a lot to do with cops, they've hardened and come to realize the value of not cooperating in the effort to jail them. To a surprising degree, investigators rely on the help and cooperation of suspects, but this help becomes harder to obtain as the criminal's experience with cops deepens. In the main, it's the "gloms" (inexperienced or first-time suspects) who confess.

The white middle class—the overclass—rarely encounters the reality of police brutality, except for such events as the campus or peace protests of the 1970s or the civil rights actions of the 1960s. When it does confront police power—at a traffic light, for example—it vociferously makes its outrage known, not only at the scene (in such original attacks as "Why aren't you out capturing muggers and rapists, instead of harassing honest citizens?") but in follow-up calls and letters to police superiors, who will know how to make these cops squirm. Cops have learned to be wary of such problems.

Directing Police Power

Cops deal with people who are in trouble or disarray and are most comfortable in that role. They are invited not to festivals or happy events, but to brawls. They observe the human animal's dark underside. Cops get called to control nasty instincts and to curb wicked appetites. They are summoned when things get out of hand. They fly from problem to problem, chasing the calls a crackling radio spews out. In order to deal with hurt children, blood, human misery, and anguish, they unconsciously grow calluses over their emotions. They become profoundly skeptical. Their temptation to cow those whose behavior they're trying to control into compliance often proves irresistible. Many of their coping strategies are hard for outsiders to understand. Civilians don't, and perhaps can't, understand cops. This is one of the most painful lessons learned by the entering recruit.

Society grants the police a monopoly on the use of violence. Only they may bludgeon, subdue, Mace, or even kill legally. This exclusive right adds enormously to their powers to search, seize, detain, question, arrest, or investigate people they deem suspicious. The borders of action are laced with stretchable legal concepts like *reasonable suspicion, probable cause, questionable circumstances,* and *articulable grounds.* It doesn't take the skills of a sophist to construct a justification for aggressive actions within those parameters.

The study of the use of police power is usually described as an analysis of the need to limit or redirect the exercise of police discretion. The phrase conceals a very bitter struggle for control, between the chief and his or her need to direct the enterprise, the cop-on-the-street's determination to maximize his or her field of action, and the civilian's concern over abuses.

There is a push—pull nature to it all that outsiders rarely get a peek at. There is a struggle between the supervisor's need to control and direct a cop's actions on the street and that rugged individualist's stubborn fight to retain autonomy. One of the comic opera aspects of this invisible battle is the administration's imposition of endless restrictive regulations (of the well-known Mickey Mouse variety) that have nothing to do with performance (like the length of mustaches and the color and state of the uniform) but that lend a semblance of sovereignty over the process.

Another one of the hidden truths about policing is that, although the brass can decide the general thrust and direction, the slug in the trenches retains the power to work her or his will in countless ways. The result is that guidelines become rough limits, within which a great deal of independent action can be exercised.

The fight for control over the street cop's actions takes place within the impenetrable world occupied by both supervisors and patrol officers. However, the battle does not distract them from the need to sustain the separateness of their corps from tinkerers and prying eyes.

Insularity

The mystery begins with the fabled insularity of the police. It is not an accident that cops speak of the "outside world" and of "civilians" with a barely concealed scorn for the uninitiated. The fact that they think of their precincts as embattled fortresses in alien lands reflects, at once, their problems with the minorities they've been sent to police and their resentment toward an overclass that has issued the *sub rosa* marching orders.

Cops understand the straightforward charter responsibilities, which, although tough to discharge, are nevertheless unequivocal and direct. The problem arises from the hypocrisy they see in a society that insists that they control "them." *Them* refers to blacks, ghetto residents, the homeless, the poor, and all others who evoke a sense of fear or unease. These orders are implicit and indirect. The laws enabling control aren't there. The facilities to which "they" might be taken don't exist. The "offenses" of the group aren't crimes, but they do offend the overclass.

How did this separateness develop? Why are the police insulated from the surrounding world? How could an agency devoted to the public's protection and service be as profoundly alienated from the people as the police are? How is it possible that an organization that inspires as much fascination and scrutiny as the police can remain a mystery to a society that constantly examines this organization's daily workings?

The Cop's Assignments

The police are the ultimate repositories of society's guilty secrets. They are there to keep order. This means making unpleasantness invisible. The underclass must be kept in its place or the chief will lose his or her job. Cops are the cleaners of society's charnel houses, and the employers don't want reports on the muck and mire dredged up in the daily rounds, unless it happens to be some juicy tidbit about the flaws and errors of the great or near great. It is the cops who are called when famous people expire in their mistresses' arms.

The message cops receive is to keep the peace, maintain control, protect, and serve. Highly visible breaches, in the form of crimes, violence, or disorder, usually result in swift retribution against a police commander asked to put a stop to them. The frantic searches, by high-ranking officials, for scapegoats, following some public disorder or series of crimes (like the Tompkins Square fracas in New York City, in 1988, and the continuing civic battles there), easily conjure up a vision of the public pressures working on these executives. It is very hard for average citizens to imagine the heat they can generate when banding together. Elected officials know that citizens' calls, letters, and nudgings at meetings quickly harden into negative feelings and reprisals in the voting booth. The people's power, normally hard to define and difficult to see, can be a fearful thing once unleashed, particularly when aimed at the police department. It is the immediate problem that the public insist be attacked, and they are usually in no mood to hear theories about how the culture of poverty produced the particular tragedy.

A society, for example, that permits scores of millions to be undereducated and unemployed will not be patient with those who call upon it to attack these ills with more equitable distributions of wealth, social programs, and other "liberal" schemes. A society that works manifest injustices on its black citizens doesn't want to be told that crime and violence are the products of such neglect. The overclass prefers to see the problems attacked through the highly visible "law-and-order" methods that promise easy solutions. They display no eagerness to hear sociological recitations. The focus is on effects, performance, and results, not on causes.

Expectations versus Reality

Lay observers believe that all of the players in the criminal justice system are strictly bound to observe laws, regulations, orders, and procedures and that the actions of all are confined by these strictures. This is not the actual case.

Discretion, the power or right to decide how to act according to one's own judgment, pervades the system. The players function as if the very laws were mere guidelines—movable foul poles, with the playing field allowing a lot of room for maneuvers. We've seen that the cop on the beat can manipulate a situation to ensure the desired outcome, without too much regard for the objective circumstances. The cop's supervisors, prosecutors, judges, defense counsel, probation officers, and others all possess considerable discretion, albeit in varying degrees.

It wouldn't be altogether absurd to believe that the disorderly conduct statutes were placed on the books more to arm cops with weapons against those they've defined as "assholes" than to accommodate citizens' yearning for tranquility. Defining behavior that disturbs the public's peace leaves a great deal to the imagination of the beholder. It would, for example, be perfectly legal to go up to a cop and, in low conversational tones, inform him or her that police officers are pigs, but it is not a course of action any prudent person would recommend. Does anyone believe that such an encounter, though legal, would end inconsequentially?

A citizen sees a cop and a guy tumbling on the ground. She hasn't seen what led up to the struggle and doesn't know if the civilian is armed, or wanted, or even whether he began the assault. The cop knows he can't afford to lose. It's not allowed. The scene is ambiguous. The observer may be watching a perfectly legitimate use of force. She takes great risks in making even civil inquiry into what the cop is doing. "Interference with the actions of a police officer" is the sort of charge frequently invoked in such situations. Cops do not tend to see such inquiries as being either neutral or innocent. If the incident turns out to be police brutality, the observer would still be far better off offering her testimony to the officer's superiors, rather than intervening at the scene.

The cop's supervisors also possess enormous latitude. They have a cornucopia of laws to choose from and finite time and human resources to deploy. So, while they piously eschew any hint that their mandate is other than full enforcement of all the laws ("We're just here to enforce the law" is one of the cleverer inventions of the police), the reality is that, by emphasizing some and ignoring others, they pick and choose which statutes to pursue. The person arrested is much more likely to have been nabbed because of policy decisions made at headquarters—in terms of which activities to emphasize and which criminals to go after—than because of the objective reality of her or his actions.

It has been said that a prosecutor could indict a ham sandwich. An indictment is a formal accusation of a crime, voted on by a majority of the twenty-three citizens who constitute the usual grand jury. It must be followed by a trial of the issues. The district attorney picks the cases to be presented to the inexperienced citizens listening to the evidence. District attorneys aren't eager to try shaky indictments. It isn't healthy for their batting average of convictions.

A prosecutor's *raison d'être* is to convict people of crimes. He or she is normally elected to office, and the campaign invariably centers on conviction rates, plea-bargaining arrangements, and other inducements to demagoguery. The easy way out is not to try potentially losable cases, even where the interests of justice cry out for running the risk.

The practical result of the latitude to prosecute or not that the DA possesses is that it allows the criminals to avoid the cost and inconvenience of a trial altogether. I can recall gathering the folders on five routine murders, where suspects were known and where sufficient evidence existed to indict, but perhaps not convict, and taking them to the prosecutor to demand action. His reaction was not adamant refusal, but gentle, and unyielding, evasion. He called for the gathering of additional witnesses, securing more evidence and allowing for the passage of time, as if it were working inexorably in our favor. The sum total of his message was that he was not going to present the cases to a grand jury, and there was no practical rejoinder available to me. The supposed killers were never even subjected to the trouble of having to make a single appearance in court. The victims—seemingly unimportant, hapless souls, usually from the same underclass as their slayers—continue to lie unavenged. The criminal justice system's practitioners can and do bury their mistakes, if they are unimportant enough to escape the interest of a powerful champion, such as the press.

Criminal investigations and prosecutions have a high perishability factor. Intensive effort, in the initial stages, frequently pays off, but the process is also heading for time zones in which witnesses die or fade away, memories erode, interest cools, consciences harden, and energies flag. There is no penalty for not bringing a case to trial, unless it is one surrounded by blaring headlines.

There is, however, a penalty for having a low batting average. Prosecutors, with the power of the state's resources behind them, have a tremendous advantage over the defense (witness the conviction rates of the accused, not to be confused with incarceration statistics), but that is not to say that "exhaust-the-prosecution" strategies, appeals, adjournments, motions, reviews, and other delays do not take their toll. The system, withal, is pathetically vulnerable to tactics that have nothing to do with the search for truth and justice.

There is tremendous dissonance between the public's expectations and perceptions of the criminal justice process and the realities that have been fashioned by its practitioners. Many of the stratagems evolved from operational necessity; some grew from the protection of turf, especially in circmcumstances involving fierce battles for scarce resources; and some were fashioned to accommodate the ease, comfort, and convenience of insiders.

And this is why we have plea bargaining; why police chiefs holler, louder and clearer than the rest, for "more cops"; and why it is easier to slough off the hard cases and simply not push as hard as one should.

Laws, in such circumstances, become almost suggestions. Orders and regulations are used to move the enterprise, generally, in the desired direction, without becoming straitjackets. The process is much more plastic and malleable than it appears. Every act of every government official is a political act (which is not to confuse the issue with partisan politics, where one person or party is favored over another). Simply stated, government officials are required to act, and these actions constitute the government's reason for being. Politics is the act of governing. In the fishbowl of public life, acts are weighed against consequences. It is always easier to see the immediate consequences, and harder to discern the eventual outcome. Most government officials, living in the here and now, rarely concern themselves with the ultimate, and deeper, consequences of their actions. This may be the classical bureaucratic blunder that undoes the sharpest and slickest, in the long run.

In public life generally, and in the criminal justice area specifically, the short-term answers prove very appealing, and executives frequently resort to palliatives to cool a hot situation. The pressures to do something, anything, quick and dirty, can be considerable. The problem arises in the waste and inefficiency introduced, which are sure to surface later. The solution that may seem unpopular in the short run, but that is believed in and based on sensible planning and thought, holds out the best hope for maintaining the long-term health of the agency.

Quick fixes rarely work. We will see many examples of how popular acts may work against the people's interests and how temptingly simple answers lead to disasters. Politicians, faced with problems, often find quick fixes irresistible. Quick fixes free them to get to the next problem but ignore the fact that another problem has been created, which will emerge later.

All of this, and what follows, is intended to clarify the questions surrounding the power and mystery of the police and how to improve a recalcitrant police system.

The temptation to believe that the police are guided by objectively weighed factors, such as the existence of the elements of a crime or evidence pointing to the accused, or that the law or the system will force the police department, inevitably, to pursue a certain course, will founder on the shoals of observable experience. The reality is that these factors do come into play, of course, but so do others that relate, much more intimately, to the personal exercise of power, cloaked in official authority. The reality of the contemporary police world is hideously complex, yet it is essential that it be understood if the thin blue line of society's first defense is to be employed for the benefit and protection of the people.

The pages following deal with the forces working within and outside modern police agencies. My aim is to promote a deeper understanding of the issues dominating police discussions. The reader will be provided with an inside look into the workings of police agencies, as well as with an explanation of how they came to be that way, and how some useful changes might be brought about to improve their effectiveness within society. Ultimately, I hope the reader will have a greater appreciation of what the real life of a cop is like and a keener grasp of what we might call the police mystique. The world of the police is shrouded in auras of mystery and mystical power. It is my objective to part this shroud and let the citizen examine exactly what it conceals.

Some wag once said that being a cop is like having a ringside seat to the greatest show on earth. The purpose of this book is to afford just such an inside view of the fascinating world of the American cop.

Readers should erase all that they think they know about the police as we try, over the succeeding pages, to reveal some of the truths, rituals, and secrets of the world of cops.

CHAPTER 2

The Police Agency

American policing is *sui generis*. Inspired, almost immediately, by the creation of the Metropolitan Police of London, in 1829 America followed England's lead by developing a local, atomized municipal police force. The rest of the world, however, went national.

Modern police emerged from the much-admired British military model, which reached its zenith of popularity following the crushing of Napoleon's ambitions at Waterloo. It is remarkable how, over a century and a half after their formal creation, police departments continue to be plagued by organizational problems that have their roots in the first days of their existence. The issues of the fragmentation of America's police and the wisdom of following a perhaps irrelevant military model continue to be hotly debated.

Foreign observers, accustomed to having their police receive their marching orders from the nation's capital, usually from the minister of interior, are shocked by the incredible fragmentation of America's police and Washington's being extraneous to the process. That our Founding Fathers were so suspicious of the encroachments of centralized power that they created a system that made city police inevitable is the hardest, and usually the first, lesson visitors from abroad must learn.

The aping, by the police, of the military's rank structure and organizational model has struck many observers as no longer relevant to the modern urban challenges facing America's cops. Although seen as an army of occupation in the ghetto, cops, functioning individually and without much direct supervision, are anything but small cogs in large organizational wheels. Each cop is the wheel.

Policing grew out of the perennial necessity to control the fractious human beast. No understanding of the functionings of the police is possible without an overview of the charter assigned to the agency; and of how it then organized itself to accomplish the mission and the uses to which the police might be put.

Police departments exist for a purpose. Their goals are described in the charter language that normally attends their creation. The mission of police departments can be summed up with the motto, "To protect and to serve."

Although the police possess great latitude, and although the law is frequently treated as if it were a guideline, rather than a stricture, the fact of the law's primacy cannot be forgotten. The police must obey the law as they enforce it or risk descending to the level of those they arrest. Although the police may pick and choose which laws to emphasize and which to ignore, they recognize the importance of avoiding outright breaches of the laws themselves. The law is the only sensible guide in a democracy, where, when it is functioning properly, questions of conscience, ethics, and morality become secondary precisely because they are embedded in the laws being enforced. Police agencies in which members work their will can become rogue departments that are laws unto themselves.

An organization may lose track of its initial goals as it takes on a "corporate" personality. Organizations frequently lose their way as they travel in time, coping with daily crises. These coping techniques may lead them astray. The hopes, fears, and ambitions of those guiding the enterprise may also compromise basic organizational objectives. Members of organizations characteristically think not only of the goals of the agency but of their own comfort and convenience, which tend to accrue, deflecting energies and resources from the areas that ought to be of prime concern. We will see how the struggle between public service and the convenience of public servants can get in the way of effective operations.

Moreover, in police agencies in particular, members may fail to give needed services or may make such inappropriate use of the operations as to deflect the department from its principal responsibilities.

Although the charter language of a police department is broad and general, it is important that the department's actions be matched against its ultimate purpose to ensure consonance. Organizations must not be allowed to stray. The charter provides the general direction, but the way may be lost among the tangle of specific individual actions on the street.

Basically, America's police are involved in three principal tasks: (1)

fighting street crime; (2) providing emergency service for injuries, accidents, illnesses, and other noncriminal events; and (3) maintaining traffic safety. These are the explicit tasks—straightforward and understood. The control of the underclass is an implied, unstated assignment that creates dissonances between the open messages about mission and the muted concerns about controlling the unsightly or unpopular.

National Police

We do not have a national police. Most of the laws enforced on America's streets were framed in state capitols. State prisons have about twelve times the number of prisoners housed in federal prisons. Policing, in America, is a local function. Our Constitution mostly reserves the police power for each of the states, which confers it on its creatures, the cities. Each city has its own police agency.

One of the outcomes has been an army of over fourteen thousand chiefs as members of the International Association of Chiefs of Police (IACP). Another has been a bewildering array of police departments—most of them the ten- or twenty-cop variety—across the land. This system makes for what our shapers treasured most: a government able to do only minimal harm.

These members of the IACP, eager to have some barometer with which to measure the incidence of crime, asked the FBI to undertake the task of gathering statistics on crime. As of 1930, the chiefs offered to submit annual totals of crimes for their jurisdictions, comprising what came to be called the "Part I Crimes of the Uniformed Crime Reports." These have changed little over the intervening years and include murder, rape, assault, robbery, burglary, theft, auto theft, and arson. Together, they are referred to as *street crime*. Drugs are, of course, an important additional factor that did not constitute a problem in 1930.

Urban cops battle street crime, rush to answer calls for rescue, and issue citations. The importance of their duties lies mainly in what they don't do, for example, fight white-collar crime, organized crime, political crime, or terrorism, which are largely left to federal units. Though there is overlap between the federal agencies and the locals, and toes have been known to be stepped on, the separate agencies have managed, in the main, to hack out a *modus vivendi* over the years.

The "feds" stick mostly to the federal crimes that municipal cops are not equipped to handle, even when, as is most often the case, the crime is covered by both federal and state statutes. Computer frauds, stock swindles, elaborate racketeering schemes, terrorist acts, and other complicated breaches of law require the expertise and thorough preparation that only the feds can bring. The enforcement of drug laws has evolved rapidly into joint undertakings between the feds and local cops, because of the escalating seriousness of the drug problem. This is the one area where task forces composed of mixed personnel seem to be working.

The state police mostly engage in highway patrol and assist small local agencies with an occasional serious crime problem. Small-town police departments are sometimes struck by a murder or a large robbery or burglary that they're unequipped to handle. The state police can step in and lend a hand.

Sheriffs have become, with rare exceptions, the nation's jailers and process servers of civil judgments and warrants, although they'll sometimes assume patrol responsibilities, on a contract or assigned basis. Their uniqueness in law enforcement lies in their status as politicians as they usually have to be elected.

All of these—feds, state police, and locals—can be described as the law enforcement community. Under the pressures produced by today's levels of crime and violence, they have had to find ways of working harmoniously together to battle the scourge produced by drugs, guns, and criminals.

Organized Crime, White-Collar Crime, and Terrorism

The continuing enterprise called *organized crime* exists wherever a demand for illegal services exists, on an ongoing basis, whether this means prostitution, shylocking, drug dealing, gambling, or whatever. Its corporate life requires that organized crime constantly seek new opportunities for growth, in order to accommodate its army of employees, arranged, as in any other organization, hierarchically.

Organized crime has branched out into such otherwise legitimate businesses as unions, construction, garbage hauling, and even hotel supplies, twisting these into crooked operations, such as "sweetheart contracts"—where a corrupt union sells out the interests of its members to obtain payments from management—or "no-show" jobs for its cronies or assigning territories and creating monopolies in such areas as the carting business.

Not every city has extensive networks of La Cosa Nostra (LCN), but the advent of heavy drug usage now offers the same opportunity that prohibitions on alcohol offered sixty years earlier. The operations of organized crime are continuing, complex, and very difficult to interrupt. Only the largest police agencies have the resources to devote to a determined attack on this evil, but their track record is pretty dismal. The fact is that only the FBI and U.S. Attorneys have been successful in penetrating and interdicting the operations of LCN.

The investigation of organized crime requires heavy commitments of scarce and valuable human and material resources. Informers, undercover operations, wiretaps, buggings, exhaustive examinations of books and records, and other sophisticated, long-term approaches are the only tactics that have any hope of working. In recent years, the FBI has been very successful in short-circuiting the workings of LCN and has sent waves of its leaders to prison.

White-collar crime—the depredations of embezzlers, stock swindlers, and other highly skilled criminals who use phones, computers, and pens to commit their crimes—is another area requiring such expensive resources as accountants, attorneys, and paper-trail sleuths who have a mastery of the arcane laws governing complex financial transactions.

Terrorism also involves penetration, high-level intelligence operations, and the devotion of rare human and expensive technical resources that are beyond the capabilities of most cities.

These three—organized crime, white-collar crime, and terrorist crime—have been left to the feds by America's police. In a division of labor that could best be described as evolutionary, the cops took the streets and the feds took the suites. The arrangement has worked very much better since the demise of the FBI's iron-willed mentor, J. Edgar Hoover, fifteen years ago, freeing that agency from the shackles of his personal, private whims and vendettas, which frequently had the agency involved in work that is now thought inappropriate, such as spying on the Reverend Martin Luther King, Jr., and developing dossiers on essentially innocent citizens who had aroused Hoover's curiosity or wrath.

The departure of Hoover enabled the feds to reach a *modus vivendi* with America's police precisely at the moment when hysteria over rising crime levels was reaching a crescendo. The cops had a full plate dealing with the horrors they encountered on their city streets.

Violence in the Streets

Street crime is the province of the underclass. It is committed by males, and it is heavily centered in the teen-age population. Most street criminals commit their first serious crime at fifteen, usually one of the offenses in "Part I." Their activities escalate rapidly from there for a decade of rising seriousness and frequency. Their names mysteriously disappear from the rolls at about the age of thirty. Some, of course, graduate into heavy-duty drug dealing and extend their careers. Most seem to slip away into a sort of criminal's elephants' graveyard and vanish from the scene, perhaps into a literal graveyard, imprisonment, drug or alcohol stupefaction, marriage, employment, or some other fate that diverts them from habitual criminality.

The criminal who most frightens America is a recidivist, engaged with drugs and armed with sophisticated firearms. Recent studies have produced rather startling new insights into the history and activities of this significant minority within the criminal class, who will receive more extended attention later in this book.

The rise of recidivists, and the menace they represent, has triggered an arms race between them and the cops, as the latter clamor for better weapons, to match the criminals' 9mm automatics, with double and triple the number of bullets commonly found in the cop's increasingly obsolete revolver.

Street Criminals

Civilians know little about crime and less about criminals. Cops don't know all that much either, because the anti-intellectual world of policing is notably hostile to research, experimentation, or analysis, cutting cops off from the scholars they need to secure crucial data and insight. Some isolated progress has been recorded, nevertheless, and the veil behind which criminals have operated has been parted a bit.

Criminals, for example, are not invariably engaged in felonious acts. They may even be the victims of other criminals, from time to time, as they get murdered or held up or burglarized. They operate in a milieu where such events are commonplace. They are basically opportunists who strike when a chance presents itself. If the opening isn't there, they go home. It isn't as planned and deliberate a process as most suspect. The question of whether a criminal will act could depend on how much trouble it will take, say, to get into your home, or whether you have a confident gait or walk in a preoccupied manner.

Hannah Arendt, the writer-philosopher, spoke of the banality of evil. The average criminal appears as a shocking revelation to an inexperienced citizen called to jury duty. The man in the dock is ordinary. The juror has no trouble identifying with him. He expected the criminal to be different, and because he isn't, the juror may be tempted to believe the guy isn't a criminal at all. This may account for some bizarre verdicts. We expect mass murderers to look distinctly and identifiably different from the rest of us, and we even tend to rely on that fiction, in order to avoid them. Unfortunately, they don't look any different from most people, especially in court, where they are presented in shirts, ties, suits, and the other accoutrements of "respectable society."

Two factors work together to create the criminal repeater: genetics and conditioning. The influence of genes is currently being probed in studies of identical twins, raised apart. The findings appear to be lending some aid and comfort to the genetic theory's proponents. The better known, and more widely accepted, influences—poverty, child abuse, teen-age pregnancies, ignorance, unemployment, welfare, racism, drug addiction, alcoholism, and exclusion—form the second, more accepted, view.

Studies that involve self-reports by criminals and criminal histories provided by police records (the only data available currently) reveal the enormous disparities in activity among recidivists. Very few repeaters commit tremendous numbers of crimes, and the majority engage in more casual, sporadic, and desultory behaviors. The challenge is to identify the small population who constitute the real menace because of the frequency of their depredations. Targeting them for selective incapacitation may well prove an effective and efficient method of combating street crime, although it will also raise serious questions concerning their constitutional rights. The difficulty in identifying these dangerous predators is, in any case, daunting. This difficulty is made even greater by the flaws of our language, which, as yet, has found no name for these unique individuals. And yet, isolating, identifying, and incapacitating them hold the greatest promise for preventing street crime.

Street Conditions

The public is also concerned about quality-of-life issues that transcend the crime question. Little old ladies get frightened when menacing hulks drunkenly ask for coins. The daily life of the city is threatened when people perceive the death of civility downtown, which is frequently the center of the action for all: symphony goers, sports fans, diners, and street derelicts. The underclass must be not only controlled but kept invisible, which means out of the busy downtown centers that attract them. The pressure on the police chief to control such conditions as aggressive begging, public drunkenness, peddling, the antics of the mentally disturbed, and other street annoyances is intense. These conditions communicate a distressing sense of decline that proves deeply troubling to citizens. The homeless now drifting about our cities, emerging like threatening zombies to accost us in the night, serve as unnerving reminders that deterioration is within the gates. The increasing population of the homeless lends a volatile new element to an already combustible mixture. It becomes as important to remove the human as it is to remove the painted graffiti.

New York's subway system, for example, has been perceived as dangerous not only because of the graffiti that seem to announce an anything-goes, all-controls-are-down sense of decay but because of the concentration of underclass members in close quarters. The combination of needy and menacing people and sights serves as a dramatic metaphor for the horrors of America's modern city life. Yet the actual incidence of crime, in the underground, is sharply lower than the levels of violence on the streets above. Cleaning the graffiti is sure to raise the riders' sense of safety.

Preserving the peace and protecting life and property assume more concrete forms when a police executive is pressured to keep these sights under wraps. The role of maintaining order frequently clashes with the exercise of personal freedoms. Police chiefs must fight to maintain a sense of balance between the interests of the demanding citizens and the rights of those seen as offending society's nostrils. These officials function between an overclass that gives them their marching orders and the underclass they've been hired to keep down.

This is one of the unspoken assignments that breeds cynicism in cops. They are pressured to keep the drunks, psychos, street peddlers, musicians, and others who contribute to what is described, by cops, as "street conditions" under wraps, while surrounded by rhetoric about "brutality" and "rights." When the poor scream in outrage, the overclass doesn't confess its complicity but piously calls for punishments or maintains an imperious silence.

The tools needed to maintain order, especially downtown, are rarely furnished. These would include psychiatric facilities where the mentally disturbed might be taken, or detoxification centers for public drunks. Peddlers' merchandise needs to be confiscated. Overlaying everything is the need for laws that authorize the cops to act. Vagrancy statutes are incredibly difficult to draw up because the courts have usually held them to be unconstitutionally vague. The police have also abused such statutes, illustrating the dilemma of providing the power to act, knowing that any power to do good may also be used to do evil. This is no reason to paralyze the government, but it is a very good reason to monitor the results and to maintain strict controls.

Informally rousting the street people is simply illegal, and doing so is the wrong message to convey to the cops. Such a message simply invites cops to adopt measures that quickly lapse into brutality and that will eventually spill over into many other areas.

Because cities are reluctant to pay for the facilities that are needed, there is no pressure to pass the relevant legislation, but there is plenty of pressure to keep the derelicts and nuisances out of sight.

Kids hanging out at night, and causing problems, require the existence of a curfew law to enable the cops to control their behavior. Curfew legislation, like laws against loitering, vagrancy, and other troubling street situations, sends chills of apprehension up the spines of many of the same Americans who call on the police to do something about kids, bums, and derelicts downtown.

Late-night revels require a noisy-party ordinance that enables the police to act, within the law, to restore tranquility.

These things cannot, and should not, be done informally. Societal hypocrisy, in pressing the police to "do something" without furnishing the tools, not only encourages cynicism but invites the police to take extra-legal measures in discharging their duties.

I can recall my wife's horror at my order to arrest street peddlers, beggars, and musicians. My view was that they set a negative tone of decay and decline in the neighborhood. One musician wandered into my office, demanding to know why the cops were constantly "hassling" him. He played drums at busy intersections. No one would tell him why he was being arrested.

"Because I ordered them to do it. I'm determined to have order on our streets, and I've instructed the cops to arrest peddlers, musicians, and others plying their trades and wares."

He looked startled. His confusion gradually gave way to a glint of recognition and surprised pleasure.

"Well, at least now I know. Thanks for telling me. The others wouldn't give me that courtesy."

He left, after shaking my hand.

We also filled the detoxification center, virtually every warm evening, with public drunks, following a terrific public battle between me and county commissioners seeking to economize and reduce the number of beds from 88 to 50. They ultimately wound up reluctantly raising it to 100, after having taken an initial vote that had resulted in six opting for the reduction and one against. The controversy proved to be a perfect illustration of the chief's need to take a systemic view. If the facility wasn't there for us, what would we do with the drunks? The catch phrase used to capture the public's imagination and gain their support was that they "could kiss downtown good-bye" if the number of beds at detox was reduced. These events illustrate the pressures operating on police agencies to attack problems for which there exist no clear-cut legal solutions. The chief becomes the instrument through which the department's actions get shaped and directed.

Preventing Crime

The frightened and impatient citizen's eyes glaze over with frustration and ill-concealed hostility at the mention of cultural, social, or, especially, economic forces channeling the underclass into lives of crime. "Action now" is the demand. Long-term strategies for the prevention of crime are lost in a desire for the prompt removal of undesirables. Suggestions that resources be spent on attacking the dropout problem or ensuring the employability of the ghetto's idle cannot compete with the demagogue's sexier calls for more cops and bigger jails. Police chiefs, sniffing the wind and sensing their advantages, trim their sails accordingly and call for more cops.

All citizens want the cop back on the beat. They feel nostalgia for those better days when the comforting presence of a cop was always nearby. The chief knows this is ruinously costly and probably only displaces crime anyway. About five cops have to be hired to keep one in a particular spot twenty-four hours a day, seven days a week. At a cost of at least $50,000 to $60,000 each, this adds up to a quarter of a million dollars to have a cop on your block every day.

Enforcement of selected laws is, within limits, a realizable objective. The police concentrate energy and resources on this enforcement mission and are able to achieve impressive tallies in target areas such as, currently, drug enforcement. Their focus is guided, to some extent, by public pressures.

Detecting and arresting offenders is another task the cops find realistically possible. They pursue it faithfully. Reports of a rapist on the loose not only will produce outside pressures to perform but will, independent of the public's urgings, get the cops' adrenaline flowing. Cops like to fight crime. Sometimes, though, the public's alarm and its pressures can produce dysfunctional results if they frighten the chief into unwise directives to subordinates. It is in these circumstances that the anxiety for success produces ghastly errors or worse.

I can recall a manhunt in the Bronx when, in addition to a lot of heat from the usual political and community figures, I was accosted by a cop who demanded to know what I was doing to catch the rapist. As the commander of police forces in the borough, I was a logical target for his questions. I briefed him about our strategy and progress. He asked about the latest incident. Fortunately, I knew the details, although not the name of the victim. I deliberately never ask for the name in such cases, lest I blurt it out inadvertently.

As it turned out, the victim was his wife. Another form of pressure to produce. I extended some fatherly advice about what his reaction ought to be (outrage that his wife had been atrociously assaulted—I knew there was sometimes an unconscious temptation either to blame the victim or to see her as "damaged goods" in such cases). We were lucky enough to have the rapist fall into our trap. He told us that a pain in his belly intensified gradually, until it became unbearable and he'd have to rape in order to experience release. With his arrest the fear subsided, until the next maniac came along. We didn't have long to wait.

The Son of Sam's first shooting occurred in the Bronx, around that time, and I can still hear the detectives reassuring me that it was a jilted lover and that they had a line on him and would be reeling him in soon. The guy on the line was me. They didn't have a clue and needed to get me off their backs. The next strike was in another borough, and it would be awhile before connections began to be made, by which time I was gone.

The pressure to produce arrests is, of course, constant, and it is healthy because it reflects the people's concern and interests. The danger comes if it frightens the bureaucracy into panicky reactions. Democracy in action means calls, letters, public meetings, and accountings. Nobody wants to even guess at the meaning of such mutterings as what will happen "if something isn't done, and soon." And, always, there is the insistent voice of the Fourth Estate.

Policing, though, is more than chases, investigations, and arrests; it mainly functions as a service industry.

Service

Police work remains remarkably unaltered from the days of the Praetorian Guard and their need to keep peace on the streets of Rome. I can almost hear the royal complaints about mobs, disorders, and the need to clean up the town. Cops, in whatever guise, were there to respond to trouble, quickly, and bring it under control. There is a wonderfully contemporary flavor to the writings of such police thinkers as August Vollmer, although they were penned more than half a century ago.

The intervening millennia might be described as attempts, by police executives, to get the cops there faster. The issue of response time continues to dominate many discussions on the question of police effectiveness. Even its definition is open to hot dispute. The breakthroughs came with the invention of the automobile, the radio, telephones, computers, and, in 1967, the omnipresent 911.

At least 80 percent of police work involves answering calls for help that have nothing to do with crime. They involve rescues, medical emergencies, and the scores of other contretemps that attend the human situation far more often than even the much heralded and feared crimes and acts of violence.

Police administrators have spent a great deal of energy on managing the service problem, torn by the dilemma of inviting the public to use the emergency facilities provided and knowing they can't possibly answer all calls and probably shouldn't anyway. Many can be handled as reports, over the phone, and others have nothing do do with the police, such as utility or phone problems. The culture of poverty carries the notion that when any service is needed the thing to do is dial 911.

Some calls are more important than others. Thus the administrators have embraced the notion of establishing a priority list for calls and screening out those that shouldn't be responded to at all.

The cop's daily task mainly involves patrolling, responding to calls, making minor arrests, issuing traffic citations, and maintaining the orderly flow of daily life without doing violence to citizens' freedoms or rights. The safe, speedy regulation of traffic flow is the third major responsibility of urban police departments. This important aspect will receive more detailed treatment later in the book.

Operational Barnacles

An unexpected crisis may incite the police agency to create a new unit or task force. This is a legitimate and frequently used approach. Pruning these units, once their usefulness has been outlived, often proves impossibly difficult. The section on the Philadelphia Police Department discusses the difficulty these barnacles produce if they're not scraped away. The constituency served will fight for the preservation of the unit even when the need has passed or the resources could be used more effectively elsewhere. Willingness to take the issue on will be a key determinant of the chief's strength and effectiveness.

I recall a police commissioner who had a passionate interest in efficiency and decided to create a tough inspections division to examine and evaluate the stewardship of commanders. Its charge was to uncover mismanagement, waste, inefficiency, corruption, and other administrative failures through audits, inspections, examinations, tests of service and performance, and other verifications.

The organization took its mandate seriously and began hacking and slashing at the barnacles. Its reports were comprehensive, persuasive, and feared. Heads rolled. Opposition, among the mandarins being scrutinized, grew. Finally the division struck at some headquarters favorites. The inspections division commander was removed by the same commissioner who'd named him, and the unit's hand was stayed.

The inspections division continued to exist, continued to issue reports (albeit of a much more tepid quality), and continued to do business, even though punishments were no longer delivered. For example, reports that contained the mildest criticisms were sent to the accused commanders for their correction and response. The paper trail remained covered. All outward semblances were observed, but nothing really happened.

What commissioner would abolish a useless unit and risk being labeled as soft on punishing wrongdoing? Elimination of the unit might have been read as being oblivious to the notion of insisting on the accountability of police commanders. Using the unit meant being very tough on buddies and cronies in the ranks and incurring the enmity of the union because of the use of spies, self-initiated integrity tests, and other hard measures of performance. The easy way out was to let the organization exist and merely go through the motions.

These tough organizational decisions involve internal and external politics. Every enclave has its adherents. Every action has its short-term fallout. Every privilege has its defenders. There are very few persons storming into the office insisting the chief do the people's business and forge a more effective agency, but there are plenty available to defend the status quo, whether it's beneficial or not.

Organization of Police Departments

The city charter responsibilities of the police usually prompt municipal police agencies to organize themselves into three columned structures: patrol, investigations, and services. The more complicated, larger agencies branch off from this basic pattern.

The Patrol Force

The patrol force will include all uniformed cops. Frequently, these are precinct forces, assigned to serve as minipolice departments for a geographical area of the city. The basic uniformed street forces are supplemented by such specialist units as traffic, canine, mounted, motorcycle, or special tactical units created for such purposes as hostage negotiations, complicated rescues, high-hazard raids, and major disasters.

The patrol force are the backbone of the agency. They are the uniformed troops, the infantry. They do the bulk of what is known as "police work": responding to calls, handling emergencies, policing events or demonstrations, and just simply being available.

Investigations

The detectives are the plainclothes personnel who investigate crimes after the fact and comprise the investigation unit. They are the sleuths of fiction who have mesmerized the public for about a century and a half. Over the years, however, they have been mismanaged so badly that a prominent think tank, the Rand Corporation, recommended such sharp reductions in their ranks as to make them an endangered species.

Police chiefs had taken to using these investigators to mollify victims, as opposed to concentrating on solving cases. It came to a choice between soft-soaping and pleasing the public, and serving them. The objective was to avoid letters or calls of complaint. It is not an accident of language that New York's detectives came to call being assigned to cases "catching squeals." They were there to silence the whining.

The salvation of the Sherlocks occurred when the same organization suggested that, instead of pleasing the public, the aim ought to be to serve it better, and that this might best be done by conducting more effective investigations and solving more cases. A solvability factor was created that virtually red-lined the unpromising cases. The detectives would concentrate, for example, on the one burglary in twenty that, because of a fingerprint or other evidence obtained, had a real chance of being solved. This meant virtually ignoring the other nineteen, following a quick inspection of the prospects of success. The irony was that this approach, although potentially alienating the department from the vast majority of its clients, actually held out the best hope for high arrest rates. In the end they'd solve a lot more burglaries this way. The fundamental reason for the delay in adopting this policy may have been the chiefs' lack of faith in the people's ability to absorb, and support, such hard realities.

Within the world of police investigations lies the murky area of vice. This is a problem area not just because it involves shoveling sand against the powerful tide of human lusts, but because it is the prime area for the temptation and corruption of a police force. Every chief appreciates this painful fact.

Any cop will agree that there is an insatiable public appetite for sex, drugs, alcohol, and gambling. This is the area blithely described as public morals. It masks a Pandora's Box of difficulties for every police CEO.

Besides the money and the temptation, there is the tremendous and disproportionate public interest in vice, which in reality represents only a small fraction of any agency's resources or expended energies. Vice titillates. There is even an element of excitement about it among the abolitionists. One only has to listen briefly to their perorations to smell something stronger than a dispassionate interest at work.

The press, always following the public's nose, eats it up. Every action stirs controversy: "Why were so many officers assigned to that vice raid when they should have been out catching robbers and killers?" "Why is the chief content to let our downtown turn into a moral cesspool?" Chances are these stories will include salacious details.

There are constituencies for every side of every question, which is why it is so important that the chief have a fixed and firmly set list of priorities. A strong moral base will lend consistency and coherence to the agency's actions.

The public official soon discovers there is a militant faction "out there" ready to march for its cause, and that a group exists for every cause. The unsteady executive who lacks an inner compass to guide actions will be buffeted to and fro.

Sex, booze, gambling, and drugs have created enough tragedies to fill libraries. Yet pleasure, especially in our pleasure-loving age, is one of humanity's most devoted pursuits. The police—frail and human, too—have suffered repeated scandals in these areas. These involve temptation, opportunity, and risk, a combination that often proves irresistible. Every police chief recognizes the agency's vulnerability to the manifold dangers of vice. Here, as in so many other situations in policing, little has changed over the centuries.

An age given over to sybaritic pursuits, where every experience is described in terms of how much joy it gave us, is particularly vulnerable to the corruption of sex, booze, drugs, and money.

Support Services

The third organizational arm, after patrol and investigations, is services. These involves the panoply of support functions needed to keep a complex organization going. They are not the sort of operations that normally grab a city council's fervent labors or support, but they are critical to the success of the police mission. Training, planning, records, computer services, payroll, research, budgeting, purchasing, personnel transactions, and such are the unglamorous ancillary functions that, although invisible and decidedly unsexy, as often as not spell the success or failure of the units that more visibly perform the police tasks.

Because the contributions of these units are indirect and often feature long-term concerns, it is too easy for political figures and even chiefs to be tempted to look elsewhere for results and starve these divisions. This is a classical administrative mistake.

Service units provide the staff assistance that, although neither visible nor impressive, spells the difference between good or bad hirings, well or poorly trained personnel, tight or loose fiscal controls, shoddy or modern physical plant, good or bad equipment, and a host of other concerns critically important to the daily workings of a police agency.

In order to accomplish the missions described in the typical charter, the police organization arranges its priorities as follows: (1) fighting street crime by making arrests, engaging in more vigorous patrol, responding to crime calls rapidly, promoting greater police visibility, and so on; (2) responding faster and more efficiently to citizen emergencies; and (3) enforcing traffic laws.

Cops and Citizens

Despite the omnipresence of cops on America's streets, the workings of police agencies have remained a mystery to most citizens. In recent years, thoughtful police administrators have seen the widening chasm between cops and the public they serve as an impediment to the sort of effective performance made possible by a true partnership.

The American public takes its information about the police mostly from television shows that convey grotesque distortions of reality and ultimately give rise to impossible expectations of the police. The cops, eager to preserve their autonomy, and believing that their freedom is tied to the public's ignorance about their workings, continue to shroud their operations in secrecy. The message of the police, especially as they have been striving for professional status in this century, has been "Leave it to us, we're the professionals; stay out of it and don't get involved or you're liable to get your socks sued off."

This fear of litigation (litigophobia?) has fed naturally into every citizen's concern about safety and the fear that comes from dealing with criminals. The separation has also fed the mystique of power that is attached to the unknown, and it has created a sort of corps of high priests of safety, while justifying increasing salaries and pensions, as well as the lavish expenditure of the city's resources on its most prestigious agency.

The chasm has continually widened between the police and the people they protect and serve. One result has been such cases as the Kitty Genovese murder, where a screaming young woman was stalked and repeatedly stabbed, while scores of citizens who heard or saw the attack cowered behind curtains and did nothing. The incident became a paradigm for the age of noninvolvement.

As crime tripled over the third of a century following 1960, and as citizen clamor for action grew, a few thinkers began to recognize the need for citizen involvement in the struggle. Witnesses and complainants were needed. Neighbors had to watch out for the folks next door. Crime prevention, through citizen involvement, gradually came to be seen as one of the more promising avenues to reducing the appalling levels of crime. At the very least, it was realized that it was necessary to suck the public into the struggle and make them more sympathetic to the plight of the police.

Gradually, a subtle, complex shift occurred. The police, sensing the need for citizen involvement and support, began to create programs intended to foster police–citizen partnerships, under the rubric of community-oriented policing (COP).

Under COP, the police reached out to embrace the people. The first efforts involved such crime prevention techniques as organizing block clubs, marking property for identification, conducting security surveys, and other defense or target-hardening approaches.

Next came teams of cops going around to neighborhoods to see what problems were troubling the residents. It became known as the *broken-window syndrome,* after a seminal article by James Q. Wilson and George Kelling in the *Atlantic Monthly,* in which they held that unattended problems like unfixed broken windows, uncleared graffiti, overgrown weeded lots, and other signs of decay communicated an "all-restraints-are-down-and-any-conduct-is-acceptable" attitude that sapped the community's morale and encouraged vandals and criminals.

Instead of prescribing quick answers, the cops shifted to focusing on consulting the citizens on what was needed and made plans to assault the problems, whatever their nature. Combating the citizens' problems often meant enlisting the aid of other city agencies, which is just what the cops did. The point was to correct the neighborhood irritant and thereby strengthen the community's cohesiveness and morale. Unattended problems conveyed a sense of hopelessness and powerlessness that led to more crime and a slow process of social dissolution.

The advent of the welcoming storefront police office, modeled to some degree on the Japanese *koban,* was intended to promote accessibility and proximity. Cities like Houston and Newark adopted this approach to further the cop–community partnership. The car, radio, and telephone all made the police more efficient, but they also distanced the cops from the communities they served. Air conditioning exacerbated the problem by allowing the cops to zip heedlessly by, windows closed, in the heat of summer, not able to hear even cries for help.

The sincerity of the movement to a citizen–cop partnership, however, might be questioned in light of the notorious police antagonism to such important symbolic groups as the Guardian Angels and volunteer bodies such as auxiliary cops. These represent the segments of the public that have been the most anxious, and aggressive, in engaging in a partnership with the cops, yet it is these groups that the cops have typically responded to most coolly. The police penchant for secrecy and hostility toward the press could also be described as telltale signs of the cops' resistance to the notion of a genuine collaboration.

In the midst of all these contemporary currents and cross-currents, it is critically important that people understand both the limits on and the opportunities for action imposed on and available to the nation's municipal police. An imperfect understanding of the police leads to the cynical evasion of responsibility by the police and may also lay the groundwork for unreasonable citizen demands and expectations. Citizens must demand openness and an accounting from their police. Settling for silence, as they did in Philadelphia, ensures the perpetuation of dysfunctional practices. Later, we will examine the Guardian Angel issue more closely, but for now, it might be wise to entertain a bit of skepticism about the depth of the enthusiasm the police are expressing for their latest discovery: community-oriented policing.

Today's police chief, pressured and harried to produce safety in an unsafe society, is increasingly reaching out to enlist the citizen's aid in the struggle. This act, however, flies in the face of police insularity, separateness, and secrecy, and it is hard to know how sincerely even the chiefs have embraced the new idea.

Partnership means that the police must surrender their long-held positions, attitudes, and actions, of being the lonely, strong, silent crime-fighters glorified by the media.

Policing is at a cross-roads. The criminal justice system is in shambles because of the rising tide of crime and violence, fueled by drugs and guns, and because of the police departments' ever-increasing ability to produce masses of arrests. Imbalances have been created as resources continue to be thrown at the police without a systemic view of the effects on the other players.

America's urban police have evolved, over their more than a century and a half of existence, into agencies assigned to battle the ills centered in our troubled cities, where the fate of the nation is most likely to be decided. The evolution of the assignment has proceeded, as these things invariably do, along differentiated lines that sometimes conform to explicitly assigned tasks, as in drug enforcement, and sometimes not, as in controlling the street people.

In the process, the cops have staked out street crime, service, and traffic safety as their territories and have tried to fulfill the explicit mandate of their charters. The implicit assignment to control the underclass continues to create serious problems.

The law enforcement establishment has had to learn to function cooperatively, under severe public pressure to perform. The police agency must be understood if it is to be controlled and channeled into activities worthy of a free and democratic people who want and need public servants to preserve their safety.

Life within the Police Agency

The police are rigidly structured, semimilitary organizations that are led by chiefs. The internal culture of the department is shaped by its workers, the environment, the tasks assigned to it, and other contributing factors such as the public's demands and expectations.

An understanding of the real workings of police departments requires a grasp of its people and the forces shaping their entrance into and their behavior and rise in the agency.

Jobs in the Police Department

The officers in a squad car, patrolling America's cities, are the street cops. They are the infantry soldiers, the slugs in the trenches. Their lives are ruled by a radio that tethers them to the citizen's call for help.

The agency is also a large corporation with many organizational nooks and crannies. Inside jobs that take cops off the street, such as training or planning, allow for different careers within the ranks. Investigators are cops on detail. The organization will find inside employment for its injured and ill. Policing is not a world of lateral entry. Everyone starts at the bottom, including the chief. One might pursue any number of callings within the agency: researcher, teacher, budgeteer, mechanic, engineer, technician, computer specialist, daredevil, or whatever tame or craven predilection he or she desires. The profession requires a bewildering variety of talents, interests, and skills. It is indeed a house with many mansions.

It was one of the oddities of the New York Police Department that the senior executives who initiated the drastic reforms of the 1970s had led sheltered lives in such cloistered halls as the police academy or the planning division during the old days of brutality and corruption in the 1950s and 1960s. Although the problems of brutality and corruption were systemic and virtually inescapable, many hid out in pristine warrens where there was no temptation to thump or steal and where everyone understood the rules of the game. The new executives emerged from these sanctuaries ready for action, untainted by past sins. The reforms that followed were made possible because of their ability to keep their skirts clean when so many others had been tainted. Their dilemma, until the denouement of the Knapp investigation and the reforms they fought for as a result of it, made for true ambivalence. On the one hand, they had to be praised for staying honest during the bad old days, and on the other, they might be condemned for haughtily avoiding the fray and sort of sitting out the struggle in the early days.

Throughout their histories, police departments have remained remarkably stable, white, male institutions.

The entrance of women in large numbers and, to a lesser degree, blacks and other minorities changed the mix, but police departments still tend to be ruled by white men, even in cities where the chief or the mayor is black.

The corporate ladder is usually climbed through civil service tests for the positions of sergeant, lieutenant, and captain. The chief's power to appoint key subordinates is either limited or nonexistent, depending on the rules the unions have been able to get carved into the organizational stone.

The cop who does not want to be physically endangered can take several paths into a safer, inside job, for example, planning, training, record keeping, or taking police photographs. Those who want action can slip into the nether world of undercover operations like vice, narcotics, or acting as decoys.

The next notch up on the ladder is detective. Detectives investigate crimes by checking records, interviewing witnesses, canvassing areas, searching for evidence, and generally undertaking the tedium and drudgery of gathering facts, tasks that are quite at odds with the flashing insights of detectives' fictional counterparts. Detectives can, nevertheless, be very resourceful and effective when pressed. This occurs in the rare cases that are important enough to generate pressure.

The Son of Sam case was solved through checking summons records for cars near the scenes of the shootings. Finally, detectives came up with a parking ticket issued to the man who became the suspect.

A vicious ramp murder-rape in Minneapolis was solved when forensic technicians pored over a vehicle for days, until they found a fingerprint that led them to the suspect. The technology allowing for the matching of a single print against existing fingerprint files had only recently been perfected. It was the devotion of scarce time and personnel resources, on a lavish scale, that made the difference. It was the sort of effort that can be expended only on the heaviest cases.

The brutal rape and murder of a young woman who worked for the U.S. Department of Agriculture in the Bronx was also solved by persistent and dedicated detectives. Over long weeks that turned into months, they furiously canvassed every tenant in a huge complex. Throughout it all, they were subjected to intense pressure from headquarters. They finally came up with a resident-suspect, who confessed and asked the investigators to apologize, for him, to the young woman's parents. Again, it was the kind of special effort given only to extraordinary cases.

Detective work is drudgery and plodding labor, but the post is prestigious, and it usually pays more than a cop's salary (usually 5 to 10 percent more) and gets the cop out of "the bag" (uniform). Detectives prefer to "get on the sheet" (make an arrest) through "hangers" (easy cases) garnered from the "squeals" (complaints) they've "caught" (been assigned).

The sergeant is the first-line supervisor: the roll caller and instructor when cops turn out for patrol, and the first boss at most scenes. Sergeants are the straw bosses on the street who arrive first, to take charge and direct operations until higher brass appears, usually in more important matters. Often students who have crammed for the test, the sergeants' greatest challenge is to transform themselves from habitual order-takers to order-givers. This is a broader psychological chasm than is generally realized. Few departments train or prepare their personnel for this pivotal and unique switch of roles. The result is characteristically low-quality supervision at a level where the opposite is most urgently needed.

The lieutenant is the shift commander, platoon leader, desk officer, or unit commander, usually the executive in charge when the captain is not working. While sergeants might lead a squad of six to twelve officers, lieutenants are in charge of all the squads working, which may be as many as forty or fifty officers. As desk officers, they occupy a semijudicial post, deciding the issues brought into the station house and recording events, in long hand, in those impressive ledgers that time has honored in preserving.

Sergeants may also command small units. Lieutenants command slightly larger ones, but it is very rare that either receive important command responsibilities, which normally start at the next level.

Captains are the true middle managers of the agency. They usually command a precinct that serves a significant geographic portion of the city. Frequently, these are tenured ranks, achieved through the competitive exams of the civil service process that also hired the sergeants and lieutenants.

Above this, the chain of power gets a little murky. Some agencies adopt the military model of majors and colonels, but for whatever curious reason, the profession's hubris never ascended to the use of the title *general*. Other departments have inspectors and chief inspectors, roughly following the British system.

Civil Service and Reform

The civil service—created to erase the abuses of ward heelers, the political bosses who hired Irish immigrants with connections right off the boats and into such city jobs as cops—has, over time, fallen prey itself to contemporary circumventers: the police unions. Thus the reforms that came with the creation of civil service were gradually coopted, reshaped, and corrupted, with the passage of time, by the representatives of the employees who sought to make the jobs as comfortable as possible. This proves a persuasive argument for the constant need of organizational renewal, through introspection and change. The civil service's inability to adjust to changing times has made it, in many places, an obstacle to reform.

Recognizing the importance of key bodies such as civil service commissions, police unions set out to capture them through the application of political muscle to the appointing authority, usually the mayor. Union coffers and support can be critical to a candidate's chances, and the unions, preferring to work quietly behind the scenes, find these sorts of payoffs very lucrative in the long run. Very few people get exercised over who is appointed to such critical posts as civil service commissions. And very few chiefs are either willing or able to take the issue on in the only forum that makes a difference: the public arena.

Thus mayors get pressured by the police union to appoint favored hacks to the three, five, or seven posts available on the civil service commissions. They are the people who will rule on hiring, promotion, and dismissal policies and regulations.

Yesterday's reform becomes today's pocket of corruption. There are no panaceas or final solutions. Currently, the pendulum has swung so violently in favor of the power of the civil service model that it needs to be pushed in the other direction—toward granting the chiefs more power, especially in the appointing process. Here, again, we find that, in desperation, city contract negotiators, anxious to save dollars for strapped municipalities, have bargained away significant managerial powers. If they have no money to offer, they find it tempting to cede such managerial prerogatives as the way in which shifts or assignments are apportioned, job titles, numbers of promotions, hours of work, type of work, vacations, weekend work, and other areas that impinge importantly on the chief's ability to run the department. The chiefs are rarely invited to the bargaining sessions, and most seem, in truth, relieved not to have to negotiate these deep and unfamiliar waters. Instead, they awaken to the reality of diminished authority at a time when their responsibilities and the public's expectations are escalating.

Appointment versus Civil Service

The issue of loyalty poses especially tricky questions. The sort of personal loyalty that engenders blind support, whatever the moral imperatives involved, leads to criminality and destruction. Yet the police chief must have subordinates who are committed to the chief's program. It is one of the axioms of administrative theory that executives must have the authority to carry out their assigned responsibilities. This means the power to reward and punish.

Executives who are locked inflexibly into a rank from which they cannot, except in the most egregious circumstances, be extricated owe their boss nothing. They earned their posts through the civil service process and will have little incentive to pursue the chief's agenda energetically.

Precinct commanders are the officials in charge of geographical sections of a city. They are, in a very real sense, that community's police chiefs. Usually, the city is divided into a number of precincts, and each of these has its commander, frequently a captain. Whether directly or through an intermediate level, the precinct commander must answer to the chief. However, commanders are granted a lot of autonomy over their area of responsibility, having a separate building and a pretty full service complement of personnel.

Precinct commanders, the captains, are very likely the most important managers in a police agency. The chief relies on them to carry out policies and programs. The commander's loyalty to the goals enunciated by the chief is usually inspired by fear of punishment or hope of reward.

If the precinct commanders have risen through a series of tests given by an outside agency (usually the civil service), and if they are mostly immune, through tenure, from punishment—except in the most serious situations—chances are that they will owe the chief's policies very little loyalty. They will frequently pursue their own agenda while paying lip service to the chief's programs.

In these circumstances, the chief lacks the responsive organizational instrument needed most: executives in key posts who are committed to the success of the chief's programs. It isn't easy to communicate to the public how their interests are jeopardized in this process, but the reality is that they do suffer. The chief's programs are visible and known and are usually subjected to intense scrutiny and criticism by politicians whose areas are affected by the police union, by the press, and by many others. All the chief's programs need is a fair chance to prove how they might result in better service. This cannot be accomplished without the cooperation of the precinct commanders.

Having energetic, responsive aides depends on the police chief's power to promote or demote and to assign or unassign. Currently, most chiefs have the second power (to shift personnel from one assignment to another) but not the latter (to promote or demote), which is left to the civil service.

The power to appoint and fire is critical to the administrative process. In essence, it translates into the power to surround yourself with people who have earned your confidence and who believe in your goals. The pursuit of objectives requires enthusiasm, persistence, and commitment. The absence of those qualities automatically results in a gradual disintegration and collapse of the administration. The civil service process simply doesn't accommodate these rarely perceived organizational needs. Civil service selects the best test-takers, not the enthusiasts or the wise employees with good and forward-thinking characters. Chiefs need appointive authority. This is the critical tool that will enable them to carry out their mandate.

Climbing the Ladder

In most police departments today, the chief plays no role in the selection of the young executives who will exercise daily supervision over the members of the department.

Cops seeking advancement do not work hard to impress the supervisor with their dedication, integrity, or ability. They study for the promotional tests instead. As they progress from cop to sergeant to lieutenant to captain, they incur no chits or personal organizational loyalties. This can be viewed as a cleansing process, as no favors are owed for one's success, but it can also deprive a worker of any sense of commitment to the organization and its goals. The ascent of police executives is entirely due to their private, lonely, individual efforts. The union, sensing the value of having workers who are neither beholden to the chief nor under the chief's direct control (in terms of tenure, promotion, salary, etc.) push to preserve this system. In their adversarial relationship with the chief, they've learned that, if you can't increase your power, the next best thing is to diminish your opponent's.

The civil service system creates major problems for police chiefs, who are trying to implement policies through functionaries whom they can neither hurt nor help. Such independence does not provide the most fertile ground for developing a team spirit and a sense of mission. Chiefs will either have to settle for working with folks who have no very special need to please them or work toward expanding the power to appoint key subordinates. Here, too, chiefs can expect opposition from the union, as it is virtually axiomatic that any reform that serves the people better is going to work against the comfort and convenience of its members.

It has become clear to today's police executives that the ability to hire, promote, demote, dismiss, or otherwise reward or punish—critical to the control and direction of the agency—must be returned to the CEO.

However, at present, the police executive corps marches, in lockstep progression, up the corporate ladder, irrespective of the qualities of mind, heart, and character that would be seen as basic to the process by any other enterprise. The chief, almost always an up-from-the-ranks insider, was most likely selected, by the mayor, for reasons either different from, or even at odds with, the qualities of perseverance, studiousness, ambition, and careerism that elevated the chief to the jump-off rank of captain. The traits that have got chiefs to the launching spot are not the ones that will get them to the top. There they will need breadth of view, communications skills, a philosophical perspective, political acumen, stamina, and wisdom. The mayor probably selected the chief for reasons having more to do with the strengths of various pressure groups than because of any considerations of merit.

There are two forces that can shape executive talent: formal education and on-the-job experience. The latter, ideally, ought to feature a program of rotation that maximizes the employee's opportunity to master a wide variety of operations and functions. It is vitally important that a broad organizational perspective be garnered through a variety of constantly rotating assignments. These rotations must be married to an ethical, intellectual, and philosophical base that will allow for the shaping of a wise and moral executive.

The anti-intellectual bias of the police world works formidably against the concept of drawing on any ideals or lore learned from a liberal arts education. Thus police departments themselves must set up programs that develop broad intellectual talents among their future leaders. In practice the system works exactly in reverse. The more promising, brightest officers are given key headquarters tasks, frequently in sensitive areas such as planning, internal affairs, training, vice, or budgeting, and are kept there as security blankets against the vagaries of fate. Chiefs cover their flanks by keeping the ablest in the most sensitive posts, reassuring themselves that the tasks will be done well. But what they fail to see is that they are stunting the developmental growth of the executive. The short-term gain is that the chief will not have to worry about the workings of a sensitive unit. The young executives experience the comfort, ease, and convenience of a familiar task and unwittingly finds themselves mired in an organizational rut. The result is usually a cadre of senior officers who are either "headquarters brats" or officers who have spent enormous chunks of time in a very small number of assignments and have never developed a sense of the breadth and scope of police activities. This narrow focus is reflected in the policies they make and in the order of their priorities. The narrowness of professional experience among this select group adds to the scorn so many rank-and-filers feel toward those who have become their leaders.

I can recall emerging from eight years in the intelligence division of the NYPD in 1965 and suddenly discovering that I knew a lot about intelligence operations, but nothing much about policing. I spent the next eleven years trying to remedy that deficiency by working in a variety of posts and frequently asking for such unpopular assignments as Harlem's Sixth Division.

Rotation results in developing the talents and experience of the best and brightest through assignments to the most important units. A two- to three-year tour of duty should suffice to maximize the benefit to the individual, while providing some value for the organization in terms of service.

Training the troops, which requires taking them off patrol to sit in classrooms, with unanswered emergency calls stacking up, is precisely analogous in that it requires sacrificing short-term goals in order to achieve a better trained force, which is, after all, a nebulous and un-measurable factor. Organizational decisions frequently come down to just these considerations, and the temptation is usually to go for the highly visible short-term gain. Thus do bureaucracies lurch from crisis to crisis.

So, in essence, police chiefs head an agency where they have spent practically all of their adult life, and where they are surrounded by old friends and enemies. A chief's selection by the mayor probably accommo-dated some narrow and probably temporary political objective, which undoubtedly did not include considerations of competence. It is no small wonder that two former chiefs dubbed these chief executives "fifty-year-old cops" and "pet rocks."

When the military or their suppliers, the defense contractors, need executives, they go to the service academies or graduate schools of busi-ness. The police world lacks such handy spawning grounds. No educa-tional institution exists for the development of police executives. Yet these are expected to move up through the ranks, without a plan of growth or the formal education required, and must successfully cope with the most challenging problems of the age.

The result is a tightly knit, homogeneous culture led by people who have been neither broadened by experience nor deepened by scholarship. The antipathy for experiments, research, study, or analysis has its roots in the backgrounds of these executives. The era of hope, the halcyon days of federal largess, in the form of the Law Enforcement Assistance Administration, was killed in 1980. All hope for federal dollars for educational or training programs died with it. The predilection that chiefs had for buying sexy police hardware rather than undertaking analytical experiments or spending the money intelligently sealed the fate of the agency, after a dozen years of wasted opportunities.

Chiefs' Selection and Tenure

Politics is the art of government. The chief's selection is a political act, and virtually everything the chief undertakes can have political implications. These must be distinguished from partisan gestures or any actions that benefit one political party over another, or one candidate or official over another. It is central to the success of their administration that chiefs be able to distinguish between an act of government as a political action and a partisan political action of any type. The first serves the people and the latter serves a narrow interest, at the expense of the commonweal.

Limiting the selection of police chiefs to insiders greatly reduces the field of qualified applicants for the chief's job. Casting a wide net ensures a tougher competition for all, insiders and outsiders, and holds the best promise for attracting top candidates. That is not to say that the selection of an insider has no value. Insiders hit the ground running. They don't need to be educated about the agency. They understand the organization and its people. There is, though, the negative baggage of friendships, antipathies, vendettas, past incidents, and the panoply of connections, good and bad, collected over long careers.

Outsiders enter with a *tabula rasa*. They have no debits or credits. They are free to make decisions without regard to politics, friendships, or obligations. It gives everyone in the agency a chance to start over. Drastic reforms are more possible. However, these new executives are saddled with the need to be educated about the culture, history, players, problems, and possibilities of the new and strange police department they've been asked to lead. If the chief's selection was fair and based on merit, the launching will be successful. Chiefs' first actions and appointments are the most important signals of their approach. This makes resistance to employing mayoral favorites essential. Such public scandals as those surrounding the federal government's Housing and Urban Development agency are invariably laced with references to favoritism. Chief executives' inability to hire their own principal subordinates and the decision to hire employees that the administration is rewarding for past services will not do much for their credibility. Nor will these executives accomplish much good for housing.

Police chiefs crave security, too, but the fight for tenure must be resisted. Tenure tends to freeze incompetents in place and puts them beyond the reach of accountability. The dangers of tenure echo the evils of civil service. (If the chief doesn't work out, the appointing authority, which is answerable to the people for its stewardship, must be free to fire the chief.) Tenure breaks the chain of accountability that goes from the people's vote to their elected representatives, who appoint the key executives who make the government work. It wouldn't be fair to hold mayors accountable if they lacked the power to ensure the delivery of essential city services.

Tenure, or the ability to remove only for cause (a demonstrably difficult process in the police world, the academic world, the judicial world, or whatever other world uses this method), undermines the democratic principle of accountability. While accommodating the security and ease of the bureaucrat, it does so at the expense of the public good. Tenure must be granted only in exceptional circumstances where it is essential to ensure the freedom and independence of the official. Judges and teachers need to be independent, to be sure, but accountability has to be included somewhere—probably in the selection process.

Mayors ought to be given courses on selecting chiefs. It is probably the most important single decision they make, and most do it with minimal preparation or thought. The results, frequently, are proof of their lack of foresight and knowledge. The course would have to extend to the development of a properly balanced relationship between chiefs and mayors. Each must understand their role.

The mayor's role is to offer direction, establish priorities, and enunciate policies. The mayor must receive a complete accounting as to the workings of the police department and be free to hire and fire the chief. Deciding on promotions, demotions, assignments, disciplinary matters, tactics, or operational approaches must be left to the chief. Governing the agency is the chief's responsibility. Role confusion leads to political interference and the poisoning of the administrative well. More police agencies have been destroyed because of political interference than by any other single factor.

Cops are drawn, for the most part, from a specific societal slice and remain in the agency for many years. The organization's powerful culture, evolving over the decades, shapes and hardens its members. No winds of change are permitted into its corridors. The few iconoclasts are sequestered, shut out, or expelled. The police value orthodoxy, loyalty, obedience, and silence. The agency is full of anomalies. On the one hand it is an absolute dictatorship, where the chief's whims are law, yet it is also a place where the lowest worker wields enormous power and a captain commanding a precinct can frustrate the chief executive's fondest dreams. The entering recruit's expectations of service and good deeds founders on the cold shoals of the secretive internal culture, the cynicism, and the unspoken assignments pushed by the overclass.

Cops people and rule their own world. This might seem a tautology, but the reality is that most organizations are influenced by countless outside forces, whereas the typical police agency is as hermetically sealed as the Vatican. The result is a powerful, self-reinforcing culture that impinges strongly on its members.

The citizens' lack of knowledge about the internal workings of police agencies leads to confused communication and results in the absence of reform.

Both the secretiveness and the public ignorance it helps to foster lead to difficulties in attracting candidates motivated to protect and to serve.

The public, as we will see throughout this work, has enormous power, but it must be directed, informed, and focused. This requires the steady flow of information to the public.

Every day, citizens are bombarded with tons of information on a wide variety of issues, forcing them to set up priorities. The quality of police service should rank high on their list of real concerns. Their safety should be a matter of high interest, even if an attack is not immediately foreseeable. It is imperative that voters understand the internal workings of the police, as well as the issues surrounding police operations, in order to secure the needed service and protection.

This understanding will enable citizens to wisely select the most important person in law enforcement: the mayor. The mayor is the one who will appoint and guide the chief of police. We can easily see the importance of the power of appointment and its pivotal relevance to accountability.

The mayor, setting the policy and pointing the way, appoints the chief and guides the chief in the proper direction. The chief then controls and directs the police department, and must have the power of appointment in order to secure the responsiveness needed to energize that department. If the chief fails, the mayor is fired, at the next election. The mayor would, and should, have fired the chief first. This is how accountability works in a democracy, but in order for it all to come together, the people must be properly informed and must vote intelligently.

The Police Organization's Internal Climate

Any organization's relations with the outside world are shaped by what's going on internally. A demoralized, internally corrupt, brutal, unfair, or badly run police agency will mirror these difficulties when dealing with clients and will not perform its duties adequately. On the other hand, the development of an internally clean, consistent, energetic police force will produce successful results on the street.

These insights tend to be clouded by the veil of silence surrounding police agencies. We need to remind ourselves of the importance of penetrating and understanding these secretive, isolated bodies. A confident, forward-thrusting department simply deals with its environment more competently. Whereas a good, tightly organized, honest department will achieve many of its aims, a confused, halting department will inevitably stumble over every obstacle.

Setting a Tone

Organizations are very different simply because of the climate and morale that attend them. The approach and competence of the chief executive officer set the mood and atmosphere of the agency. Imagine an organization driven by the CEO's belief that "yes" ought to be the answer to any suggestion that doesn't raise any solid objections. This would be an organization where ideas are adopted unless good reasons can be raised for rejecting them. Imagine a different scenario, where the leader's view is cautious and suggestions are generally rejected unless compelling reasons are raised for their adoption. Both are organizational models that exist in real life. Whichever approach seems better, it is undeniable that different climates are created by each, even though most police organizations are usually driven by identical outward constraints, such as organizational structure, mandate, manuals, and even types of personnel. The first type of organization might be full of excitement, innovations, experiments, confusion, and debate, whereas the other might be placid, unified, monolithic, stolid, and predictable. Each has its strengths and weaknesses.

Convinced that organizations thrive on the excitement of change, I ran the Minneapolis Police Department, for nine years, determinedly on the "yes" model. The sort of complaints that were generated centered on such comments as "confusion," "going in a hundred different directions," "the agency can't assimilate all the changes fast enough," "too open, freewheeling, and unstructured," and "short-circuiting the chain of command." Internally one rarely hears the positive side of either approach. People tend to respond to the irritants in any system they're working in, but there is no doubt that the "yes" model does require a tolerance of ambiguity.

Organizational messages are transmitted most eloquently through actions rather than through the most pious memos or fervent orders. Members check to see what gets done and how it is accomplished, and then they respond accordingly. Cops will translate organizational messages into situationally relevant symbols. They will adapt their behavior to conform with what's expected or permitted and will avoid what is rejected.

Every agency has its own set of rules, and these tend to be pretty standard. The only way workers have of differentiating between what is tolerated and what is forbidden is to watch how their colleagues act and how the administration responds. Usually the screw-up symbolizes the lowest level of accepted performance. The screw-up becomes the cynosure of all eyes as fellow workers watch to see how the organization reacts to his or her fecklessness. Separating the criminals, the unfit, the psychos, drunks, and thumpers from the ranks—they usually comprise no more than 1 or 2 percent of the force—is the clearest message an administrator can transmit about the kind of organizational climate the chief wants to create.

Policy and Practice

Virtually all agencies have written procedures calling for truth, beauty, and justice, yet the internal daily reality of agencies may be out of sync with these noble ideals. The mere existence of explicit rules doesn't ensure that they'll be followed, or enforced by the administration. Written guidelines may not even reflect the administration's true thinking. The employees tend to respond to the value system transmitted in the daily actions of the hierarchy rather than to written policy.

Brutality, corruption, and other dysfunctional acts are influenced by the climate within. If, after selectively hiring the most qualified candidates and training them comprehensively, a CEO's policies reflect favoritism, racism, or any other counterproductive "ism," these negative practices are going to surface on the street in various forms. A police department's first order of business is to get its internal house in order through the creation of an organizational climate that fosters integrity and effective performance.

How is this done?

A Whistle-Blower

Policies and practices that reflect a sound value system are needed. A case study will illustrate the point. The chief of the Washington, D.C., police received an anonymous letter alleging over a dozen specific wrongful acts in one of his units, as well as complaints directed against one of his commanders. It seemed clear that the writer had inside knowledge. The department's manual of procedure required officers to report wrongdoings, and it expressed a firm determination to uproot mal-, mis-, or nonfeasance, meaning criminal or noncriminal wrongdoing or failing to do what was required.

This letter, however, instead of being referred to the internal affairs unit for thorough investigation, was sent to the commander in question. He focused all of his energies on identifying the writer, taking few pains to conceal his anger at the temerity of the accuser. He finally succeeded and discovered that the writer was the wife of one of his detectives. The inquiry now bore in on the husband, as he was within the commander's grasp and the wife was not. The harassment continued, by supervisors and cowed peers, even as evidence appeared that the husband hadn't even known about the letter and that its contents had not even been based primarily on information he had furnished. His wife had been an avid listener to the banter of his compatriots and fancied herself something of a writer. To compound the difficulty, she was a buff (someone fascinated by police work and drawn to its practitioners).

The letter was dotted with specifics, relating to cops conducting personal business during office hours, deliberate misclassification of arrests to secure greater credit for crime clearances, possible favoritism in assignments, and other charges relating to wrongdoing in the unit and the commander's tolerance of it.

The husband was ultimately driven from the agency, following a series of harassments, transfers, and official and collegial acts that wound up sending him to the hospital with chest pains. This is a classic example of the immense pressure that can be generated in a hermetically sealed society ruled by immutable codes of silence and behavior. The full force of the agency, formal and informal, is brought to bear on the "snitcher," regardless of orders outlined in the written policy.

The handling of this case illustrates the power of unwritten organizational messages. The chief's decision to send the letter to the accused commander very clearly revealed his attitude toward whistle-blowers. When he later accepted without question a totally self-serving, self-exculpating, superficial, and even outraged, report on the items cited in the letter, from the very commander accused of the wrongdoing and his key subordinate in the matter, he demonstrated the agency's attitude more forcefully than any speech or order could have done. The troops watch in fascination and fear and absorb the inherent message.

It was one of many curious anomalies in this case that the officer ultimately driven to quit was recommended for discipline and was duly informed, but he was never notified that the one sensible supervisor involved in that tangled web recommended that he not be punished for exercising what in essence was the fundamental constitutional right of free speech—exercised, in this case, not by him but by his wife.

The record of the case, as revealed in the lawsuit that followed, demonstrates the organization's priorities. The specifics of the letter aroused little interest beyond an airy dismissal of the accusations. Some clearly perceptible umbrage surfaced at their having been raised at all. It appeared that the bosses were very interested in communicating to the writer of the letter, and all other cops watching, what would happen to those who dared point out errors. Notwithstanding the existence of all the right messages in the department's arsenal of orders, the real priorities in this case were conveyed in the actions initiated and encouraged by the very supervisors accused of wrongdoing.

The resolution of the case simply extended the illustration. The cop's marriage disintegrated, but his lawsuit prevailed as the city made a whopping settlement, choosing to avoid the exposure and risk of a trial. The key commander was elevated to police chief in the summer of 1989, and the policies exemplified in the case received the reward that citizens had come to expect from a city administration wrapped in scandals.

How an organization responds to criticism becomes an important index to its approach. Is it self-protective or open-minded? A good litmus test is its relations with the press. A chief who believes in the public's right to know, and who sees the press as the essential conduit for disseminating information, will run an agency very differently from the more journeyman executive, who tends to be at war with the media. A healthy body should not only be receptive to examination but should even welcome random, independent audits, as well as opportunities to attack wrongdoing in the ranks. Yet, most cops—chiefs or officers on the beat—nurture an inbred suspicion of the press.

Organizational auditors will search in vain for directives calling for, or even remotely suggesting, the toleration of corruptive or brutal acts. Yet agencies exist where such responses are woven so deeply into the organizational fabric that they seem to suggest a conscious and deliberate policy of encouraging such abuses. This is why one must observe the organization's behavior, in addition to reading applicable written memos, orders, and reports.

The level of difficulty in reaching a chief reveals the openness and accessibility of an agency. If one can get to the chief without having to maneuver a gauntlet, and if the chief opens his own mail, receives calls, and ensures a responsive answer to every question raised, then subordinates must behave in kind. The organizational message is transmitted downward from the chief to the street cop. How, in such circumstances, would it fare for a commander if the chief were told by a citizen that she or he was unable to get through to the commander? The chief's response would not only be a message to the agency but would serve as a model for the behavior of all subordinates. A citizen with a valid point is far more likely to get something done in an open and responsive system than in a closed and defensive one.

Other Messages

Even the car a chief drives conveys a message. A big, heavy, impressive vehicle and chauffeur tell the troops that the chief is "getting his," in the form of perks, and the cops on the street are tempted to translate that into how they can "get theirs." They might wind up sleeping on duty, accepting freebies, or hustling. Such time-worn images of petty chiseling as the cop taking an apple off the fruit stand and sauntering off without paying are translated behaviors. If those at the top are getting unjustified benefits, those at the bottom will compensate. "Flashing the tin" was, for many years, the way New York cops got into movies free. Moving out of the city to distant suburbs, where they had no official authority, and the soaring flight of admission prices did more to reduce this practice than any passion for honesty. Even in Minneapolis, theater owners and sports executives regularly sent me passes, which I returned with lectures about the messages such actions conveyed. Boozing it up at the local gin mill "on the arm" proved the path to alcoholism for legions of cops. Very little has been said or written about a culture that turns cops into a corps of petty chiselers. This behavior colors the cop's view of the world, promoting cynicism and encouraging shortcuts and circumventions that automatically find their way into official actions.

Conversely, if the street cops get the shiny new cars and the high rankers get small, used, rented, functional vehicles, a totally different organizational message is transmitted. This will reflect a spare operation where the priority is centered on serving the people and giving the cops the tools they need to do it.

The ease with which even sensible executives can fall into the trap of using luxury vehicles was brought home to me when I saw a chief I respected driving a very fancy limousine. I asked about it, and he boasted that it had been confiscated from a drug dealer, so it wasn't costing the taxpayers a cent. Then I remembered the siren voices of my own associates, who'd tried to tempt me in precisely identical circumstances. I quickly declined the offer of a fancy confiscated car and asked them to have the narcotics unit use it in its operations. I thought no more about it until my friend drove by in his jazzy car.

Shaping the Recruit

The internal culture impinges importantly on new entrants. If brutality is condoned or corruption is widely practiced, the pressure on the recruit to go along is irresistible. Quickly, the entire body is infected by the virus. The culture shapes and controls the development of its workers. In order for the agency to be healthy, strong, and honest, the administration must create a culture in which the department's code of ethics is reinforced, through the daily actions of the top executive.

Personnel decisions are the most eloquent policy statements any police department can make. Disciplinary actions reflect reinforcement of the values at work. If a cop is punished for overzealousness, the troops will absorb the meaning. If discipline is inconsistent—in terms of failing to convey an unwaveringly clear view of what is right and what is wrong—cynicism will develop. Favoring friends and punishing enemies will destroy morale.

Every hiring and every firing strengthens or weakens the agency's value system. If the feckless are separated and the dedicated are hired, a definite view is expressed. If dismissal is used as a tool of control, to establish who the boss is and to silence critics, then the onlookers will get the message and tailor their responses accordingly.

Cops on the beat, dealing with a sociopath or a nasty drunk on the street at three o'clock in the morning, must know, for certain, exactly how the agency will react if they give in to their frustrations and "thump the asshole." Different departments respond very differently. At different times in their histories, the same agencies also respond differently. The cops can usually guess what the reaction at the top will be, yet within this potpourri of possibilities, we can bank on the existence of documents in all departments that require strict adherence to markedly similar codes of conduct. The orders are the same, yet the behavior is different. The variable is the organizational climate created by the actions and reactions of the administration in power as it deals with its problems every day.

Corruption

A store's door is tried and found open; officers loot the place. A cop is sent to guard a DOA, and cash and jewelry mysteriously disappear. A motorist is pulled over, and a large bill is attached to the license. Prisoners regularly complain that more money was taken from them at the time of arrest than was returned on release. All of these are emblematic of an organization that fosters corruption.

Brutality and corruption do not always coexist. Organizations that tolerate the beating of demonstrators or criminals—and state, in their internal investigations of charges of brutality, that the force used was measured, appropriate, and legal—may set their faces hard against corrupt acts. Tough law-and-order departments, for example, preach and practice aggressive tactics. The line between aggressiveness and brutality may be as thin as an extra blow. The key lies in the treatment of the case internally. How the chief responds will convey the message to the troops.

It is not too grand a statement to say that chiefs' control over their agencies is determined by how they respond to the 1 or 2 percent who test the outer perimeters of their tolerance on the issues of brutality and corruption.

Corruption, for example, is one of those peculiar human conditions that inevitably exist where aggressive controls for its exposure are absent. Unpopular, proactive, self-initiating integrity tests raise the hackles of the cops coming under random scrutiny, but such tactics—which may include the use of spies—are essential to maintaining a climate of integrity. Honesty, like nature, abhors a vacuum.

Most chiefs are products of their agencies. They've come up through the ranks. They've formed friends and acquired enemies. Yet, their actions must reflect blindness to these factors, as well as to sex, race, religion, or national origin, if they are to have honest, vigorous agencies. In an absolute dictatorship such as a police department, the character of the chief is the central determinant of the agency's health.

An instrument of justice cannot itself be unjustly constituted. If minorities and women are excluded, the organizational message is that the institution is racist and sexist. To police a society of diverse cultures and races, the police need to be understanding and sensitive to cultural variation. It is not a coincidence that most riots have begun as a result of an encounter between a white male cop and a minority teenaged male. The presence of minority members in uniform communicates an eloquent signal to the communities served by that department, as to its attitudes toward and concern about broad questions involving social justice.

Developing Personnel and Distributing the Risks

Every police agency has its pluses and minuses. Some assignments are sought, others are shunned. A hierarchy of status develops in which every assignment sends a different signal. One may connote favored status, another scorn. The internal integrity of the department requires that assignments be distributed evenhandedly and be perceived as fair. The inclusion of an appeal process, where the agency really listens and responds to complaints, is an essential safety valve, whether the final response is the one sought or not.

The organization should reflect a concern about the development and growth of its members. Such progress is made through formal instruction and the collection of varied work experience. This can be accomplished through extensive programs of classroom education and through a structured program of rotation assignments calculated to broaden the grasp of the worker. These policies need to be widely understood, which is why having them in writing makes so much sense, providing it is understood that consistency between word and deed is absolutely essential to the healthy functioning of the body.

Change is unsettling, and even such patently useful practices as a rotation scheme that changes the worker's assignment every several years is likely, in the short run, to be resented and resisted. The benefits usually become obvious long after the anguish of the change has been left behind. Too many cops, at all levels, spend most of their careers pigeon-holed, doing things they do well, without ever being forced to master the many other tasks of their profession. Chiefs need to learn that while their short-term interests may be accommodated by leaving an effective worker in a key job in place, that individual's interests and the long-term interests of the department are best served by suffering the inconvenience of making a change.

Rotation not only contributes enormously to the growth of middle managers—the lieutenants and captains who have so much to do with the agency's daily workings and who really represent its future—but also encourages fairness by distributing safety risks more equitably. Many agencies, for example, assign cops to dangerous areas for long periods, while their colleagues are sequestered in "country clubs" indefinitely. Over the course of the years, one may face thousands of dangerous situations while the other has had a career of relative safety (called "having your ass in a tub of butter for twenty years" by street cops). It can also be argued that personal growth and development require change, not monotony.

When union contracts allow the most senior members to choose the tours they want to work, the old, experienced hands wind up working the day shift, Monday to Friday, which is the time when they are least needed. The greenest rookies end up working the graveyard shift, when the most knowledge and experience are needed in order to cope with the serious problems that arise at night.

Agencies that aspire to more effective service must strike at such counterproductive privileges, which were adopted to ensure the ease and comfort of the senior cops. The union, by fighting for such perks, is essentially putting the comfort of its members above the public's safety.

The Effects of Waste and Inefficiency

The chief's toleration of waste and inefficiency not only affects the areas directly involved but creates a momentum and the encouragement of careless practices. Attacking these problems is obviously desirable, but in practice it almost certainly means making the lives of the workers less comfortable. Making people work harder, smarter, and faster sounds like an ethic everyone can embrace, but the specifics of such objectives usually involve discomfort for the workers. This leads to the dissatisfaction of the workers and their allies: the unions, notably, and politicians and other supporters.

The incredible range of problems cited in reports following studies of large police departments like New York's or Philadelphia's illustrates the difficulties facing reformers. The problems are not mysterious, yet definitive action is wanting. Reforms engender tremendous resistance. Unfortunately, wasteful practices have their constituencies. Costly overtime policies enrich the ranks. One-person patrols mean splitting up close partners. Precinct consolidation is bound to anguish neighbors who treasure their local station house. Even the wearing of name tags raises alarms about reprisals as cops hide behind the claim that the people they arrest will take vengeance against them or their families, a palpably spurious claim. However straightforward and desirable a reform may be, the experienced police executive must anticipate a battle to implement it. Organizations must be wrenched from their habitual comforts in order to put an end to wasteful and inefficient practices.

A Case Study of Philadelphia

Shaken by the horrifying results of a bombing and a shoot-out with MOVE, an obscure urban cult whose name implies a return to Africa, the mayor of Philadelphia appointed a reform commissioner in 1985 to revamp the city's police.

The MOVE group had created, in their communal home, an anarchical situation that threw the neighborhood into turmoil. Loudspeakers blared noisily and incessantly. Unsightly sanitary conditions attracted rats and alarmed surrounding residents. Clashes with the police produced such tragedies as the shooting death of a cop. The terror and confusion continued, month after month. City officials were deluged with demands for action.

Finally, a police department accustomed to autonomous, unmonitored actions attacked and bombed the house, creating an inferno that destroyed an entire city block. A furious gun battle took a score of lives, including some of the children of MOVE members. Despite the danger posed by the group, the police overreaction created a dramatic shift of public attention, from the irritations produced by MOVE to the actions of the Philadelphia Police Department.

The new police chief convened a task force to study the agency on May 5, 1986. It consisted of prominent, respected figures in the city's public life, including lawyers, scholars, prosecutors, criminologists, and other experts.

The task force's report provided a revealing glimpse of what an investigative group would find in a large urban police agency that hadn't been subjected to tough scrutiny or reform. The report illustrates the enormous difficulties confronting reformers. It also demonstrates the depth, extent, and intractability of the largely invisible, but frequently felt, problems facing many large police agencies in America today.

The task force found an agency in trouble, in terms of management, personnel, equipment, physical plant, training, and various other critical areas. Perhaps in order to blunt the effects of harsh criticism on an already demoralized force, the report blamed these serious shortcomings on a public that hadn't insisted on police accountability. The agency's managers were faulted for fostering a history of favoritism, brutality, and corruption. The organization sounded painfully like Brand X, yet it is clear that Philadelphia's department was not dramatically better or worse than most other police departments. Without scrutiny, review, and accountability, these secretive agencies tend to go their own way and do their own thing. Despite its gentle, generous approach, the task force was horrified by what it found.

The report's introduction paints a bleak picture of a citizenry fed up with and resigned to poor service. The police agency revealed a pathetically small, eager cadre of professionals within the ranks, anxious to nurture what seemed to be a forlorn hope for better days and a desperate need for sweeping changes. The majority were content to get along as they always had.

A number of deficiencies were discovered, such as the failure to hold commanders accountable; the absence of any history of reform by the agency's key figures; fragmented neighborhood political power, which resulted in confused messages to the police about what level and kind of police services the area needed; interference by the union; and the absence of outside review. Not having a system of reporting to the public allowed the agency to lose sight of its objectives. Such devices as annual reports and strategic planning would have forced a focus of attention on what the agency should have been doing and where it ought to have been going.

The task force found the usual flight to the suburbs, population decline, growth of the underclass, and a centralizing of problems within the city. There was a need to establish a mission for the city government and its police. For the city, the task force suggested economic revitalization (service industries), restoring civility between citizens who had forgotten the importance of common courtesies on the street, maintaining a climate of tolerance in the community, and addressing the problems of poor neighborhoods. The task force understood the importance of manners and sensitivity in citizen exchanges, as well as the awful problems of the poor.

The report concluded that the Philadelphia police mistakenly saw their mission as protecting society at whatever cost. Because this mission implied the use of questionable tactics, cops sensed that the public would prefer not to know how order was maintained. Secretiveness and autonomy were the natural results, and the MOVE fiasco was the inevitable consequence of such an approach.

This view of themselves, as "crime fighters" exclusively, got in the way of the many service functions the police perform, which usually elicit the most public sympathy and support. A new strategy for the police would have to encompass a partnership with the citizens and emphasize community-oriented police approaches to their tasks.

Cops needed to be on the street, among the people. Reliance on special units had to be diminished. Instead of creating elite cadres to softsoap the people, the report called for the use of generalists and the elevation of the levels of service from the lowest patrol ranks. Historically, every time a problem arose, the police department had created a unit of specialists to cope with it. This had the effect of inviting the general force to ignore the difficulty because it was now the province of the specialists. As the experts dealt with the crisis or, as seems more likely, the nature of the problem shifted, the organization failed to adjust. New units were created to cope with the new problems, and the organizational barnacles accrued.

The organization had to be decentralized and had to recruit quality local people. It needed better facilities and better managers. It needed everything but money. It suffered from all the disabilities of poor leadership listed elsewhere in this book.

The task force noted that the problems of allocating personnel had shown up in reference to areas and shifts. Cops had not been apportioned on the basis of neighborhood's real needs but had been distributed according to formulas that accommodated the comfort and ease of the employees. This is typical of organizations that evolve into self-serving operations. Cops needed to interact with citizens, on the street, at busier times. A statement from the chief to the troops, reflecting a reorientation toward providing citizens with needed services rather than only concentrating on fighting crime, was needed. For example, the report called for the return of the foot cop to promote closer citizen contact, especially downtown. These findings flowed right into the mainstream of the community-oriented policing programs that were rapidly gaining ground among police scholars. Predictably, by failing to identify its basic objectives, the agency had gone astray.

The task force also cited the absence of any reevaluation of units that had been created *ad hoc* to solve some temporary problem, but that had never been dismantled. Such an absence reflected a loss of focus on the basic objectives of policing. Many other examples of police inefficiency were discovered by the task force. More expensive and more highly trained cops were being used for clerical and administrative jobs that could have been done by less costly civilians. The absence of prioritizing and screening calls to 911 forced the agency to respond to everything, and quickly, without distinctions concerning importance. All of these practices had resulted in inferior police service.

Programs relating to officer stress, physical fitness, or drug addiction were either inadequate or nonexistent. Equipment, the physical plant, and related facilities were found to be neglected, obsolete, lacking, or unusable. The department needed better qualified personnel, at all levels; new cars, computers, and better radios; and all manner of equipment and modern buildings and related facilities, such as training sites, firing ranges, and support systems.

Citizens had lavished money on their police force but had got a poor return on their investment. Too much had been spent on personnel and too little on equipment and management. Organizationally, management style had developed to reflect the wishes of the central authority. Initiative and individual development of talent had suffered. The department was probably still feeling the aftereffects of the long period of Frank Rizzo's control, both as police commissioner and as mayor. The task force's findings, without ever saying so, clearly reflected the effects of Rizzo's many years of ruling the agency.

The task force also found a need for better selection, training, evaluation, and promotion procedures. The absence of even a high school diploma, or its equivalent, as a prerequisite for employment, as well as a too-brief probationary period of six months, served as impediments to attracting and keeping the better candidates.

A curious reflection on the tension between serving the people more effectively and providing for the comfort and convenience of the cops was included in the report. The task force called for establishing and communicating a philosophy of policing that put its first emphasis on protecting and serving the citizens within the confines of the law.

Although not intended as one of the task force's concerns, corruption within the agency was compelling enough to force the group's attention to an examination of the issue. They called for the development and communication of a set of ethical standards for supervisory responsibility in order to monitor the corruption problem and to allow for the provision of resources to attack it. It would not be enough to leave corruption problems to the internal affairs division alone. The code of silence had to be broken. The guidelines would, of course, have to be followed by tough, determined action.

Brutality, the other major problem of urban police departments, also came to the study group's attention through scandalous disclosures and incidents. They called for control of the use of force and firearms. There needed to be greater accountability to the public, through the chief, and better training of all personnel. To promote better treatment of the poor and minorities, the task force suggested recruiting minorities.

Police tradition and habit, along with the self-perpetuating errors and abuses that had accrued over years of mismanagement, had combined with union and civil service pressures to promote hostility and resistance to reform.

The tone of the report can be characterized as affectionate, hopeful, and supportive, even as it attacked the awful reality of the brutal and corrupt operations, the mismanagement, the archaic practices, the poor personnel, the substandard equipment, and the rundown physical plant of the Philadelphia Police Department. The hopes and good faith of the group are evident throughout the report, as they struggled to identify glimmers of light in the darkness. It is clear that they wanted to function as positive reformers. In the end, they centered their hopes on the new reform chief, who'd made such impressive initial strides but who departed soon after the report came out to accept a lucrative job in private industry. As an outsider who hadn't been tainted by the MOVE fiasco, nor by identification with the *ancien régime,* he'd been able to attack the problems free of any constraints from the past. He was succeeded by an up-from-the-ranks insider. It seemed a case of a chastened mayor, reaching desperately for reform, initially, following the MOVE tragedy, and then lapsing into business as usual with the second appointment.

This brief overview of the police, by a knowledgeable group, clearly shows the problems facing America's police executives as they try to turn these agencies into instruments of service. The public's indifference and ignorance play into the hands of the enemies of reform. Lack of interest creates a political vacuum that is usually filled by those seeking to promote private gain over the public good.

The report demonstrates the need for knowledge, examination, and reform. To assume complacently that the lessons apply only to Philadelphia is to miss the larger point of the current crisis in urban policing. No police chief would, or should, have been amazed by the appalling disclosures offered by this study. Recent analyses of the New York Police Department, by a State Senate Committee and by another body commissioned by the mayor, uncovered similarly serious problems. Miami, Boston, and Washington, D.C., have also been rocked by disclosures of wrongdoing and mismanagement.

Americans invest billions in their internal system of protection and emergency service without demanding much of an accounting. A heavy price—in dollars and lives—is exacted for such neglect. It should not take urban cataclysms to spark examination and reform.

Every reform gores someone's ox. Those hurt are known, visible, and angry. Those who stand to benefit face a potential, not-yet-felt benefit. The people rarely have lobbyists pressing for the general good. The need for voters to be a lot more choosy about their elected officials ought to be self-evident.

Even unpopular reforms and unwanted changes will gain the grudging respect of the workers in the long run. They will be able to see, very plainly, what has been accomplished and will have little trouble figuring out the motive. They will grumble and bitch and moan, but their actions will reflect pride in an agency whose workings they can respect.

Tightly closed and isolated organizations, like police departments, are like cultural hothouses in which the prevailing climate produces more intense effects than might occur in more open operations. Most organizations are penetrated or bombarded by outside influences, which work against the development of the exotic factors that reinforce and intensify organizational myths and rituals. The police world resists such penetration very successfully. The result is that the pressure on the entrants to conform to a twisted value system is pervasive and incredibly intense.

Responsiveness

Rumors and conjectures are the hallmarks of secretive or confused operations. An open system provides information freely. It is clear that most arguments for secrecy are really attempts at self-protection or self-aggrandizement. Very few secrets are really needed, and even in these special cases, the necessity for maintaining them is rarely prolonged. Articulable grounds should be required for every organizational secret.

We all fancy ourselves effective communicators, yet the process is terribly difficult. We all know what we think and mean, but misunderstandings nevertheless abound. The need for simplicity and clarity is not always perceived. Either police executives, as a class, must develop into clear, effective speakers and writers, or they will be misunderstood, and their agency will consequently work under many misapprehensions. Police executives must also work on developing effective listening skills. Of course, if their thinking is clouded or their priorities are confused, their talks and writings will mirror these conditions.

As mentioned earlier, an internally just system will not allow petty tyranny to exist. Supervisors have to be perceived as wielding power justly, and as being held accountable for its use. The expression of personal pique or of tempting vendettas in disciplinary actions undermines an honest administration.

A precinct commander in the Bronx lost his post and ruined his career when he disciplined two officers for what turned out to be personal reasons that had nothing to do with their performance. The cops had immediate access to my office. Their complaints were investigated. The inquiry turned up a classic example of petty tyranny. The discipline was rescinded and the captain was immediately removed from command. He enlisted the aid of a local politician, a state senator, in an attempt to secure an injunction barring his transfer. A steamy Bronx courtroom became the arena. The judge, an obvious ally of the state senator pressing the suit, gave me a very hard time on the stand. In the end, he was not able to circumvent the law, and the decision stood. The captain left the department and the cops got on with their lives. The case illustrates the struggle that is often necessary to uphold honesty, but the final effect on officer morale is more than worth it.

Morale

Little needs to be done to promote the officers' morale. The spirit of a group is more importantly affected by the group's objective situation than by the ministrations of the most devoted entertainers. People know whether they're working in an honest organization and whether the chief is a cheap politician or a determined public servant, and this knowledge will decide morale more conclusively than any palliative or program intended to lift workers' spirits. Workers can see through transparent efforts to cajole them easily. They can also, when tasting the fruits of victory following the sweaty, painful ordeals that such wins always seem to require, appreciate that morale flows from successful operations, solved cases, and other products of hard, effective effort.

The police are workers like any others. They respond to effective leadership and honest policies. The quality of their service is importantly influenced by factors within the agency that the public doesn't readily see, but that they can certainly affect. The isolation of the department makes penetration difficult, but penetration is still possible as well as essential.

It cannot be overstated that the most important factor in determining the organizational climate is the character of the chief. An honestly run agency will serve the people better and make the workers happier.

The police are the protectors of our safety and the preservers of our rights and property. If this salt shall lose its flavor, wherewith will it be savored?

CHAPTER 5

Cops

It would be hard to imagine a job more written about, and less understood, than that of a cop. The cop's world has been combed over by novelists, playwrights, screenwriters, television producers, and the inquisitive press, yet the practitioner and close observer knows that the world occupied by America's cops remains *terra incognita*.

There are many good reasons for this continuous isolation of the police. Cops resist intrusion in various ways. They reveal what they must, when they must, and slip and slide or simply stonewall the public and the press the rest of the time. Those who study the police are put off by the long stretches of boredom that constitute such a large chunk of what is called *police work*. As the repositories of society's secrets and the wielders of power, cops have an understandable jealousy about protecting their turf. The probing media are usually resisted, often subtly, and are seen as the enemy. Cops are expert feigners of cooperation, while in reality they do their best to deflect probes.

The depicters and moviemakers tend to focus their representations on the juicier public-relations aspect of the job. Many cops wind up laughing up their sleeves at the ersatz images their manipulations manage to produce on the screen. Cops understand that the reality of their daily work is guided by complex and sometimes conflicting explicit and implicit messages that are more confusing than photogenic. What they see on the screen—an image they are happy to promote—is the heroism and terror that form an infinitesimal part of their lives. Still, they are flattered and pleased by the simplistic heroic visions being communicated to the public they serve. Cops use a coarse expression for this technique of evasion, which reveals their cynicism and hardheadedness; they call this "pissing in their pocket and telling them it's raining." Cops can manage to get a lot of folks to look up at the clouds, as they spin their webs with insouciant looks.

Some cops, though, adopt the media's image and act out the impulses of such avenging angels as Clint Eastwood's "Dirty Harry" or Charles Bronson's character in *Death Wish*. The simplistic, idealistic view offered by these dispensers of perfect justice proves irresistibly tempting to some cops. The results are very often tragic, either for the cops or for their targets. Controlling these would-be heros may very possibly be a chief's greatest challenge. Turning Rambos into servants, rather than masters, of the law is a trickier business than might be expected. The theory that "we're the good guys, they're the bad guys, and anything we can do to get them has to be okay" dies hard.

Stability and Homogeneity

Police agencies are peopled, overwhelmingly, by cops, even in inside or clerical jobs that might be handled by civilians instead. Civilianization became, in the 1960s, one of the main issues surrounding debates on police reform. It was perfectly obvious that many tasks in the police department could be handled by lesser paid civilians rather than cops. But this meant risking the admission of outsiders into the cops' exclusive club. After over twenty years of backing and filling about "going civilian" or abandoning that program, most police agencies remain predominantly staffed by cops. This domination by long-term insiders strengthens the isolation.

Cops usually spend about a quarter of a century at their jobs. It is a remarkably stable occupation. They come to stay. This makes the screening of applicants critical. For most of the entrants, being a cop is the focus of career aspirations. It will probably be the best job they've ever had or could ever get. Losing it makes other employment difficult and almost always leads to a real decline in earning power and status. Most cops come from economic levels that limit the choices available very strictly. They usually lack the skills or education that would make them marketable.

The police ladder, from rookie to chief, is almost invariably made up of cops at different stages in their careers. This ladder greatly strengthens the bond that holds them together. It promotes the isolation and insularity of the agency and tempts everyone to adopt an "us-against-the-world" view that can cause many problems in the agency's performance.

Change and reform, in such circumstances, do not come easily.

Cops are welded together by dangerous experiences and shared secrets that produce a strong bonding effect. Theirs is an institution that, despite being on permanent public display, has successfully resisted intrusion and study.

In addition to the various financial benefits, cops find certain lighthearted aspects of the job enjoyable. They get to work outdoors and are usually subject to minimal supervision.

Expectation and Reality

Entering cops are shocked by the contrast between their expectations of the job and the reality. They focus initially on fighting crime but soon discover that policing is mostly a service industry. About 80 percent of their work turns out to be responding to accidents, injuries, illnesses, and citizen emergencies that have nothing to do with crime. Before they decided to become cops, most people asked themselves whether they'd be tough enough, brave enough, strong enough, and hard enough for the job. They should have been asking themselves whether they liked helping people or not. Dealing with the fractious human beast on a daily, nonstop basis can be exasperating.

The importance of this disparity between reality and expectation suggests that employees may be entering the profession for the wrong reasons. Somehow, no one wants to publicize the unglamorous service dimension that is, far and away, the major part of the police job, maybe because it makes cops look too much like nurses or social workers and too little like the macho characters found in the fiery imaginations of youth. The recruitment mystique sets the rookie up for a shocking discovery: Policing isn't much like what they've seen on television. Even though many of the recruits have links to the department through fathers, brothers, or relatives "in the job," they are mostly useful as encouragers and general prodders, rather than as divulgers of the profession's secrets. The rationale for not explaining the job clearly to rookies is that they'd never believe it anyway, so it's best to get them in and let them gradually find out what it's all about. It is one of the curiosities of the profession that cops always grouse about the job and counsel casual acquaintances against taking it, but they invariably encourage their relatives and loved ones to enter the department.

In most cities, recruits come from a blue-collar or civil-service family of workers who haven't quite made it into the middle class. They come from homes where the topic of college is rarely, if ever, brought up. The job becomes a path to middle-class security and respectability. The recruitment pool tends to represent a very specific slice of the socioeconomic-class pie.

Weeding Out the Unfit

The usual gauntlet begins with filling out an application, taking a written test, and submitting to a medical examination. Then entering recruits must take a qualifying physical test of strength, coordination, agility, and mobility. All of these tests must be job-relevant because, in the past, they have served as artificial barriers to the entrance of women into the force. When the police had to prove that their daunting tests were really related to the everyday activities of cops on the street, they discovered that they couldn't. It was especially difficult to prove when so many beer-drinking cops lapsed into appalling physical shape soon after successfully entering and still managed to perform acceptably. However, there is ample room for legitimate doubt on this score. It is hard to believe that many of these out-of-shape hefties could rush up flights of stairs or chase fleeing felons. Because the departments didn't appear to be ready to fire their physical misfits, they were left with no argument for excluding women, however passionately they may have wanted to. In the end even the title *policeman* had to give way to the androgynous *police officer*.

The really critical winnower, though, is the long and thorough background investigation. This inquiry typically results in a half-inch dossier of employment, school, military, and personal history. It is here that the agency really relies on weeding out the unfit, through discovery of behavior patterns in school, work, or personal life that presage failure in a job that requires optimal performance and superior personal characteristics. There is often a multiple-choice psychological screening test, although no one really expects these tests to identify the psychopaths. At best, they've proved occasionally useful ancillaries to the background check.

Some agencies use lie detectors, which actually measure reactive and physiological changes induced by our having been conditioned to tell the truth, thereby producing involuntary nervous reactions when we lie. The devices really measure such physiological changes as increased sweating, a quickening heartbeat, or an involuntary reaction of the nerves. Tying these to truths and lies is another matter altogether. The pattern of the questions is critical to measuring reactions to the known, and expert operators are essential to any hope of success. Even under the best of circumstances, these devices are not infallible. In fact, some consider them about as useful as witchcraft. The results of these tests have never been considered reliable enough to be admitted into a court of law as evidence.

A practice that has been gaining wider appeal recently is the use of drug testing. These tests have proved effective in weeding out drug-addicted candidates and even in discouraging many addicts from applying. Traces of marijuana can show up in urine samples as late as three weeks after use. Other illegal drugs vary in their duration in the system, but they all leave traces for at least a few days following the drug's use.

A wrong assumption made about the police is that they're not very adept at weeding out the palpably unfit at the entrance level. On the contrary, the thoroughness of the background investigation nearly guarantees that new recruits will be qualified for the job. The background investigators (other cops trained for that purpose) find out an enormous amount of information about a candidate's life. Those later found to be unfit are usually exposed because of a predilection for brutality. They tend to be veterans, shaped by the agency rather than by their genes or preentrance proclivities. Most of the brutes I encountered, in three police agencies, were probably formed and subtly encouraged by the agency's culture. The background check tends to exclude the feckless, the irresponsible, and those with poor or unstable school, work, or military records. So here we can see a clear illustration of the difference between people's illusion about the importance of identifying the psychologically unfit, on entrance, and the reality that the organization shapes these people, and all of its other members, into what they ultimately become.

In recent years, a great deal of energy has been spent on demands to screen out the potential brutes before they enter the police department. But this reasoning fatally ignores the shaping nature of the institution itself. The brutes have not slipped through the agency's filter. Rather, they've been shaped by the organization's culture. The usual scenario goes something like this.

An act of brutality occurs, an investigation is launched, and the accused cop turns out to be some type of sadist. Predictably, demands for psychological screenings are made to identify others who may be potentially unfit for service. The odds are great that the officer was acculturated and shaped by the organization's own pressures and policies. An organization that condones, or subtly encourages, brutal measures will take normal employees and strengthen their aggressive instincts to the point where someone eventually goes over the line. Some may have had proclivities in that direction, in the way of aggressive youngsters recruited into any activity, but these tendencies could easily have been channeled into productive and positive pursuits by a more salubrious organizational climate.

Meat Eaters and Grass Eaters

The thumpers and thieves (the sadists and the thieving cops who practice ham-fisted methods or who would "take a hot stove") imitate the on-screen images they find so appealing. They are often tough, brave, and assertive cops. Yet they can also be sadistic leaders who set a tone that virtually coerces the timid majority into going along with them. Nobody wants to be called a wimp when the fur starts to fly. The organizational climate of a particular department is decided by how effectively the chief meets this challenge. His would not be the first department taken over by these kinds of tough characters. During the New York Police Department's Knapp Commission investigation in 1972, the distinction between these leaders and the rest of the herd was conveyed in references to "meat eaters" and "grass eaters."

Acculturation

If the organization blinks at chargers of brutality and routinely exonerates accused cops, the rank and file will perceive this unwritten message and tailor their actions accordingly. In such a climate, even the reluctant recruit is carried along by the terrific pressures to conform to the expectations and actions of his or her peers. Although rarely comprising more than 1 or 2 percent of the force, the "meat eaters" can dictate prevailing attitudes, unless the chief moves quickly to keep them on a short leash. This is not easy.

Cops want the support of their commanders and their chief, and they are not forgiving if they don't get it in all circumstances. Right or wrong, they want the support of their bosses. This is, of course, unreasonable, but clubs tend to be clubby, and clubbiness breeds the sort of camaraderie that engenders the expectation of shared experience and overlooked misdeeds. The union becomes the instrument for the application of pressure on the chief to be a "regular guy," which really means joining the conspiracy of silence and secrecy about how cops really dispense justice.

Surprisingly, pressure is often exerted to encourage the violence found in the more aggressive cops. Our societal belief in avenging angels and the pure justice they dispense dies hard. Shrill calls for law and order, to "clean up the mess" or to adopt "no-nonsense measures," are little more than thinly veiled invitations for the police to do whatever is needed to get the job done, without too much regard for constitutional limits. The drug hysteria, with the attendant shrieks for tough actions like roundups and sweeps, illustrates the point clearly. The police unions, eager to protect their members, often work to thwart the disciplinary process used to curb the excesses of police wrongdoers. The scared public can frequently be convinced by demagogues to sacrifice law in exchange for safety. Such trade-offs almost invariably ensure that they'll wind up with neither.

So entering cops are, in a sense, admitted into a secret society where a code of loyalty, silence, secretiveness, and isolation reigns. They work around the clock and begin to socialize mostly with other cops, usually members of their own squad, thereby promoting even greater parochialism. Cops themselves reinforce organizational myths and rituals. They talk about good "stand-up" cops who don't turn in their buddies, about "assholes" and civilians and how to deal with them. There is a prescription for every situation.

Cops either possess or develop, as a result of role assignment (a not-to-be-underrated force), the courage to risk physical harm. They learn how to cope with moments of sheer terror that create urges in the rest of us to flee for our lives. Cops are physically brave and live with the absolute certainty that this is the prime value of their existence. *Coward* is such a powerful epithet that, even in a profession accustomed to the rawest language, it is a word that is used very sparingly.

On the other hand, cops seem to have no appreciation of the value of moral courage, if they are, indeed, even aware of its existence. Policing is not a profession that cherishes the iconoclast. It values conformity. Very rarely will a cop stand up and voice disagreement with colleagues on questions of police mythology. Assertions of commonly accepted truths—that the chief is a psycho or that the job sucks and that morale has never been lower and that they're all going to hell in a handbasket—are simply not challenged. Cops accept the myths circulating around them because resistance carries a risk of ostracism.

One of the theories that police work supports is that courage comes in many different forms, and that it is wise to think about what types matter the most in which circumstances. Bravery and cowardice, the *mater* and *magister* of police lore, do not succumb easily to compartmentalization. The cop who'll charge a murderous, knife-wielding brute wouldn't dream of contradicting another cop who asserts a commonly held opinion in a public setting. The citizen who throws herself across the gate of a munitions plant and goes to jail would be terrified at the prospect of a bar brawl. The person stoically facing certain death from some dread disease might blanch at either prospect. Courage has many dimensions, yet it is generally considered a single quality.

If cops are to develop the moral courage it takes to cleanse their agencies of corruption and brutality, they are going to have to learn that courage takes many forms, and that the type needed for such reforms is different from the street heroism they value so dearly.

Training recruits in the importance of moral courage, such as is so piously and consistently included in the widely ignored code of ethics that every police agency adopts as its credo, is as important as teaching the recruit to cope with street dangers, yet police training usually neglects this critical aspect. In fact, it might be held that the opposite message is being transmitted, that the thing to be is a "stand-up guy." The similarities of the value systems of the police culture and the underworld can be striking.

The cop's isolation begins early. Entering recruits, fresh and eager, approach the field with all the enthusiasm of breathless acolytes. They have come to serve humankind. They see themselves earning plenty of psychic income. The rookies are suffused with altruism and expectations of appreciation. The thrill of discovery is accompanied by an intense need to share new experiences. One's friends and relatives are the natural audience. Newly initiated recruits long to discuss the wonderful secrets they are now privy to. Cynical older cops look on with knowing glances and say nothing. The probationers will learn soon enough.

Rookies

Recruits are hired and soon discover that their role is to control fractious and rebellious souls who resent their very presence. Rather than appreciation, young cops encounter hostility and resistance. The need to preserve order and their own authority dominates every aspect of the job. Others are watching. It's a damnably difficult, slippery business, and rookies don't receive a lot of preparation, in terms of formal education or training. They see many of their colleagues escape into the "refuge" of the fire department, where the challenges are merely raging infernos. The appeal centers on the fact that firefighters have to deal only with objects (fires), whereas cops have to cope with troublesome people.

Chastened by the discovery that their ministrations are not welcome, and finding themselves challenged at every turn just to maintain control, young cops make another disappointing discovery. Nobody understands them. Not their friends nor their loved ones. Certainly not any outsiders, who laugh in all the wrong places, offer sympathy where condemnation is clearly demanded, and tend to look askance at what are demonstrably necessary measures to get the job done.

Cops are never told to be silent or to keep the agency's secrets. They never see an order upholding the code of silence that guides their working lives. There is no need to be explicit. The reactions, body language, whispered asides, and other rites of initiation convey what is expected. The reactions of those normally confided in reinforce the notion that the cop will be understood only within the ranks. One of the curious fallouts of this reality is that cops will not seek counsel from any outsiders. Every successful counseling program for the police is run only by cop counselors. Given the tensions of the job and the predilection toward alcoholism and other dysfunctional forms of escape, the need for these programs is obvious.

The tragedy is that society reinforces this seclusion and secrecy. Recruits have been entrusted with a secret, unmentionable mission in addition to explicit ones: They must keep the underclass under control, and society doesn't care to receive progress reports. Society is concerned with how well the police are performing when it is directly affected. It's the methods that society would rather not know about.

A disturbing discovery for recruits is that they need to deaden their feelings in order to perform the job well. Such an approach is essential if they are to deal with the broken bodies of children, handle smelly DOAs, and wallow in puke, gore, urine, brains, and offal with any degree of effectiveness. The trouble is that feelings cannot be turned on and off like tap water. Shutting them off means distancing oneself from all emotions, both good and bad, private and public.

Conservatism accompanies the cop's development because conserving the mandated status quo is a cop's first duty. One day cops must arrest abortionists, and the next they are ordered to protect them and to arrest those who interfere with abortions. The same holds true for flag burners. The cop's role is to conserve, not to question. The adoption of a questioning or philosophical view might well get in the way of effective functioning. Yet the value of independent reasoning cannot be overstated, especially in a democracy. The cop has to be ready to shift and act, not to reflect or question. The dilemma is extended by the horrors produced in this century by people who just followed orders. But cops must enforce the law. Until their conscience is egregiously offended, and they are forced to quit, their only feasible alternative is to do what they're told.

The sense of "us and them" that develops between cops and the outside world helps to forge a bond between cops whose strength is fabled. It is called the *brotherhood in blue,* and it inspires a fierce and unquestioning loyalty to all cops, everywhere. It is widened by the dependence they have on each other for safety and backup. The response to a summons for help is the cop's life line. An "assist police officer" call is every cop's first priority. The ultimate betrayal is for one cop to fail to back up another. This is another method of pressuring conformity, as this support is withheld from the few organizational pariahs.

I was reminded of this recently when I drove to pick up some food while vacationing in downtown Miami. A white cop, standing on the sidewalk, was surrounded by six white guys, and there seemed to be some sort of a confrontation going on. The cop's body was stiff with tension.

I watched the scene carefully, from about fifteen feet away, planning my action. I'd have to let the cop know I was on his side when I intervened. The whole scenario played over in my head. There was never a doubt that I would get involved, although I knew nothing about the controversy taking place. Somehow, the event, whatever it was, dissipated, and they all left the scene. At sixty, I was relieved to have been spared the need to jump in, but my training and instincts allowed for only one possibility. I would help the cop in just the way I'd expect to be helped by any other passing cop in a similar situation.

The world of the police, shaped by isolation and dependence on each other for safety, might be likened to a latter-day Atlantis because of the mystery in which police operations are shrouded and the public's ignorance about the internal realities of the police world.

Cops develop codes of behavior that might strike observers as extreme or even simpleminded. But they have strong roots in a cynical view of the human animal and in the certain knowledge that they're on the side of the angels. Their value system treasures toughness and a rough, unspoken appreciation of platonic love. Any cop's wife can attest to the depth of feeling that develops between partners. We will see, later, how this factor complicates the issue of women entering the ranks.

Evidence of the extent of police insularity can be found in such simple exchanges as occur between two New York cops who establish that they're in the same organization through a series of oblique, coded questions. These messages will be understood only by other members. "Are you in the job?" is a common question. It seems to suggest that no other possible employment could be contemplated. And the answer can't be "the seventy-sixth precinct" but has to be "the seven six." Like most other secret societies, the cops have developed their own argot.

The upper echelons of the police world are no more welcoming of public interference than the hardening young entrants. They don't want their actions to be probed too carefully. The police do make mistakes but feel that they can't afford to admit them. The stakes are too high. There are criminal and civil liabilities to consider. Cops, who depend on contrition and confessions from suspects, share a repugnance for admissions of guilt. Although they are contemptuous of such purgings, they are quick to recognize and exploit their value when dealing with suspects. The public is not terribly understanding of errors, although the possibility that they might be more tolerant than most chiefs expect seems at least plausible.

Cops are acculturated through actions and lore. They'll be told, by the senior cops who initiate them into the profession's rituals, that if questioned about the source of their wetness, the appropriate response is to deny it's raining. There is a common belief that even obvious facts can be beaten back by determined, hard-faced denials. Cops have seen too many repent of their soul-cleansing admissions of guilt in the dock to have any illusions about which is the better way, in the long run. They'll go to some lengths to avoid the same errors, even while continuing to cajole damaging statements from their targets. They've seen contrite murderers ease their minds with soul-clearing confessions, only to repudiate and challenge them weeks or months later during the trial. Cops exploit the criminal's instinct to unburden himself or herself at the emotional moment of arrest, but they also learn the lesson that such an outburst is almost invariably regretted later on, when the loss of freedom becomes the principal concern. This lesson strongly reinforces the cops' code of silence.

Although there is a good deal of formal training offered by police departments, a surprising amount continues to take place through the process of initiation conducted by senior officers. The use of field-training officers (FTOs), senior cops who are seen as models worth emulating, as formal tutors of recruits simply invests the practice with the blessing of official sanction.

A great deal of the cynicism created in cops can be seen in the time-hallowed advice given to the rookie by the "hair bag" senior cop, whose first words are usually held to be "Forget all the bullshit they gave you at the police academy, kid; I'm gonna show you how things really work here on the street." The use of FTOs is a way of trying to turn this inevitable and invariable practice into a positive.

Additionally, there has been little movement toward higher educational standards for police officers. What little enthusiasm existed for it, as a step toward professionalization, was beaten back by the claim that higher requirements would exclude minorities. The result has been a continuing reliance on a high school diploma or its equivalent for a job that is tremendously powerful and complex. Unions, curiously, have fought the raising of educational standards because they are, institutionally, driven to protect the interests of their existing members, rather than of potential ones.

One reason for the lack of an advanced education in the police force can be traced to class differences. The job peculiarly belongs to the upper segment of the lower class, who generally don't send their children to college. Cops come from hard-working blue-collar families. In the offering of an attractive job that pays psychic as well as quite impressive real income, forces such as the police union, allied politicians, and other friends and protectors are marshaled to keep the prize under the control of the class that owns it.

The cop, then, not only has enormous power but is likely to lack the philosophical, ethical, cultural, and intellectual base needed for its wise employment. The cop is not alone, however, as the other participants in the system suffer from similar gaps in their training. In the cases of judges and prosecutors, for example, the problem centers on lack of street experience rather than lack of formal education. Judges and prosecutors are simply lawyers who have been trained for their trade. They've rarely been exposed to the ethical or philosophical challenges involved in untangling messy human problems on the scene, nor have they had much opportunity to develop the "street smarts" that characterize most veteran cops. The difference between education and experience is illustrated by the gallows humor of the police, who hold that a "conservative is a liberal judge who's been mugged."

The Conditioning Process

Most people contemplating a career as a cop naturally begin to question their toughness. This seems like a relevant question for a generation fed the police rubbish that flows from the tube. Yet nothing could be further from the truth. Who could possibly hold himself or herself equal to the ersatz heros of the silver screen?

The funny thing is that the question of toughness is really irrelevant. First of all, policing is not as dangerous a profession as is commonly supposed, and it's becoming less risky all the time in terms of the number of officers killed, notwithstanding the very serious violence surrounding the drug wars. The number of cops killed in the United States has steadily declined over the past sixteen years, from about 120 a year to about 70. As shootings by the police have been reduced through administrative controls and reviews, violence against the police has begun to decline dramatically as well. The belief that violence engenders violence does have some validity.

Second, enormous backup and support await a cop in trouble. Dangerous calls draw the response of hordes of cops. Especially risky operations are often left to specialists. Every tragedy is, of course, highly publicized, giving credence to the television depictions. The death of a cop is a tremendous civic tragedy, but it also provides a spectacle for exploitation by the union, politicians, police brass, and others. One of the really gripping photos of the 1988 presidential campaign was former NYPD Lieutenant Matt Byrne giving candidate George Bush his son's shield. Officer Ed Byrne had been gunned down in the drug war.

Once the decision has been made to become a cop, the next transformation to take place comes with role assignment. The badge and uniform confer not only the trappings of office, but the expectation of performance both within the cop and by the organization the cop has just joined. It is remarkable how humans adapt to role assignment. We tend to underestimate the psychological importance of this adaptation. Once I put on the badge and uniform, I was expected to run toward things I'd formerly run away from. This expectation, and the very strongly conveyed sense that anything less was simply unacceptable, creates a mind set that infuses cowards with courage. I suppose that, above all things, humans fear humiliation most. Appraisals of courage, in all things, permeate the police culture. One of the blind spots of such appraisals, though, is the stark and consistent emphasis on physical courage. A colleague used to call the vast majority of cops the "grass eaters," "tapioca" because they had no flavor of their own but merely reflected the prevailing view.

Training contributes to the shaping process. This takes place in the police academy and continues throughout a cop's career. Role models are everywhere, reinforcing and reiterating values. Older cops tutor their apprentices in how to assume control. Cops are taught to take charge in all situations. They take assaults on their authority very personally because they see their effectiveness rooted in the question of who's in charge. Thus we see a clash between expectations and reality as recruits begin to see that their preconceptions of "the job" were well off the mark. The process of adjustment begins. Cops have not been launched into knight errantry but have been recruited to control obstreperous human behavior and keep everyone in check.

At the other end of the organizational scale, we find the recruit grown older, and possibly evolving into the agency's next chief.

Chiefs

There is no way to enter the elite world of an executive cop except through the bottom rungs of the organization. No Ivy League graduates will be found in prominent police posts. No police colleges exist that will produce a corps of executives. Chiefs are, indeed, fifty-year-old cops who have climbed the corporate ladder successfully. If they are gifted, their experience may comprise only a few long-term assignments in key posts, which have deprived them of the well-rounded experience that their new position requires. Their education is frequently confined to the rote memorization required for promotional exams.

Although a bachelor's degree is becoming a more common requirement, cops often obtain a sort of general-equivalency degree from an institution that makes generous allowances for life and work experience. These colleges usually require that a majority of the courses be in police science. So even where an effort is made to broaden the executive through general education, the emphasis is placed on the vocational aspects rather than the liberal arts courses that are so desperately needed. Chiefs identify with recruits because they both came from the same roots. The chief's skills and outlook match those of the entrant. They are links in the same chain. The chief's skills have been developed for the climb and for the stations along the way, but ironically not for the summit.

As departmental chief executive officers, chiefs need a moral perspective to guide them through the countless decisions they will be asked to form. They need a vision about the types and numbers of personnel required. Should the agency emphasize a greater use of civilians? What about a rotation program? Should educational entrance requirements be raised? Are there too many supervisors? Have some of the upper echelon executives outlived their usefulness? What about recruiting blacks and women? Precinct consolidation? How should the chief handle the thumpers in the ranks? The disciplinary actions will be very strictly watched by the troops. If the chief lets the brutes get away with their actions, the rest will get the message.

Equipment is an easy area for a careless chief to ignore. One can always put off the purchase of new cars by putting a few extra thousand miles on the current fleet. The acquisition of computers might be postponed until the next budget cycle. The troops can make do with the current radios for a while longer. Rationalizations are easy in this area in the short run, but they carry negative long-term consequences for performance. America is awakening to the decline of its infrastructure, as well as to the dumb decisions made to postpone upkeep and repairs.

Maintenance is even easier to overlook. Simply prolonging the periods between repairs, upkeep, inspections, and preventive replacements frees up money for more urgent purposes. It is a tempting road to follow. However, balance must be struck between the agency's long-term needs and the present crisis that must be attended to. Skilled chiefs are jugglers who can't lose themselves in the problems of the present if they hope to forge a successful department.

The physical plant is another area of concern for the chief, but new buildings tend to be such long-term projects that few executives feel tempted to improve their successor's lot.

The "awhile longers" produce sporadic failures and attack morale, but the absence of a direct cause-and-effect relationship between a crisis and the decision, taken long ago, to forego expenditures in that area is not likely to be identified as the villain. An operational failure because of a breakdown of equipment—or the simple lack of the necessary tool or facility—is rarely traced back to the decision, taken months or years earlier, to put off the repair or purchase of the needed items.

In addition to internal questions, the chief must deal with all the various publics, the press, the other players in the criminal justice system, politicians, and hosts of special-interest groups.

Chiefs are decision machines. They attend meetings and conferences, take and return calls, receive and answer mail and report, and are bombarded by a steady stream of visitors, all demanding a portion of the dwindling resources. Neighbors want cops on the streets, but chiefs know they need a well-trained force and that in order to have one, they have to move cops off the street and into classrooms. The mayor receives a call from an angry constituent and wants the chief to deal with it. The downtown council is nervous about youths hanging out and the steady influx of dangerous street people. A particularly violent crime panics the public. The automatic reaction is to look to the police chief for guidance and protection.

A chief's daily fare is composed of town hall meetings of angry citizens demanding action, foaming editorials decrying an action or a failure to act, a nervous mayor's insistent summons, a council's brutal cross-examination, or calls and letters from disaffected citizens anxious to air their grievances. These cannot be shrugged off if the executive is to avoid the charge of cavalierism. They cannot be succumbed to if any hope of controlling the agency is to be retained. They must be absorbed, processed, evaluated, and responded to, reasonably and respectfully, in a firm and direct manner that encompasses the chief's view of what the right thing to do is, regardless of the consequences. This is much easier to describe than it is to do.

Pressures have been known to panic chiefs into such unwise actions that a results-at-any-cost posture gets translated into quick action at the operational levels that doesn't take legal niceties into account. The message is transmitted subliminally but clearly to the cops, and the outcome may well be a questionable arrest or an illegal action.

The awful holocaust, following a long series of battles, disputes, and controversies, between the Philadelphia police and the urban cult known as MOVE resulted from executives' succumbing to demands for action. It provided a classical example of how an inappropriate response might be triggered by insistence that something be done. The temptations of quick action and surgical strikes frequently lead to such debacles as Philadelphia's.

Another pressure on the chief is the issue of information. The public has a right to know and a need to protect itself from attack. In the circumstances, for example, of a serial rapist or killer, the strongest instinct of the chief is to say nothing. Why stir up a hornet's nest of public indignation or fear? The silence is justified by the rubric that this is a "confidential and continuing investigation," but the silence is quickly seen as a transparent effort at the old bureaucratic game of covering flanks. The excuses, developed over the decades, are ingenious. One, frequently used, claims that the police didn't want to alert the criminal, allowing evasion of a trap or plan of attack. Meanwhile, though, random serial killers (like the Son of Sam) or rapists continue to strike at unsuspecting, unprepared victims who might have been more cautious if they'd had any prior warning. The fact is that these serial criminals, who strike at strangers when the opportunity arises, operate in very definitive patterns that would have enabled most victims, if they had been alerted to the dangers, to avoid the circumstances that made them vulnerable to attack.

Secrecy

The overwhelming majority of attempts at secrecy in the bureaucracy are, in my experience, pathetic attempts to keep the public from discovering the department's many warts and failings. There are, of course, legitimate grounds for secrecy, but they are rarer than the public realizes or than police executives would allow. A hot continuing investigation, the setting of a trap, withholding the identity of a child victim or the victim of a sex crime, and withholding the name of a victim pending the notification of relatives—all are good reasons for secretiveness. There must be logical, articulable grounds, beyond the shopworn bromides, on which to predicate confidentiality. Unless there are good, explicitly described reasons to withhold information, the police executive must recognize the right of the public to be informed. An enormous amount of mischief is caused because chiefs in this country lack the requisite faith in the wisdom and strength of the people. Therefore they withhold information about such things as the dangers produced by a cat burglar operating in their area, a team of muggers striking repeatedly, or the tactics of any of the serial criminals who strike randomly at strangers when the specific scenario that triggers their assault arises. Though chiefs may rationalize that secrecy protects the public, in reality its function is to protect the chiefs and their departments from scrutiny, while depriving the public of the opportunity to protect itself.

In order to perform their job adequately, chiefs need to be effective communicators. They have to be clear thinkers with a set of internalized priorities that allow them to decide on their areas of emphasis. They need a philosophical and ethical perspective that will enable them to decide the thorny daily issues of command. Every demonstration, for example, involves the rights of the protesters, the rights of those being picketed, and the rights of the general public, to name only three—there are inevitably others. Striking the proper balance is the challenge.

The reforms needed to improve the agency will involve serious battles. How chiefs marshal their allies and obtain the public's support is crucial in determining the strength of the department. The skills chiefs need, the questions they face, and the actions they take are unique, rarely based on prior training or preparation. Precedents established by other police chiefs are mostly useless. There are enough differences in every case to make precedents irrelevant, except as the most general guides. It may sound hyperbolic or silly, but I've never seen a problem precisely replicated in usable form. Adjustments are always needed, even if prior experience can, and should, be drawn on.

Pressures on the Chief

Even police chiefs do not always understand the nature of the pressures working on them. They feel them and resent them, but find it hard to understand that pressures are a necessary part of public life. In the privacy of their councils, they can be heard, inappropriately, railing against politicians or citizens who are doing nothing more than demanding better performance. Their hostility toward the press and the all-too-evident relief with which they embrace retirement demonstrate their failure to recognize that pressures are real and permanent fixtures of a democracy and that the only real complaint can be directed at their appropriateness. The job of the chief is to decide how most productively to respond to pressures. Caving in to any element when logic and right dictate another course will ensure the defeat of the administration and the agency. The pressures ought to be seen as the water's weight against a submarine's shell as it sails toward its objective.

The direction of the agency is set and the speed is determined by the chief—easily the most important member of any police agency. The talents needed to succeed are rarely the ones the mayor appointed the chief for. Chief executive officers are frequently the key operatives in any organization. But because of the myriad of choices about what to emphasize and what to overlook, as well as the hundreds of problems from which to select the most important, it is the police chief who absorbs and directs the central responsibilities of the department.

In order for chiefs to be able to perform their duties successfully, they must have the power of promotions. The ranks above captain are known as the senior staff. The critical question concerning them is whether they've been appointed by the chief or have climbed the ladder through civil service tests. In the latter case, chiefs find themselves surrounded by key aides they haven't appointed and whom they cannot demote without a formal process based on specific acts of serious wrongdoing. This stultifying straitjacket—the product of earlier and, at the time, necessary reforms—proves a very serious impediment to change or progress.

In agencies where chiefs get to appoint their own key aides, they are usually forced to choose these aides from the ranks of captains. That is exactly where these aides would return, at the stroke of a pen, if the chief is displeased with their performance. This is the key to a system that makes the NYPD commissioner a very powerful executive.

Like any power, the power of promotion can be abused. But that is no excuse for abolishing it. Chiefs have no other way of maintaining control over their executives. Chiefs would be rendered powerless to supervise the executives' actions, and the executives would know it.

The reason that so many police departments seem to stumble from crisis to crisis, and that they often get bogged down in repeated failures is probably that not enough attention was paid to the selection of the police chief. As a privileged insider, it was easy for me to see chiefs' flaws in any of a dozen small-to-horrible mistakes made by their departments and later reported in the daily press. The fault usually lay in the person at the helm, not in the stars.

Between the Recruit and the Chief

Between the recruit and the chief are patrol officers, detectives, first-line supervisors (sergeants and lieutenants), middle managers, and senior staff—all cops.

Cops on the street hurry from call to call, bound to their crackling radios, which offer no relief—especially on summer weekend nights. That is the time when the ghetto throbs with noise, booze, violence, drugs, illness, blaring TVs, and human misery. The cops jump from crisis to crisis, rarely having time to do more than tamp one down sufficiently and leave for the next. Gaps of boredom and inactivity fill the interims, though there aren't many of these in the hot months. Periods of boredom get increasingly longer as the night wears on and the weather gets colder.

Cops complain about the pace but they love the action. They all want to work in their state's big city, which frequently draws its recruits from suburban departments. The cops' grumbling conceals their love of action and the search for adventure that drew them into police work. They also love the power and autonomy, as well as the challenging variety of their job. It is important work and they know it. Gaps that occur during the day allow for coffee, a smoke, and the yarn swapping and rehashing that cement partners into intimates. When all else rots, your partner will still be there. So much has been shared. The partners have been bonded by moments of danger or glimpses into life's foremost secrets. This is deepened even further by those savoring aftermoments that transform an event into a common vision.

The summer has an explosive, electric quality that fills the cops with apprehension. It is a mixture awaiting a spark that will galvanize thousands into the dreaded riots. Usually riots are composed of thousands of individuals chasing their own fantasies. This haphazard action is controllable by the police. However, if that force were unified or focused, chaos would result.

The challenge for the larger society is to understand the institution of the police in order to be able to make sensible decisions about it. The challenge to the cops is to open the agency and develop a common sense of purpose with the public they are hired to protect and serve.

CHAPTER 6

The Slippery Slope of Crime, Arrests, and Statistics

As America nears the end of the twentieth century, street crime occupies a high, and sometimes the highest, place on the public agenda of concerns. The problem festers in the core cities, where all of society's difficulties seem to be centered.

Drugs, alcohol, guns, and the problems of the poor produce ever-escalating numbers of murders, shootings, rapes, and other crimes. The prisons burst and demands continue to be made for tougher measures. There is little discussion of, or seeming concern about, the underlying conditions nurturing the growth in crime.

Even independent chiefs, long accustomed to going their separate ways, are forced into new directions.

The tremendous public pressure triggered by escalating drug trafficking and its contribution to rising violence is forcing formerly warring agencies to find ways to work together. No one wants to be blamed for the failures everyone is looking at every day. As a result, it would not be too fanciful to call this era the Golden Age of Law Enforcement Cooperation.

There is, to be sure, a Tower of Babel flavor to all the diffused activity, even allowing for the heightened cooperation. One of the daunting tasks facing the much ballyhooed drug czar, William Bennett, Jr., on his appointment in 1989, was to coordinate the wildly scattered efforts against illegal drugs. Most believe he'll fail, just as the U.S. Attorney General failed to merge the Drug Enforcement Agency into the Federal Bureau of Investigation in the 1980s. The united front masks real turf jealousies.

Contradictions dot the landscape of law enforcement in America. Pressures force warring agencies into frightened cooperation, yet they guard their preserves zealously. No serious student of the field believes the new drug czar will achieve true operational coordination, yet the differences will be muted and papered over while the real cooperation will take place on the streets, where the arrests are being made, even as organizational changes are resisted and behind-the-scenes battles for resources rage.

So the city cops are left with the task of battling urban violence. What does this mean?

Nothing is simple in the complex world of the police, not even the straightforward notion of crime.

Crime, for example, usually means street crime, which is defined as the eight offenses listed in the Uniform Crime Reports, Part I Crime. The first four (murder, rape, assault, and robbery) are crimes against people, and the second four (theft, auto theft, burglary, and arson) are usually called property crimes. The list of eight Part I crimes has remained largely unchanged since it was devised over fifty years ago, although some revisions are currently under way in the manner in which crime statistics are compiled.

No one really knows why crime goes up or down or, for that matter, whether it fluctuates at all, as over 50 percent of street crimes go unreported. The most important contemporary determinant of crime, illegal drugs, is not even part of the Index. Crime statistics have proved most useful in comparing a city's current experience against its own history, rather than in attempting intercity comparisons. Cities are so different and so many factors are unknown that the frequent efforts at intercity comparisons founder on the shoals of the unrevealing and inconsistent figures produced. When we speak of a rising or lowering crime rate, we are referring to a city's experience this year versus the same city's crime incidence the year before.

A crime is an act, or omission (failing to file a tax return, for example), forbidden by law and punishable by a fine or imprisonment or both. Crime is not an inadvertence, nor is it an accident. Society wisely requires that evil intent accompany most actions defined as crimes. Where an evil intent is lacking and a tragedy results (manslaughter, vehicular homicide, etc.), the law usually requires evidence of "a reckless disregard for the circumstances, or a wanton indifference to the consequences" or some other condition that establishes negligence or irresponsibility of a very high order. Courts have spent decades refining the meaning of such phrases.

Crimes are usually either felonies or misdemeanors, and the distinction is the amount of punishment, with the more serious crimes (felonies) receiving more than one year in prison and misdemeanors usually carrying a sentence to the county jail.

Crime Statistics, Arrest, and Reality

The crime statistics that create so much fear are compiled in two ways. One is through the FBI's Uniform Crime Reports (UCR), an annual statistical compilation of street crime submitted by the nation's police chiefs. It is based on the crimes reported by victims to police agencies. The second is through a survey of a statistically significant sample of 49,000 households, by the Department of Justice's Bureau of Justice Statistics (BJS).

The reports seldom jibe, and most students of crime tend to be skeptical of the findings of both. As we mentioned in connection with the UCR, probably fewer than half the crimes committed are reported to the police. Not all shoplifters are reported or arrested (some stores have a policy of just showing or shoving the thief out); most rapes are not reported (there is still a social stigma attached to this crime, although the police have become a lot more sensitive about handling it); the homeless and drifters rarely report robberies, assaults, or other crimes that are accepted as part of their daily lifestyle; many burglaries (of a garage, for example) are not thought to be worth bothering the police about; arsons may be seen as accidents and go undetected (this is, of course, true of other crimes as well); hence not all failures to report can be blamed on victim indifference. However, murders and vehicle thefts do tend to be faithfully and accurately reported. Thus it develops that, of the eight crimes comprising the UCR, we can safely rely on only two being consistently reported to the police.

The semiannual survey by BJS has other flaws, notably human memory and its failings. Many people forget crimes that occurred to them or to members of their families during the preceding six months. Crime is more of a commonplace in the ghetto than is usually supposed.

The overall result is that, when such factors as possible fudging of the figures to put a better face on the crime picture are factored in, we can say only that the most widely used indexes on street crime in America are seriously flawed on several counts. Nevertheless they are the only game in town and they do have their uses. They confirm the plight of the poor and the deep involvement of the underclass, as perpetrators and as victims, in street crime.

The problems associated with understanding the different indexes of criminality in our society, however, don't end there. Different police administrators take different views of statistics. Although conventional wisdom may hold that chiefs ought to be painting the bleakest possible picture in order to get more help, the negative pressures emanating from rising levels of criminality seldom tempt them to take this tack. The chief's efforts to put the best possible face on the crime picture illustrates the importance of subtle organizational messages.

In the police bureaucracy, no one ever says, "Let's get the crime figures down by misclassifying the events reported to us." Bureaucrats prefer euphemisms and evasions. King Henry, after all, didn't say, "Why don't you guys kill Archbishop Thomas à Becket for me?" He said something like, "Will no one rid me of this pest?" A nice nebulous injunction that managed to convey the desired meaning without his risking incrimination. The modern approach is to retain "plausible deniability." In this non-risk-taking age no one wants to take the chances connected with cooking the books.

Police chiefs might complain that the statisticians are being altogether too finicky in classifying a broken door as a burglary (which would get it into the Part I Index when it might easily have been rated as a destruction of property, also a crime, but not part of the crucial Index). When chiefs convey these subtle messages, the number crunchers scurry to please. The result? A declining level of crime—which is not really accurate.

In New York City, for one, the practice had developed such exquisite refinements that when, in 1966, the newly elected Mayor John V. Lindsay ordered honest crime-reporting, burglaries soared 250 percent and robberies rose almost as much. Again, the only Part I crimes not importantly influenced were the two hardest to manipulate: murder and auto theft. All the others had been subjected to a process laughingly called *canning*—as in tossing the reports into the garbage can before they were tallied.

The point is to recognize the malleability of seemingly immutable crime statistics. The usefulness of the figures, even when honestly compiled, is centrally related to the user's understanding. I can recall asking a commissioner of a major urban city how he honestly felt about the crime statistics that his department was spewing out, oozing comfort everywhere, and that frankly made me skeptical. His answer was, "They're suspect."

Even in the seemingly stable and predictable area of homicide, the facts can get slippery. A recent medical examiner, again in New York, came a cropper over mishandling his office. Among his peccadillos was the charge that he had been too accommodating to detectives eager to have suspicious deaths ruled suicides or accidents or as having occurred through natural causes. I can vividly recall my colleagues, when I was a detective, buttonholing medical examiners with the plea, "Ah c'mon, Doc, we don't want to create a mystery out of this, do we?" Difficult as it may be to believe, a lot of folks went to the grave, in New York City and elsewhere, classified as having died in circumstances quite at variance with the facts.

The crime trend seemed to have stabilized, but at a very high level, in the 1970s, only to explode in the mid-1980s, reaching record levels in 1988. Alarm over the violence resulted in a 150 percent increase in the prison population at a time when reported crime had flattened out. The panic induced by the rises in the 1980s pushed the numbers of those in jails much higher. Since the late 1960s, the number of the nation's prisoners has tripled, and the number of those under some sort of supervision resulting from a conviction has soared. All of this flies in the teeth of the commonly held belief that we are all softheaded and softhearted about crime and that our judges are wimpish, woolly-headed liberals who enjoy springing predators. The overcrowding has now, in fact, reached such appalling proportions that these same judges, in the name of promoting minimally humane conditions, have had to sign orders to reduce the congestion, loosing a dangerous band of predators on society. It is a good illustration that the complexity of our criminal justice system is such that every time a finger is pressed on a serious problem, two unanticipated new problems are bound to pop up.

Clearly, it wasn't the intent of these judges to sic a gaggle of monsters on a helpless citizenry, but conditions were crying out for a remedy. The communities could have built more prisons or adopted alternative methods of control, but too many preferred to posture and declaim rather than undertake difficult correctives. Despite all the rhetoric, few public dollars have been spent on prison construction in recent years, and the American people are notably impatient over such sensible proposals as sentencing guidelines (about which more later), which they regard as too soft.

In studies concerning murder, which is the most serious of the street crimes and one of the two consistently recorded accurately, blacks were cited as the killers more often than whites, for example, in 10,228 of the 17,859 cases where the offender was known (national 1987 statistics).

Over half of the murders were with firearms, and 7,807 were with handguns. When accidents and suicides are added, handguns kill over 20,000 Americans annually, or about 40 percent of the total slain in the sixteen years of the Vietnam war. No other industrialized nation suffers remotely similar carnage. The wild trafficking in drugs brought record numbers of murders to many cities in 1988. The connection was made through the presence of drugs or drug paraphernalia, the existence of drugs in the system of the deceased or other victims or the perpetrator, the statements of witnesses, or other evidence.

Murders, for example, reached a national level of 18,673 in 1983; 17,260 in 1984; 17,545 in 1985; 19,257 in 1986; and 17,859 in 1987. These numbers reflect a high, but seemingly stable, level, which rose to 20,675 in 1988 as a result of the crack epidemic. However, for the same period, between 1983 and 1987, motor vehicle theft, the other most recorded statistic, rose 28 percent. Even here, though, a cavil may be in order because these statistics are so importantly influenced by the technological race between manufacturers and car thieves. One carmaker was widely accused of having given up the effort to make cars harder to steal through the introduction of antitheft devices. The results was a disproportionate ratio of that brand's cars being stolen. Even in the areas where we might most trust the data, cautions are in order because of the complexities that surface as we look more closely.

Street crimes create the greatest fears when they involve stranger-to-stranger violence, and one serial murderer can terrorize an entire community, as the Atlanta child murderer and the Son of Sam illustrate.

Underscoring everything is a highly mobile population where traditional values such as a close-knit family appear to be in decline, while hedonism is on the rise. Such value shifts have a lot more to do with crime trends than the number of cops hired.

Politics and Crime

The politics of crime doesn't end with what gets recorded or "canned." Not all crimes are equal. Here, as with everything else in life, some are more equal than others. One of the harsh discoveries made by cops, early, is that everything, except for the selfless acts of one such as Mother Theresa, is, ultimately, rooted in dollars and cents. Thus the murder of an important citizen is going to get more attention and effort than the killing of a poor, anonymous citizen. When we speak of the squeaking wheel getting the grease, we recognize the squeaks as being produced by power, whether this means money, media attention, celebrity status, or whatever grabs the chief's attention. Both the Knapp Commission inquiry and the Kitty Genovese case were launched by front-page articles in the *New York Times*.

Police cynicism, a much studied and frequently cited phenomenon, is fed by the fudging of crime figures; by dishonest efforts to get crimes classified as accidents; or by the unequal treatment of victims.

Powerful people or institutions can get the mayor on the phone, and this spells both trouble and work. Even the anonymous citizen can get more action than the herd by knowing how to apply pressure through a call or letter to the appropriate mover or shaker. This matters more than is generally supposed. The police bureaucracy avoids a lot of work because a complaint, or a demand for action, has been sent to the inappropriate place or person, where it is lost. One of the vilest epithets in the New York cop's lexicon is *letter writer,* because this means more questions to answer and more work to be done.

It is inefficient and probably impossible to investigate all crimes. Only a few are realistically solvable. The clearance (arrest) rates for property crimes hover between 13 and 20 percent; the rate for violent crimes against people is much higher, because the victim has usually seen the offender. The arrest rate for robbery is a low 27 percent as opposed to a high of 70 percent for murder. The figures on murder are getting worse because of the increasing incidence of such stranger-to-stranger events as drug murders, gang killings, and the busy activities of organized crime, known to the FBI as LCN (La Cosa Nostra).

Concentrating on those cases that are most likely to lead to an arrest holds the best promise for raising the clearance rate. In any population of crimes, promising leads are going to exist for one or two that hold out the promise of identifying and arresting the culprit. The overwhelming majority of the others are not worth investigating simply because they constitute a diversion of resources that might be spent more profitably by being concentrated on the more promising cases. A perfect system, free of pressures and interferences, would function on the basis of such objective factors.

But poor people matter less than rich people. Prominent ones count more than the faceless weak masses. Notorious cases get more attention than the humdrum. The public get more frightened by crimes that might easily have happened to them or their loved ones than by accounts of such predictable events as bums and druggies wiping each other out. A murdered prostitute accepting rides with strangers doesn't provoke the alarm created by the murder of a young woman by a stranger as she gets out of her car to report for a job interview. Citizens project themselves onto the TV screen, identifying with the victim, and if they can't discern possible avoidance strategies the chief is going to come in for some grief, even when the victim is "unimportant." The police chief has to be sensitive to the symbolic value of a crime, too. The disappearance of a little boy, the killing of a stalked and screaming young woman, and the murder of senior citizens in their homes by burglars are examples of the kinds of cases that grip the public's imagination.

Criminal justice is a minefield of assumed, and sometimes incorrect, citizen notions. It is important that we bring precision to the process to help clear up some of the complexity and confusion. People are always saying they've been "robbed" when they've actually been burglarized, a totally different crime. The former involves a mugging or a holdup, and the latter occurs when criminals break into a home. Citizens love to read "Mugger Faces 20 Years" but don't want to consider the more sensible complexities of sentencing guidelines.

Arrests and Effectiveness

Very few meaningful arrests are made by the uniformed street cops. Their visibility tends to displace, or perhaps even prevent, crimes. It is through such operations as decoys, where the cops replicate the victimization experiences of the citizens and offer themselves up as the targets, or undercover work or sting or stakeout tactics or through the investigative efforts of detectives that the important felony arrests are made. Some of these tactics attempt to anticipate the commission of a crime and deflect it from the citizens, and others necessarily follow the event after it has occurred.

Stakeout units are good examples of the tortuous turns even straightforwardly aggressive tactics can produce. Some crimes can be anticipated with pretty accurate certainty. If a liquor store or candy shop has been held up six times in a year, an analysis of the events will reveal approximately when the next assault will take place. The cops actually become, if anything, too skilled at this game.

Once a pattern is analyzed, it becomes a simple matter to station two protected, trained, and heavily armed cops in the back of the store, connected to the clerks through electronic devices. The cops leap out, at a signal, and surprise the intruder. Prearranged reactions having been settled, the employees rarely suffer injury even when gunfire ensues, although few police operations are entirely free of risk.

Stakeout units can be quite effective, as we've seen, but, as the scenario actually plays out in real life, the robbers are frequently killed. Most of them are black. To the minority community, it looks like summary executions. Detroit, which once had a unit called STRESS (Stop The Robberies, Enjoy Safe Streets), disbanded it because of the toll it was taking and the public furor that attended a series of highly publicized killings of robbers.

With black males comprising 6 percent of the U.S. population, yet occupying over 40 percent of jail and prison space, and with the leading cause of death among young black men being murder, it is little wonder that racial controversy attends any program that aggressively attacks street crime. What never gets asked is what conditions of life existed for these men that made their failure inevitable. The usual answer is to get the police to clean up society's failings.

In murder, for example, 48.1 percent of 1988's victims about whom detailed data are available were black. Of the thirty-four largest cities, the nation's capital led, with a murder rate of 59.5 per 100,000 inhabitants. Next came Detroit with 57.9 and Atlanta with 48.8. Last was Honolulu, with the very low ratio of 3.3 per 100,000.

The fact striking us in the face is that blacks are disproportionately involved in street crime—as both perpetrators and victims. To speak baldly of these things is thought to be playing into the hands of racists, but they seem to have little trouble securing or inventing their own material. Meanwhile, not only does the plight of the blacks go unaddressed, but society has a ready-made excuse to avoid mentioning it altogether. Current policies play into the hands of racists and their "lock 'em up" rhetoric. Until whites awaken to their complicity in the creation of an underclass, crime and violence will continue to escalate.

Decoy operations are often seen as entrapment, even though they rarely come close to it. Sting operations are also attacked for producing inducements to burglary and theft, since they create a market for stolen goods. Entrapment, though, is inducing the innocent mind to commit a crime it had not contemplated, and the availability of a "fence" is not sufficient to justify a break-in. Just making the commission of the crime easier, facilitating it, is not considered entrapment.

Fears of long, hot summers encourage chiefs and mayors to tread lightly on such aggressive police tactics. The underclass in the ghetto are restive, and never more so than during the hot summer months. Chiefs, who fear riots, know that stakeouts, decoys, stings, and such might easily spark the precipitating incident.

Though racial issues become embroiled in defusing the underclass, charges of racism have at times had a self-defeating effect. In Los Angeles, the police were forced to abandon choke holds, not because they were ineffective but largely because of a stupid remark made by the chief following the death of a black man who'd been subdued with the grip, which temporarily cuts off the flow of blood to the brain, causing the suspect to pass out. The chief created an uproar when he blurted out that blacks were somehow physiologically different from "normal people" in the flow of blood to the brain. The resulting clamor was so intense that an aggressive agency, and an aggressive chief, had to abandon the practice. The irony might well rest in the officers' having to resort to deadly force in subduing violent suspects they might have controlled through using the hold.

Debates in the field do not center on whether the police ought to or ought not be aggressive. Everyone pays lip service to the notion of police aggressiveness. After the law-and-order rhetoric has received its customary obeisance, the talk begins to focus on specific tactics and their appropriateness.

A tough law-and-order administration will focus on making more arrests even if it means overwhelming the rest of the system. A public-relations-oriented operation concentrates on what might be called touchy-feely programs intended to reassure folks and get them feeling better, such as detectives coming around on every crime reported or opening up storefront ministations. A service-focused agency will work hardest on response times, making sure that every call gets answered and that there are no backlogs. Every police agency adopts either an authoritarian and aggressive arrest approach or a watchman (lots of patrol and watching) model or a service posture. Usually the choice reflects the chief's philosophy.

Each of these approaches, and others, represents a choice for the administrator to make, and the decisions are neither obvious nor automatic.

We think of crime as immutable, yet we have seen it go unreported, get mangled by police policies, or be given different weights. The slipperiness or plasticity of the crime issue doesn't, however, end there.

The Shifting Sands of Crime

Even the definition of what a crime might be evolves with time, changing mores, and shifting interests. When I became a cop in 1953, rape was forcing sexual intercourse on a woman "not his wife," and no conviction could be had on the "uncorroborated testimony of the female." This was the only serious crime for which such an absurd condition existed. Even in 1989, in Minnesota, adultery was described as sexual intercourse with "a married female, not his wife" and continued to be labeled a crime. Thus a married man was exempt if his relations were with an unmarried female.

The statutory changes reflect the shifting opinions of the electorate. The public's new consensus tends to stir legislative action. In the areas of domestic abuse and drunken driving, for example, current attitudes have been reflected in the laws passed and in the actions of our criminal justice system. Shifting attitudes toward marijuana have also changed both the law and the actions of law enforcers. When it is perceived that enforcing a given statute is no longer fashionable, the very faddish agencies that constitute America's police will concentrate their efforts elsewhere. They have an enormous potpourri of laws to choose from and know how to follow the election returns.

Our legislatures make the rules by which we live, and we call these rules *laws*. State legislators like to do popular things, which leads them to search for a consensus or even tempts them to occasional demagoguery. Except for broad constitutional limits, legislatures have free rein to decide what is or is not a crime. They usually have little trouble identifying *mala in se* crimes (those acts so inherently evil, such as child murder, that they prove repugnant to all of us), but *mala prohibita* crimes (acts that are not, to the eye, clearly wrong but that are prohibited nevertheless, so as to provide for an orderly society, such as traffic regulations and tax laws) give them pause. Abortion is a good example of the tangled web encountered in trying to interpret *mala prohibita*.

Causes of Crime

We know who commits street crimes and why, but it is harder to understand why Minneapolis, for example, had a record number of crimes in 1987 and experienced steadily declining rates throughout 1988. We don't know why two young men, similarly situated in all respects, will choose radically different paths. The scholars searching for causes have focused on genes and conditioning as the prime factors. Not all of the poor, or even a majority, become criminals, but nearly all street criminals are poor.

The conditions of life and the number of our poor, the genetic secrets waiting to be discovered, the number of homeless on the city's streets, drug abuse, the number of single-parent or no-parent families, the flight of stable families to the suburbs, the government's economic policies, racism, the mobility and passion for anonymity of our rootless population, a shifting value system, the divorce rate, and such nebulous items as might be called the waning "altruism factor," along with others—all probably contribute to the crime rate.

Other issues add to the dilemma of the police in combating crime. Unenforceable, unpopular laws tend to be breached often, by many, and give the police enormous trouble when they are required to apply them. This is most evident in vice or drug operations, which are fed by strong popular demand. An arrest merely begins a gauntlet where the outcome is not likely to result in imprisonment. Wherever there is a demand for anything, a supply will follow. The variables are the risks, which will only determine the costs. Drugs will be out there as long as there is a demand, and effective interdicting operations by the police probably only drive their price upward, forcing addicts to commit more crimes to support their habit.

The rate at which the public reports crime may be more a reflection of the levels of confidence in the police than of the relative incidence of crime. The result is such absurdities as a higher per capita rape rate in Minneapolis than in New York or Newark.

No one is paid to think for, or administer, the criminal justice system. Activity in one sector frequently results in unintended surfacings elsewhere, as the various players look after their fiefdoms. If a pin map of the city were to be drawn showing the highest incidence of crimes, fires, ambulance calls, or other indicators of urban dishabille, the poorest sections would have the clusters, yet the resources are not distributed accordingly.

The crime picture is loaded with just such complexities as these. The obvious conclusion is to make certain that, in a free society, a rational consensus develops around what shall be prohibited and allowed, in order to prevent the hypocrisies inherent in such efforts as Prohibition, where attempts are made to control behavior that is favored by so many as to make enforcement impossibly difficult.

Weather and Crime

The police work curve normally follows the weather pattern, with the summer months forming the hump, in more ways than one. Heat and police problems proceed in tandem. Warm weather promotes outdoor life, drinking, and fractious human animals rubbing against each other, usually in greater numbers than the cops find desirable. Heat raises temperatures—psychological as well as environmental. Harsh winters clear the streets. Warmth causes the homeless to emerge and wander about. Arrests of twenty of these derelicts in Minneapolis revealed that half had serious criminal records. The urban homeless commit, and are the victims of, a lot of crimes. Heat brings the miserable out of their roach-infested, overheated cubicles.

The daunting winters of Minneapolis were the city's foremost asset, worth about five hundred cops. They enabled us to undertake vast training programs from November 1 to May 1. The result, when coupled with the nation's hardest entrance requirements (a two-year college degree in police subjects, a tough basic-training course, and a demanding licensing exam), was one of the best trained agencies in the nation.

Sunbelt cities are burdened with the problem of police busy-ness all year round. Frostbelt towns worry about the summer, when the stacked calls and delayed responses fray everyone's nerves and politicians get angry calls from constituents complaining that the cops have been called but haven't arrived. The pressures pile up, and worried officeholders, not the steadiest of persons in the best of times, harangue police chiefs.

This is where the chief's mettle is tested yet again. Chiefs are either going to accommodate the comfort and convenience of their colleagues, or they are going to work the troops weekend evenings, get those with inside jobs out on the streets in uniform, curtail summer vacations, go to one-person patrols, or take any of the other score of tough decisions that will stamp them as managers and gain the hatred of subordinates. That is the usual trade-off.

Additionally, executives will demonstrate their skill as planners if they schedule hiring and training to produce a hump of workers during the busy summer months. This is a tougher balancing act than it appears to be and requires tight planning, preparation, and timing. Such factors as retirements, deaths, and resignations have to be calculated in such a way as to produce the lowest personnel levels at the beginning and end of the year, when the cops are least needed, and to go over the limits during the summer.

Service is the police agency's principal *raison d'être,* notwithstanding the glamor and pizzazz surrounding the crime issue. However, delivering better and faster service frequently puts the chief at odds with erstwhile buddies who then have to speed from call to call. That is what "serving the people" ultimately gets reduced to, a choice between the troops and the people.

The politics and issues surrounding street crime and the criminals who perpetrate it are much more complex than any casual observer would be led to believe by the rhetoric of the participants.

Crime statistics are mere symptoms of the underlying social and economic conditions that spawn and drive criminal behavior. It makes no more sense to go from criminal to criminal, ignoring the causative factors, than it does to quarantine the ailing without analyzing the symptoms and trying to devise a general cure.

Street Criminals and How They Got That Way

The frightening volume of crime and violence in late-twentieth-century America, featuring guns, drugs, and terrifying acts of bloodshed, is produced by street criminals. Their activities have popularized a word, *recidivism,* that, but for the fear street criminals have managed to spark, might have remained esoteric, just as graffiti might have remained but for the efforts of ghetto artists.

Recidivism

Some glimmers of light are being shed on the mysterious activities of criminals that may reveal their differentiated behaviors and allow the development of a strategy for coping with their assaults. Policing's traditional hostility to research, scholarship, and experimentation has delayed and confused the process. There is a reluctance to "play with people's lives" or to take such risks as not arresting some people while booking others for the same crime, or saturating one area with cops and leaving another area uncovered.

Analyzing crime and its perpetrators requires enlisting researchers, scholars, and experimenters to gather and evaluate data, to study the events and people involved, and to prepare theories based on the principles discovered.

Successful experiments require taking risks. The medical profession has done a good job of convincing us of the necessity of such "games" of research, but the principle hasn't spilled over into policing. It is not an easy connection for chiefs to make.

That cops and chiefs play with lives, through seat-of-the-pants, intuitive policies, rarely gets mentioned. Few chiefs would agree that neglect or wrongheaded programs are treatments, too, but they are. This is illustrated by such traditional responses as the hands-off attitude toward such chronic police problems as domestic violence.

The few studies actually conducted have led to shocking disclosures that have changed the face of American policing in such areas as domestic violence, drug enforcement, drunken-driving programs, and investigative and patrol techniques. Yet the system remains determinedly resistant to scholarly intrusion.

Recidivism is one area that has received, and continues to receive, the attention of the few scholars still active in the field. Studies show that the criminal repeater is a complex creature who looks very different from what experience and personal observation have led practitioners to suppose. Career criminals have, within their ranks, a minority of about 10 percent who are serious repeaters. These recidivists commit many times more crimes than the majority of criminals, who are also labeled recidivists, but who strike more randomly and less often. Serious repeaters reach such totals as fifty robberies or two hundred burglaries a year each. The other 90 percent of the criminal repeaters function much more casually and sporadically.

Most of the data provided by police records and self-reports collected from offenders by scholars indicate that many offenders drop out of a life of crime around age thirty. They usually commit their first serious crime at the age of fifteen. Those who stay tend to remain active criminals until forty and beyond. These are the most serious cases.

Recidivists have several things in common: bad family influences such as poor parenting, poor communication, parental delinquency, and discord in the home. Early antisocial behavior, such as lying, stealing, fighting, or use of drugs or alcohol is an indicator of future problems. Other characteristics of a recidivist include poor school performance, low IQ, and unstable employment.

All criminal repeaters commit a variety of crimes, depending on opportunity and risk. They are not specialists.

Almost half of urban males are arrested for nontraffic offenses before the age of eighteen. The U.S. Bureau of Justice Statistics estimates that 83 percent of children who were twelve years old in 1989 will become victims of actual or attempted violence if crime continues at current rates. The numbers of both perpetrators and victims among those living in poor neighborhoods are, of course, much higher. There are theorists who hold that black youngsters in the ghetto are far more likely to be arrested, for identical events, than their white counterparts in the suburbs. This theory raises the question of whether a criminal's career may not be launched by an early arrest that, having blemished the record, makes it easier to lapse into criminal conduct later, as there's not much to lose. Once a criminal record is acquired, it becomes a permanent albatross around the carrier's neck.

Predictable and expected factors, such as starting crime at an early age or the high frequency of offenses, prove the surest indicators of serious future involvement in crime. The most important predictive dimension is the frequency of past criminal acts. The importance of having the offender's juvenile record available at the time of the first adult arrest is critical, yet it is mostly forbidden by laws intended to protect the young offender.

None of the predictive scales are infallible. The better ones tend to be so cautious, or so broadly encompassing, as to nullify most of their worth. The search for a magic formula holds only the promise that we may come up with a workable, if fallible, system.

The predictive scales developed to identify future menaces include such factors as

1. Prior conviction for some charge.
2. Prior incarceration.
3. A first conviction before age sixteen.
4. Served time in juvenile facility.
5. Drug use in preceding two years.
6. Drug use as a juvenile.
7. Unemployed most of the last two years.
8. Seriousness of current crime.
9. Frequency of criminal acts, which is a particularly critical factor.
10. Higher age of active criminals (thirties), which is a predictor of future dangers if this is not the first arrest (the older the recidivist, the likelier that he or she will commit future crimes).

The evidence indicates that a thorough probation report and the use of sentencing guidelines that include these factors should help to identify and isolate the offender who represents the greatest future danger. But much more needs to be done in this area of recidivism, which might well be described as still being in its infancy.

How do we select, for monitoring, the recidivist who represents a threat of future harm to society?

What about the ethical implications of, in a sense, anticipating future criminality and punishing it in advance?

One answer might be that every sentence currently being handed out takes future dangers into account. Those persons felt to be most dangerous are imprisoned for longer terms now. Our system has always included this consideration of future risk. Now it is being discussed more openly, and the search for a workable formula is more serious.

The first question, how to select the recidivist to target for special attention, is harder, and it has to include not only those pinpointed for selective incapacitation but also those who ought to be the continuing focus of police interest and who ought to be flagged for intensive legal investigations, commensurate with the risky prospects they face of prolonged confinement.

This is really what all those "repeat offender" and "career criminal" programs are all about: selecting and targeting for especially vigorous and attentive investigative and prosecutorial treatment those criminals identified as menaces. When one of those on a list (compiled on the basis of the seriousness of the criminal record) gets arrested, he or she is not treated routinely but is singled out for the sort of treatment reserved for the important cases. Most of these serious repeaters are involved with drugs.

Over half, and sometimes as many as three-fourths, of offenders picked up for serious street crimes of all kinds have evidence of drug use in their blood or urine at the time of arrest. The dramatically escalating homicide rates are blamed on drugs, and a significant number of victims are found to have drugs in their systems as well. Drugs encourage violence because of the economic dilemma of the user (the relative cheapness and availability of crack has, ironically, eased this problem), because of the pharmacological effects of drug on behavior, and as a result of battles for control over the drug market and similar monetary factors. There is a strong correlation between drugs and crime. The more drugs used, the more crimes committed; the fewer drugs used, the fewer crimes.

Studies are revealing that even those forced to enter treatment programs—as a condition of their probation, for example—can experience success. They must be carefully monitored through weekly tests—and must be forced to stay in treatment or returned to prison. The longer they remain in treatment, the greater is the prospect of abstinence, whether they entered the program voluntarily or not.

Despite the temptations inherent in these data, not a single major police executive has advocated the legalization of hard drugs as of 1989. Police executives consider the risks to our moral fiber to be unacceptably high, and although they are well aware of their failing efforts in the "drug war," they prefer to go on fighting it.

They are not sanguine about England's prescription (medically monitored and controlled heroin maintenance program) nor about some of the Scandinavian countries' more permissive attitudes toward drugs.

Experts believe that crime can be reduced through three strategies:

1. Prevention, which is dependent on such "upstream" questions as prenatal care, parenting, education, and family influences.
2. Career modification through treatment or rehabilitation.
3. Incapacitation by putting the recidivist behind bars.

Here we will deal only with the latter two as the first involves heavy-duty social engineering, which is discussed elsewhere. Suffice it to say here only that the first strategy invites us to examine how the pregnancy of a black teenager, or her brother's dropping out of school, plays into the hands of racists eager to see their stereotypes confirmed. It is a tragic irony of our age that the black youngster who is most defiant and rebellious, and who is most involved in drugs and other self-defeating activities, is, in the long run, the racist's strongest ally.

Given the challenge that serious recidivists represent and the opportunity for lowering crime rates that neutralizing them offers, it is small wonder that the few scholarly data existing in the field of policing have been focused on this menace. The task of positively identifying and isolating these offenders from their less dangerous criminal colleagues has proved very difficult, but the effort is clearly reflected in the sentencing-guideline formulas and the many programs adopted by police agencies across the country to target the repeat offender. The origins may be found in such seminal studies as Marvin Wolfgang's analysis of a large cohort of juveniles in Philadelphia. His work, and that of others, has contributed to the development of the indices listed later in this chapter.

Washington, D.C., has been pursuing a highly touted repeat offender program (ROP), and Minneapolis, with its Top 40 Program, concentrates on a group of criminals thought to represent a disproportionate risk to society's safety. These programs, although usually somewhat distinct, generally share such features as the compilation of a list of the most serious, currently active recidivists (as reflected in arrest and conviction records) and monitoring their activities and targeting them for special attention. Thus, even when such targets are arrested for a minor violation, they can count on its being treated as if it were a major one.

Once identified, the serious career criminal should, in the fashion of the serial killer or rapist, be incarcerated for a long period, for society's safety.

The enormous swelling of the prison population has, however, mostly occurred haphazardly, tending to focus on personal violence offenders and sometimes being informed by the sentencing guidelines in the few states using this approach. These states, still using primitive filtration systems, are, nevertheless, light-years ahead of the troglodytes who simply make huge numbers of arrests and stuff everyone, indiscriminately, into overflowing prisons. The federal government's adoption of sentencing guidelines may speed their spread across the nation, but their critics simplemindedly attack these guidelines as being soft on crime. Now that the courts are ordering large-scale releases to ease overcrowding, it is more imperative than ever that the real menaces be identified and incapacitated.

It is becoming clearer that the differentials in offender behavior, in terms of the frequency and seriousness of the crimes and the future prospects for offending, cry out for the adoption of a variety of approaches. Alternatives to incarceration are essential strategies for coping with the majority of offenders, who represent no serious risks for the future but who must be controlled and must experience some consequence for their actions. These are the more casual criminal majority, who drift in and out of crime and who offer the best hope for career modification without extended incarceration. Society will have to develop the maturity to accept occasional failures in terms of both release mistakes and jailing errors. It is a lot cheaper to use alternatives than to build prisons, and the risks are probably not much greater.

A recent federal study of eleven states showed Minnesota to have the best record of keeping released prisoners from returning. The low recidivism rate was related to the various programs and monitorings possible in a system that is not bursting at the seams and forced to release prisoners almost indiscriminately. Minnesota ranked forty-ninth in a recent study of per capita incarceration rates in the United States. When possible, it has used other approaches than incarceration, such as probation, community service, fines, and other treatment or restitution models.

With prisons stuffed to bursting, drug-related arrests swelling, and demagogues calling for mandatory sentences and other draconian and impractical measures, serious imbalances are being woven into the penal system. The criminal justice system will require still more early releases, without creating the additional prison space required to handle the volume.

The challenge is to identify the really dangerous 10 percent of the criminal population and to imprison those predators for the safety of society.

Putting the recidivist behind bars through selective incapacitation poses such risks as

1. The high possibility of error.
2. Ethical questions concerning the punishment of future conduct versus the need to protect the public.
3. Disparities in sentence and treatment that will promote a sense of unequal justice.
4. A possible severe impact on minorities.

All of these factors deal with the arrested offender. In reality, the decision to arrest is anything but automatic. A study found that the factors affecting whether a person is arrested or not include

1. The seriousness of the offense.
2. The hostility of subject (the attitude test).
3. The decision of victim (to arrest or not).
4. Stranger-to-stranger crime (these crimes are perceived as more serious by the system).
5. The officer's prior knowledge of the offender or the situation.
6. The socioeconomic background of the neighborhood (we saw earlier that blacks in the ghetto are more likely to be arrested than whites in the suburbs).
7. Alcohol use in interpersonal disputes.

These are the formal and informal criteria that have evolved, over the years, as a result of police behavior. In order to target the serious criminal, an eighth point—what we might call the *societal menace factor,* as represented by the serious recidivist—may have to be inserted.

The pervasive influence of drugs, certainly acknowledged but not even remotely appreciated in its full dimensions, has led to a number of valuable findings:

1. As drug use increases, so does criminal activity.
2. Juveniles who use drugs commit a disproportionate amount of juvenile crime.
3. Drugs and crime tangle. It is hard to isolate cause and effect or to identify which came first, addiction or criminal acts.
4. Drug users arrested, for whatever crime, also tend to traffic in drugs.
5. Treatment works. Duration is the key.
6. Urinalysis is effective in detecting use.

A lot of this appears to be self-evident, yet these findings constitute the most important new discoveries in the field and hold the hope of developing rational approaches to the challenge posed by the recidivist.

Recent surveys also indicate that the overclass is distancing itself from hard drug use at the same time that the underclass sinks deeper into its despair. The implications of such a trend for the criminal justice system are profound. The dominant class tends to address the problems that pinch its feet. Its indifference is fatal.

The overclass is most directly affected when its children are in danger of being hooked on drugs. Murders, gun battles, and atrocious crimes seem distant affairs. The overclass mostly picks its way around these problems. If it doesn't see its interests as directly threatened, it goes on to other concerns, leaving the underclass mired in violence and enslaving addiction. I had the distinct impression, when I commanded the Bronx forces, that the overclass was perfectly satisfied to have the ghetto residents stupefied on alcohol and invisible. There is no reason to suspect that it will feel any different if the stupefying medium is drugs. The isolated act is not enough to galvanize the overclass to action, and it seems safe to guess that, by the time the underclass is finally moved to massive disorders, it will be too late to address the root causes of violence and crime.

We cannot, however, ignore the threat posed by those already shaped into criminals, nor the need to separate them from society.

Predictive tests, which form the basis of incarceration decisions, must be used with great care. They have to focus on serious criminals, as indicated by records and objective factors.

The process must be restricted to only a few recidivists. If extended to all, or most, or indiscriminately, the result will be the total breakdown of the system that is so evident in the major cities of our nation.

Thoughtful scholars have suggested that, among the factors connected to their use, predictive scales:

1. Identify a small target group.
2. Emphasize prior criminal conduct.
3. Define as "dangerous" someone who has been convicted of a crime as an adult.
4. Include the use of juvenile records if an arrest follows graduation from the juvenile system.
5. Show that the predictive scale relies more on arrest and indictment information than on job or marital data.
6. Must show the potential gain, measured against the burden imposed on the defendant. It is always tempting to "lock them all up" without weighing the costs and benefits.
7. Be used to target people for investigation, as well as sentencing.
8. Limit the punishment by the seriousness of the offense.
9. Emphasize that the heightened risk of a long sentence (the possibility of an error) imposes an obligation to investigate more thoroughly.
10. Encourage the system to use bail more than preventive detention.
11. Encourage the system to focus on past behavior, not future conduct.

America, with its frontier tradition and gunfighter psyche, has always been a violent society. Our murder rates are much higher than those of other modern nations. Yet even we have been shocked by the recent carnage, which has not only greatly increased in volume but produced such bloody scenes as shock the conscience of jaded viewers. The American people are frightened.

At the center lie the serious recidivists, who, although found to constitute only a tiny fraction of the criminal population, represent a disproportionately high danger. They are becoming the focus of the system's attention.

It is these predators who represent the real challenge. Early intervention, forcing change in their behavior, and simply warehousing them in prison appear to be the three strongest possibilities for success. The first involves social and economic policies we seem to be abandoning, rather than considering. The criminal justice system is beginning to concentrate its energies on the second and third possibilities.

The system for identifying the recidivist is in its primitive stages, but scholars and thinkers have provided some valuable insights into the possibility of fashioning programs that obtain real results in the fight against crime. The sum total of the results to date, however, is probably limited to the modest findings contained in this chapter.

The sad, and not very obvious, fact is that cops are irrelevant to the crime rate, although they have a lot to do with it after the crime's committed. The prevention of crime is possible only in a society that has worked to make itself safe through policies of inclusion and social and economic justice, or because total control is possible. Yet cops are not interested in theories about preventing crime. Their desire—a perfectly logical one—is to promote arrests, to increase their own numbers, and to push for programs that at least hold out the prospect of increased public safety, such as those that target the recidivist or that promote arrest or response efficiency.

Incarcerating serious recidivists will pay off in reduced crime by their being otherwise occupied. The identification of recidivists, though, has proved elusive. One can almost tally the crimes avoided through warehousing the real repeaters, but how do we cull them from the group of more casual offenders, especially when we haven't even come up with a useful label for them?

CHAPTER 8

Service and Traffic

Although there won't be many movies or television series on the service and traffic functions of the police, a pretty persuasive argument could be made that policing is fundamentally a service, not a crime, industry.

Practically all of the work of the police gets funneled through 911. Even when a citizen rushes into a police station to get a cop, chances are that the cop on the desk will dial 911 and have a car dispatched to where the citizen needs it. This makes analysis of what constitutes the daily fare of police operations a simple matter of analyzing 911 calls.

About 80 percent of the calls to 911 are for such noncriminal police events as illnesses, accidents, injuries, and the other difficulties that attend humans in disarray.

In the ghetto, the police are used as a service, whatever the circumstance or relevance. Many inner-city dwellers have even learned to lie in order to get a speedy response from cops who have tired of rushing from one call to the next. They'll report "shots fired" or "officer needs help" when a drunken male is at the door, threatening to break in.

In the more affluent sections, citizens seem to have precisely the opposite approach and either hate to bother the police or don't want them intruding into their affairs. Unfamiliarity with police practices inhibits their use.

Most police chiefs bridle at the 911 tail that wags the dog of the departments. Any citizen with a phone, or access to one, seems able to marshal the energies and forces of the department at will. There is a real fear that the troops on patrol are really being administered by cranks, psychos, drunks, kids, idiots, or pranksters who have nothing better to do than harass the cops.

Service

Nine one one, the emergency number now in general use and first proposed in the 1967 report of the President's Commission on Crime, is today the conduit through which the police receive the great bulk of their assignments. The development of this simple device proved both a method of helping the people get faster service and an invitation to call. Policing is a labor-intensive occupation, and the really important technological innovations might be said to be the auto, the phone and radio, 911, and, recently, the computer.

People want to see more cops out there, on the street, in patrol, and in uniform. The chiefs usually translate that into hiring more personnel, but the real challenge is to manage the enterprise so that the number on patrol is maximized. The citizen who dials 911 wants the cops to come, and quickly. The seconds become interminable agonies.

Old people fall out of bed and lie helpless on the ground. A family member can't get a response to frantic knocks and fears the worst; this becomes a "check on the welfare of . . ." call and is really aimed at finding DOAs before the odor becomes overpowering. Johnny is having another of his rowdy Friday-night parties, and the cops have to be sent to break it up. A thoughtless motorist blocks the driveway. False alarms, lockouts, and other screw-ups prompt citizens to grasp the phone and dial the cops.

Nine one one is accepted as one of the givens of modern life. Citizens automatically reach for it when in trouble. It leaps to mind whenever police, fire, or ambulance services are needed. It has become, in a very short while, the people's lifeline.

The early years of 911 weren't easy. The telephone company (it was then only the monolithic American Telephone and Telegraph Company) resisted the new burden mightily. Because its exchange boundaries didn't coincide with political geographics, huge technical problems were created. Five one six, for example, was the area code for two huge counties: it wouldn't do to have Nassau's emergency calls for help wind up in the Suffolk County's Emergency Dispatch Center.

Citizens asked about finding the eleven on the phone dial, so we all had to learn to say "nine one one," instead of "nine eleven." There was a raging debate about whether citizens should be advised to call about anything or only when genuine emergencies occurred. Would they be able to tell the difference? And everyone wanted his or her own easily remembered three-digit number for whatever service was being provided. It is easy to forget the early struggles once an approach achieves general acceptance, but the early days of 911 were anything but halcyon. Its spread, nationally, was hampered by the cost of implementing it and the phone company's early resistance. In the end AT&T became a very effective champion of the cause.

Improving the police service means responding more rapidly and effectively to citizen emergency needs. The response must be discriminating and differential. Not all calls should be answered at the same speed, and some shouldn't be responded to at all. A department that sets out to respond to all citizen calls will be at the mercy of anyone with a quarter or a phone.

Prioritizing Calls

What the great variety of calls suggests is the need to construct a priority system that creates the needed distinctions. A great many calls, such as the reporting of a loss or a theft for insurance purposes, can be handled over the phone. Cops have a strong tendency to cowboy down the streets, if allowed to, and tough controls have to be imposed to ensure orderly, measured responses. Police chases are currently in bad public odor because police caravanning and wild driving, in questionable cases, have produced some highly publicized tragedies. I can recall the calls and letters from outraged citizens, which lasted for months, over a chase in which the suspect crashed into a young female medical student, paralyzing her. The event was perceived as having been triggered by the police, who were chasing a man who had committed an armed robbery and who, as he fled, entered a highway, heading into oncoming traffic. The police must either chase or risk losing the chance to capture a dangerous criminal. Knowing that the police will chase gets a lot of otherwise nervy people to pull over on the highway. The issue is one that doesn't appear likely to go away. It looks as if it may join the pantheon of questions surrounding aggressive police tactics. This is another of those perennials that periodically surface and that require a reasoned, brief, and persuasive response from the chief.

Communicating the Service Message

Communication gets to be a problem in the area of the expectations raised by 911. The public are invited to call and expect a cop to arrive quickly. It makes no sense, though, to have cops respond helter-skelter to an open garage door and a bike missing. The public has to be educated to differentiate between a genuine emergency and the slow response dictated by a low-priority call.

The most urgent thing is to establish a system that ensures a response, within six minutes, to real emergencies. This requires distinguishing crises from less serious events. The system must then be tightened to ensure wide compliance.

The letters that littered my desk usually began with "I dialed 911 and the police took twenty-five minutes to get there." If the expectation of service is raised, the failure to deliver exacts double penalties.

Police chiefs must first get it very clear how they want their department to respond to calls to 911—a more difficult challenge than it appears, on the surface, because of the political and public pressures surrounding these issues—and then make certain that the system works.

Next comes the tough part of educating a public that receives endless messages throughout the day. The chief's message must be simple, brief and direct—and it must be repeated *ad nauseam:* "The police will respond to your emergency and get there within six minutes. Nonemergencies will not receive the same fast response, and calls that require no response at all will be handled over the phone." If all calls are responded to on the same levels of urgency, then the sheer volume will degrade the operation disastrously. It is only by sorting out the truly urgent that a response fleet is able to function effectively. Cops will, of course, take the calls more seriously if they know the more important ones are being dispatched on a first-priority basis.

Because police work is mainly a service business, the quality of that service is going to establish the agency's reputation.

Response Time and Technology

Studies show that the longest time gap between a citizen's perceived need for a cop and that officer's arrival is the time it takes for the citizen either to get to a phone or to find another way of contacting the police. Often the citizen has been confused about which number to call. "Easily remembered seven-digit numbers" for calling the police—all the rage in the 1960s—turned out to be an oxymoron. I can remember asking the Philadelphia chief what his department's number was, while inspecting his brand-new communications center in 1969, and getting a stricken, puzzled look in response. The delay may be caused by any number of factors, including the citizen's reluctance to "bother the police," the need of a family member or witness to calm down or for a victim to wash up (the first urge of rape victims, and a great mistake, especially as the DNA technology enabling identifications through sperm becomes more promising, although it has stumbled recently), or the simple availability of a contacting mechanism. This latter point is the one most dramatically addressed by 911, which not only makes access easier through an easily remembered, universal number that requires no coins in public phones, but which also constitutes an explicit invitation to the public to call their police.

Today 911 has added such refinements as an automatic number identifier and an automatic location identifier, which provide the emergency dispatcher with the phone number and location of the device being used to make the call. These not only help ensure an accurate response but virtually eliminate false alarms. Both are expensive features, however, and their cost has stood in the way of their universal adoption, notwithstanding their obvious value.

Mechanical devices prompt false alarms. Human interaction allows for monitoring, filtration, evaluation, and judgments that mechanical devices don't permit. Drunks, kids, mentally disturbed people, and pranksters can be weeded out through conversational exchanges. In a time when the fire department has been bedeviled by pulled boxes (kids yank the arm and disappear, forcing the engines to come running), the police department, with its human-voice phone interactions, has had no significant false-alarm problem, except in the area of the mechanical devices that trigger a recording into 911, which seem to be set off by any vagrant wind or wisp of smoke. A fight for legislation to forbid these in New York City failed; the one in Minneapolis succeeded.

The new 911 is married to computer-assisted dispatch (CAD) through a terminal in the cop's vehicle. The officer can also use this device to secure information on driver's licenses, warrants, dangerous locations, or "wanted" information. The list of available services is expanding as the police refine their ability to handle citizen emergencies and the technology being used.

Repeat Calls

In the beginning, victims screamed and cops came running. The ensuing years have been little more than refinements of this hare-and-hound chase. With the advent of 911, citizens called faster and cops scurried to respond more rapidly. It soon became a pretty mindless exercise. Thoughtful administrators began to see the need to develop systems of prioritizing responses. Even these systems, however, didn't materially ease the burden. The volume overwhelmed many agencies, some of which experienced as much as a doubling of calls, virtually overnight, as they went to 911.

Every approach seemed to center on answering more calls faster. As the process was mechanized and was made more efficient, the human factor inevitably diminished.

One day a scholar asked, "Where are you running to? How do you know you're not responding to the same chronic problems week after week, with different cops, who aren't talking to each other?" An analysis of this simple proposition produced the startling result that cops were, in many cases, doing just that. A few locations were generating multiple repeat calls, week after week.

Might it not make better sense to analyze the calls, evaluate the problem, diagnose the issues, and prescribe a more permanent solution? Mightn't it be best to visit Johnny on Tuesday morning and warn him that his weekly rowdy parties would, next Friday, result in his arrest? Shouldn't the narcotics squad concentrate on an apartment that produces calls as a result of deals gone bad?

The police discovered the need to be more discerning in their responses and created a unit to diagnose the chronic problems and devise long-term solutions. One of the surprising fallouts was the discovery of the creative talents of the cops assigned to devise new approaches to long-standing, festering sores in the neighborhood. The section dealing with Minneapolis's experiment (RECAP, for *R*epeat *C*all *A*nalysis *P*rogram) describes the cops' ingenious prescriptions for some of the problems they analyzed.

The 911 printouts also provide a vehicle for random inspection of the police service, to establish its quality and to detect possible areas where responding cops are failing to record events that require documentation.

In one case, a string of violations was observed and compiled on a notorious bar, leading to a hearing before the licensing authority that resulted in a suspension of the right to operate. Another bar was closed following a raid prompted by an analysis of repeat calls to that location. A twenty-four-hour convenience store attracted large groups of kids who created noise, vandalism, and littering problems for the neighbors. A few curfew sweeps and pickups of youngsters out past the permitted hours cured the problem.

A mentally disturbed citizen regularly marched into a restaurant with his hair and beard covered with feces, to wash in the bathroom. He was brought before a judge and committed for observation.

Many of the city's problems are chronic and require devoted individual attention. Neighborhoods can be destabilized by one wild family. A cesspool of a bar can become a center of problems for the community. The issues have to be fought with the discrimination that the modern-day requirement of handling thousands of problems uniformly and swiftly will not allow. Efficiency does require fast, standard responses, but these must be accompanied by analysis and diagnosis of and prescriptions for the few chronic problems that require individual attention.

Most revolutionary ideas in policing have their roots in such obvious and simple questions and answers.

The issues surrounding service are not, however, exclusively restricted to questions of policies and programs.

A Cup of Coffee

Practically everyone believes giving a cop a cup of coffee is a pretty innocent act, and it is true that it doesn't rank up there with drug dealing or child molestation, but it isn't quite as free of harm as some apologists would allow.

A cop on patrol receives two calls: one for a disorderly person in a coffee shop (one that accommodates the cop with free coffee) and the other for your heart attack. The question then becomes whether you want the cop's decision clouded by considerations that might not include only the relative importance of the summons.

Training

Technology has helped, but policing remains a very primitive business that mostly centers on the human animal in trouble. This requires a wide variety of responses and a broad, general range of skills. Police work is wonderfully varied.

Training, which everyone supports in the abstract, nevertheless involves taking cops off the streets and placing them in classrooms, where they can't answer the stacked calls and the insistent pressures to respond.

Not only does the service function require speedy responses, but the cops must be able to cope with the unexpected—from the delivery of a child, to applying cardiopulmonary resuscitation, to stemming a flow of blood, to some hair-raising rescue effort. The key determinant of how effectively cops function is the amount and kind of training they've received.

The life of the urban cop may be easy to describe, but given the complexities masked behind the designations street crime, service, and traffic safety, the reality requires the possession of myriad skills, as well as dedication, energy, and interest. The third factor, traffic, invariably gets even shorter shrift than service, but it remains an important area of police operations.

Traffic

Enforcing traffic regulations is an unpopular task in the police world. It brings cops in contact with the overclass, in a negative context, and it makes the enforcers more uncomfortable than they look. Yet it is a key task because the public's safety is much more tied to accidents than it is to crime. We kill about twice as many people with cars as we do with knives or guns. Effective enforcement has been demonstrated to reduce the number of deaths, injuries, and accidents on the roads. The incredible impact of the organization called Mothers Against Drunk Drivers (MADD) in reducing the annual toll of killings on our highways is further testimony of the efficacy of enforcement and education. As enforcement activity (summonses for moving violations at high-rate accident locations, arrests of drunk drivers, etc.) tripled in Minneapolis, deaths due to accidents were reduced more than half, and injuries and accidents declined dramatically.

What is not generally appreciated is how a tough, "no-breaks" traf-fic-enforcement policy can affect street crime. The street criminal is fre-quently part of the burning-rubber, squealing-wheel set that produces anarchy on our streets. The dangers involving motorcycle gangs can most effectively be controlled through no-nonsense enforcement. Carefully tar-geted stops produce suspects with outstanding warrants, result in the arrest of those who have committed other crimes or who are on their way to or coming from such sites, and lead to the discovery of evidence or contra-band. There is no better way to convey the image of an aggressive law-and-order posture than through the highly visible operations of a tough traffic-enforcement program.

Traffic E's

Enforcement will not, by itself, produce safe streets. Its usual part-ners are education and engineering. No group illustrates the former more eloquently than MADD, and nothing demonstrates the force of the latter better than the photos of a collapsed bridge.

MADD has alerted the public to the menace posed by the drunken driver through a remarkably effective educational campaign intended to pressure the system to get tough with these criminals. The collapse of a bridge in Connecticut demonstrated the importance of engineering.

Although the police are principally involved in enforcement, they must work closely with the engineer and participate in the educational effort. The three E's—enforcement, education, and engineering—are interdependent.

The three E's can produce safer streets, but they require commitment and the expenditure of funds and resources that the government is all too often tempted to put into showier projects.

The controversies surrounding the spending of funds on the mainte-nance of roads and bridges, raising the drinking age to twenty-one, lower-ing the speed limit to fifty-five, and requiring the wearing of helmets or even seat belts illustrate that even proven methods of saving lives aren't easy to adopt. One of the painful ironies is the number of paraplegics being supported in our hospitals with taxpayer dollars, because they re-fused to wear helmets. People take even essential encroachments on their freedoms—including the freedom to self-destruct—seriously.

Despite their attachment to the crime-fighter image, cops feel comfortable in the service role, too, where they are summoned and asked to help. Traffic enforcement, though, is an uninvited intrusion. It pits the cop against an unknowable array of potentially powerful, frequently skilled, occasionally educated, and almost invariably vocal citizens. The initial contact is bound to be tense, and the aftermath, in the form of letters or calls to superiors or politicians, may be worse.

I've heard police chiefs speak longingly of abandoning the field altogether. The growth of ancillary forces, such as meter monitors, traffic control agents, and school-crossing guards, is a result of this attitude. This does result in cost reductions, but at the expense of retaining control of the streets. In such areas, the chiefs are simply communicating the antipathy of the troops toward a distasteful task.

It is a mistake for the police to seek to abandon this field, despite all of the pressures and temptations. Traffic enforcement is an important element of promoting public safety.

The traffic function includes such allied factors as police visibility and the "broken-window" syndrome, in which unattended symbols of decay or neglect convey a message of irreversible decline and promote an "anything-goes" air of abandon. Widespread violations of traffic laws create a sense that the controls are withering. A tough enforcement policy communicates a sense of order, discipline, and structure and conveys the message that the cops control the street.

Handling traffic is both a subtle and an ambiguous undertaking. The lives saved, injuries averted, and accidents prevented don't produce an identifiable and grateful supportive constituency. It is easier to identify those who are angered by a ticket they received. It is anything but easy to treat all violators equally, and nowhere is this more clearly and convincingly illustrated than in the "professional courtesies" cops extend one another on the road. Cops do not give other cops tickets. This "courtesy" undermines the credibility and integrity of the entire traffic-law-enforcement effort.

A tough program communicates the vigor of the police agency and its determination to maintain standards in precisely the same way that a no-nonsense approach to street crime convinces everyone of the department's goal of having a clean and livable city.

Service and traffic law enforcement are among the less heralded operations of police agencies, yet they easily dominate the bulk of the responsibilities.

"To protect and to serve" is frequently the motto; yet not much gets said about the latter. Crime is sexy and exciting. It captures the headlines and mesmerizes lots of cops, who adopt the image, irrespective of the realities they face every day.

Improving the ability of the police to respond to and handle citizen emergencies—of a noncriminal nature—is one of the key tasks of today's police administrators.

CHAPTER 9

Management Problems, Concerns, and Opportunities

Americans are used to hearing pleas for more resources from their bureaucrats—whether they be pentagonites, academics, welfarists, or police chiefs. Like Oliver Twist, they ask for "More, please sir, I want some more." Yet my experiences and observations have taught me that the crisis is not one of money, but one of management.

Often we read about a plea for more funds, usually coupled with the threat that something cherished will be threatened with extinction if the funds don't come through. Six months later the press reveals, of the same needy organization, indictments reflecting collusion, payoffs, double billings, or other frauds. The inevitable inquiry shows that the organization was awash in resources, most of which were being wasted or worse. Secret funds are discovered. Excessive billings come to light. Extravagant expenditures are exposed. It should come as no surprise, although it did to them, that the task force studying the Philadelphia Police Department concluded that the one thing the agency didn't need was more money.

Between the lines and behind the figures lurk bloated bureaucracies busily tending to their comforts, accommodating friends and allies, limited only by the depth of the taxpayer's pockets. Stated simply, I have never seen a police agency that didn't have far too many supervisors or that worried much about waste or costs.

The Transit Police and the Minneapolis
Police Department

From the date of my arrival as Number Two in November 1976 until my departure in September 1979, not a single promotion occurred in the three-thousand-member force of New York City's Transit Authority Police Department (TAPD). At the end of my stay, after deaths and retirements had whittled the supervisory levels considerably, the agency still had too many captains, lieutenants, and sergeants. Those above, the deputy inspectors, inspectors, deputy chief inspectors, and assistant chief inspectors, had been trimmed to a mere handful of three inspectors and eight deputy inspectors. They've had a good time filling those ranks, which oversee large operations or clusters of commands, ever since.

The Minneapolis Police Department (MPD) had, in 1980, about a 42 percent ratio of supervisors to cops. Reducing the inspectors and captains from 23 to 12 and the lieutenants from 112 to 38 still left, by 1989, too many supervisors in the ranks.

Supervisors, like all employees, try to earn their pay and justify their positions. They tend to be proud and dedicated employees. They demand reports, inspect operations, ask questions, intervene, issue orders, and require accountings. Because few have any real appetite for uncovering wrongdoing among their colleagues, they normally eschew that particular role. Ironically this may be the only role where they might actually be of some use and the one invariably cited by chiefs urgently pleading for more promotions. History has demonstrated that blessed little wrongdoing will be uncovered by these supervisors, unless they are flogged into action by the chief.

The interventions of supervisors often prove paralyzing rather than energizing. Cops have to spend their time preparing largely unnecessary reports or otherwise accounting for their actions in redundant ways. The police bureaucracy lives and dies by reports. Documentation is the staff of government life, and nowhere is this truer than in the police world, where records become the lynchpins for trials, dispositions of property, the deprivation of freedom, and other important events. There is a tendency to require a report whenever something exceptional occurs, and these documents simply keep being generated well past the point of need. Police executives must train themselves to think, "Is this needed? Do I read and use this report? Who does? Can we live without it?" That orientation will lead to the elimination of a lot of paper. Workers need to feel useful, and supervisors do this by getting involved. This predilection for intervening and requiring reports has led to the latest wrinkle in managerial innovations: flattening the organizational pyramid, for which we may read, "Get rid of more supervisors."

Such management wizards as Lee Iacocca gained fame and fortune by counseling the removal of organizational layers of management types and reducing the distance between the grunt in the trenches and the general at headquarters.

We've seen how the dead hand of civil service and its lock-step progressions up the corporate ladder have paralyzed police chiefs' opportunities for action by saddling them with aides they could neither promote nor demote. No corporate head would, or could, survive having key subordinates foisted on her or him by outsiders.

Many police departments are staffed, at the upper reaches, by civil-service-appointed executives who will not bring the enthusiasm and commitment a CEO needs to get the job done.

Executives choosing their management team use personal observations, annual evaluations, and the daily interactions inevitably connected with close contact to measure the characteristics sought. The chief usually has no trouble identifying the most promising young executives, but a lot of obstacles exist to block the chief's ability to act on that knowledge.

Management's purpose is to get things done through the efforts of others. It involves hiring the right people, assigning them tasks that are related to the purposes of the organization, creating the units that best fit the needs of the agency, providing usable, modern equipment, and housing staff in an efficient physical plant. This may all seem obvious, but the obvious isn't always accomplished.

For example, try asking workers in any organization what the agency's top three priorities are, and you're likely to receive quite a range of guesses. Effective management requires clear objectives and clear language.

Police Work

The recent craze over management by objectives (MBO) proved a sensible reminder of the importance of an organization's sticking to its last. MBO taught us the foolishness of believing that any administrative fad would replace the hardheaded management that comes from recognizing problems, prioritizing them, and finally attacking them. It is not only legitimate but essential to resolve the question of how any action relates to the organization's purposes. Over the years, irrelevancies accrue simply because of the pushes and tugs of various groups with widely different goals. The ship has to be kept on course, and the course is protection and service. MBO basically asks managers to identify where they want to go and requires the development of a plan to get there.

While serving as Bronx commander of the NYPD's forces, I began an extensive swimming program for thousands of ghetto kids. I asked the cops assigned to the task to wear uniforms every time they were out of the pool.

One officer asked me why. I answered, "These kids will be throwing bricks off the roofs at the cops in a couple of years, and I'd like them to have one positive association with the police floating in their memories."

However, the police commissioner at the time was less sympathetic and urged me to abandon the program. "It isn't police work," he said.

I'd whine and plead and evade until the moment of vagueness that I could cite as reluctant tolerance arrived, whereupon I'd make a hasty exit.

Was it police work?

The objectives of the agency were clear enough, but couldn't some of them be realized indirectly? Mightn't they contribute to future safety? I thought so, but they disbanded the program within minutes of my departure from the post.

Motivating Workers

Positive reinforcement and the wonders of participative management are often extolled. Ours is an age when workers are to be stimulated, led, inspired, guided, and listened to, as opposed to driven, disciplined, or directed. The current rage is to speak of quality circles, where workers discuss how to do the job better, team-building models, and other plans that include the worker's participation. And it is true that management ought to care about its workers and include them, to whatever degree possible, in the decision-making process.

What gets ignored in this equation, however, is that a lot of work is unpleasant; most of us would rather turn over in bed or go to the beach than get up and head for the office; it is more fun to play golf or tennis than it is to do most things defined as work, and few people die saying they should have spent more time at the office.

This suggests that there is going to be some resentment or resistance to any job, and there are going to have to be controls and standards. Workers are motivated by positive factors, such as inclusion, raises, recognition, praise, and rewards, but they are also motivated by such negatives as dismissal, reprimands, and fear. As Robespierre said, "Virtue without terror is powerless." This is an age, however, in which words such as *terror* or *power* are not in vogue. The degree to which fads guide action is enormous.

A close examination of any successful organization will reveal that its employees are motivated to produce by fears of dismissal, anxiety over loss of status, the desire to avoid failure, the need to escape the boss's wrath, and a lot of other negative factors modern management tomes don't consider worth including in the managerial "age of positivism."

The focus of the negative discipline ought to be directed at the very few who consistently perform badly. They are the standard for the lowest acceptable level of performance, unless management demonstrates that their performance is unacceptable.

At the other end of the scale, we need to employ reinforcements and rewards. Including the workers gives them a stake in the action. The point is to use both poles, the negative and the positive.

Worker Ownership of Projects

I'll always remember the day I called members of my staff into my office to discuss a specific project. As I contemplated the problem, two solutions flashed in my brain. Privately I exulted. I'd now show them why I was the chief. An eloquent voice urged me forward. As I started to speak, a tiny, feeble message in my mind struggled to be heard: "Are you here to show them how smart you are and how well you can solve a problem? Will they adopt your solution when you arrogantly pronounce it? Is this sensible management?"

I stopped myself in my tracks and asked for suggestions. A spirited discussion followed, out of which one of the participants offered a useful point. I was impressed. What did the others think? They liked it. Why not put Alice's point down?

The discussion continued, and soon Point Two was raised. It was quickly recognized as the missing piece. The providers glowed with pride. Was there anymore? No, that seemed to be it.

I thanked them all and said that, as Alice and Harry appeared to have furnished the answers, we'd now have to get busy to implement them. They left with a sense of ownership in the project.

How valuable it is to curb the ego. How useful it can be to nurture the egos of others. Manipulative? Certainly, but to a valid organizational purpose, taking into account both ethics and the needs of others.

The Japanese in their American-based plants beat back the United Auto Workers' attempt to unionize the employees by using policies that demonstrated concern for the workers. There were company picnics; uniforms the workers might wear or not, depending on their choice; swimming pools; and other amenities. The workers could rotate assignments as they chose, make suggestions about doing things more efficiently, or choose more convenient hours of work. There were no layoffs. It was a wonderful example of worker–management cooperation. Firings and disciplinary actions were minimal and were reviewed by committees of peers. It was the best modern example of the positive pole at work.

Managing

How does one develop a managerial perspective that works? By hearkening, again, to the Bible, rather than to one of those faddish tomes so much in vogue among all managers, police or civilian. A quick glimpse at the *New York Times* nonfiction best-seller list will reveal today's fashion in the organizational suites. The Bible says, "Get wisdom, and with all thy getting, get understanding." But where?

My experience suggests that the answer lies in reading: Shakespeare, Machiavelli, Ibsen, the Bible, Tolstoy, Dostoevsky, Melville, Milton, Kipling, Kafka, Joyce, the Greeks, and others who have offered insights into human psychology, human nature, greed, pride, ambition, and flaws of character. The key to managing people lies in an understanding of the human being. There are no shrewder observers than the artists who have made human studies their life's work.

Any given formula may have its successes—for example, MBO, participative management, and quality circles—but the principles guiding administrative actions ought to encompass a broad grasp of the complexities behind that most complex of creatures: the human being. Poets have a deeper understanding of management than successful bureaucrats writing about their own experiences.

The connection hasn't been made yet because the synapse is too remote, yet the British ruled their empire with graduates in the classics from Oxford and Cambridge, and although they sometimes exploited cruelly, they brought a civilized perspective to imperialism that was altogether lacking, for example, in the Spanish or Portuguese models.

Managing and the Persona

So much of our personality gets in the way of achieving what needs to be done. Taking a press commentary personally will encourage paranoia and work against the public's right to be informed. Arrogance engenders resentment and hostility. Eschewing credit does not lead to its loss. Self-congratulation discourages praise, as others will see no need to add to such tiresome exercises. There is much toughness in humility, only it isn't always obvious. I can recall the soft, gentle tones of New York City Police Commissioner Pat Murphy conveying steel-hard messages to old hands. There was no bluster, threat, or stridency, but the content, and his actions, conveyed the toughness eloquently enough. There's no tougher approach to anything than to ask gentle questions. It is no accident that the exemplar of this method, Socrates, had to be executed. Remembering that public life means service, rather than the defensiveness that comes with thin skin, is a very hard lesson to master. The inducement to self-pity is often overwhelming. There is a delicious temptation to blur the distinction between personal interests and the people's interests.

The chief needs to be mercilessly introspective. This was brought home to me again recently when my wife, reading a book I was writing about my handling of a Bronx incident, reminded me that the failure was mine, and that I was just offering a lot of excuses. She was right and I added an epilogue acknowledging my fault. Flatterers lead one astray. Harsh truths, such as are contained in press commentaries or the union's newsletter, and even reversals, such as tactical defeats on key points, ought to be welcomed for the insights they afford into our foibles. Character is built by avoiding self-pity and learning from criticisms. In public life, defeats are rarely permanent. The point is to put the persona on the shelf and to remember what the purposes of service are.

In deciding how to run the agency, police chiefs must decide whether they're going to serve the people or accommodate the comfort and interests of their colleagues. The two notions are irreconcilable. Choosing the people means earning the undying enmity of colleagues. Pat Murphy was very likely both the best and the best hated chief the NYPD ever had.

Developing Managers

The education and training of police managers, nationally, has been not only appallingly deficient, but wrongheaded. In common with most American education, the system, such as it is, is vocationally centered, with lots of courses on what can only be called the oxymoron of "police science." Law, procedures, regulations, and technical requirements are heavily weighed. The emphasis, a not-altogether-mistaken one, is on developing an effective technician. These skills are essential, but they must be accompanied by an understanding of the broader context within which events take place.

The trouble lies in two areas: education and experience. To take the latter first, most bright young stars get placed in key jobs and are kept there because of the nervousness of the chief over taking a chance with a sensitive unit. Often there's been a scandal or some atrocious press commentary, and the chief, wanting no recurrence, installs one of the best and brightest as commander and, remembering the sting of the pain, keeps the person there forever, even through what may turn out to be several promotions. This process will, of course, narrow the experience base of the fledgling executive, even as it ensures that a tough job will be done well. These are the trade-offs that always attend these things, which is why it's so hard to find a villain in the drama of why police departments don't produce cadres of tough, smart young managers, and why it's so important to avoid the extremes of too long or too short a tenure, however tempting either may be.

The second disability comes from a failure to prepare managers for the world they will discover as they enter a senior position. There, as they wield greater power, they will encounter difficult choices that require a philosophical and ethical base and perspective. Liberal arts is the handiest path to the development of the needed wisdom, yet courses in language, history, English, communication skills, philosophy, or art, as mentioned earlier, get pretty short shrift in the hardheaded world of the police.

The ability to get up and speak effectively in front of a group; skill in dealing with the press; a grasp of the issues needed to cope with unions, prosecutors, the various publics, and others—all should be provided through arduous preparation and training. Yet, there is little evidence that American policing is even aware of this challenge, much less rising to meet it. The result is chiefs and senior executives who are clearly out of their depth in dealing with complex public issues and who, rather than show it, retreat, like their subordinates, behind the agency's veil of secrecy. One of the consequences, here and elsewhere, has been the phenomenal growth of the public relations industry.

One of the requirements of accreditation by a national agency trying to raise the standards in police departments is the appointment of a press information officer. I balked at this provision, insisting that the police agency be open, accessible, and responsive—which meant that reporters would contact the police employee handling the case in question, rather than some slick flak paid to cosmetize the issues.

Private industry, well ahead of the police in this and other, worthier, areas, has for years used the skills of experts whose stock in trade is polishing the corporate image without enormous regard for the substantive problems being masked.

Major-City Chiefs

Over a period of nine years, I met regularly with the chiefs of America's fifty largest cities through an organization called the Major Cities Chiefs of Police. They were honorable, dedicated men (there had been a woman, the Portland, Oregon, chief—the first such daring appointment—but she'd been forced out, after a brief tenure, amidst a controversy in the 1980s) who cared about their responsibilities, yet their eyes glazed over with hostility and boredom at any mention of managing better, eliminating waste, and getting more out of what they had, rather than asking for more resources. Tenure was another favored topic.

These were not executives who read, wrote, or commented meaningfully on the world around them, although they were widely experienced and had a lot of important observations to make. They had all grown up in determinedly anti-intellectual environments, and the conditioning had stuck. Now, mired in the complex problems of today's age, they were unable to think systemically, or to provide the insight the nation needed in order to understand and attack the crime and violence that threatened the country's very existence. The analogy between the chiefs and Vietnam generals suggested itself with perennial hardiness.

The Urban Generals

Why did America's generals keep assuring us we could win and never furnish us the insights that, through the exertions of countless demonstrators and thinkers, we ultimately came to accept as the political and moral realities of Vietnam?

What pressures operated on our military that forced or tempted them to twist easily observable facts into upbeat scenarios colored with roseate hues?

Whence the self-hypnosis that grips so many in public life? What has any of this to do with life in America as we ponder the twenty-first century and the appalling escalation of urban carnage?

The Vietnam analogy may be useful as a reminder that those who don't learn from history are fated to repeat it. The moral similarities between Vietnam and the war on drugs is striking.

The police chiefs are under intense pressure—from the press, the public, mayors, council members, and other frightened or interested citizens or groups. Every community meeting is dotted with harsh judgments and unanswerable questions. The crisis, though, also serves as a vehicle for additional resources, and the temptations of power, money, or sex frequently prove irresistible to those at the centers of action. Whereas cops on the street might be bought off by money, their chiefs more often succumb to the temptations of the trappings of office. It was a cynical secretary of state who said, "Power is the ultimate aphrodisiac." The drug war is at once their greatest curse and the most promising opportunity to enhance their kingdoms. Realpolitik involves such ambiguities.

So they give us body counts.

The capital's police try to wriggle off the petard on which they're hoist by pointing to over forty thousand drug-related arrests in two years, piously enunciating they can't be blamed if this number overloads and wrecks the system. After all, they're doing their job. Don't blame them if nothing works.

What might?

The capital chief's answer is "More cops."

The scene is replicated in Los Angeles, New York, and Chicago and points north, south, east, and west. Is there a haunting echo of other generals asking for more time, treasure, and personnel?

A few of us went to Washington to beg our leaders to put some funds into research, experimentation, evaluation, and study of the drug problem. They were about to heave a large chunk of cash at the difficulty. Across the hall, Ed Meese captured the headlines and interest. Our small band contented itself with a couple of bored reporters.

We'd been given leave, by our colleagues, to speak in their name, but only on the condition that we refrain from any attack on the monies heading their way, which would most likely be wasted on time-and-a-half expenditures to get additional cops to make still more arrests. We had to promise. Thank God the question never arose. Instead, our plea sank to the bottom, unheralded and unheard.

Yet my colleagues know we are losing the war. If one listens carefully to their analyses, the virtues of treatment and education will be extolled, over enforcement. The system collapses under the strain, yet the urban generals cry for more.

The drug problem shifts under our feet as we discuss it. Some educational programs appear to be working. Good results are reported for some treatment approaches. Drug testing gives us a way of monitoring compliance. Prevention hasn't even been thought about. The race question becomes another of those unmentionable factors, despite the obvious implications of enslaving large numbers of blacks with still another drug.

Maybe the Vietnam generals were never sufficiently introspective to examine their role philosophically. They were there to do a job and they tried their damnedest. Oliver North was a hero of that struggle. Typical of the good soldier, he was brave, patriotic, faithful, and true, but did he have a perspective about democracy and its demands on our hearts and minds?

The chiefs have been given their role assignments, and they're going to carry out their orders faithfully. The results will tempt the suspicion that the solution, if it comes, will not emerge from their exertions.

Public life requires wisdom and character as much as it requires duty and courage. We have repeatedly discovered that we can't afford super-patriots who envelop themselves in the flag while inviting their friends to plunder the poor's housing. Police chiefs have to learn that it is the people's interests they serve and that this might be done by taking a more sophisticated view of U.S. Supreme Court decisions, and by thinking systemically about crime, violence, and drugs and of their obligation to report what they see and to call attention to the inequities and injustices that produce so much misery and crime. Their duties go beyond the simpleminded notion that they're only there to enforce the law.

It's really a pity that my colleagues didn't read the Greeks or Shakespeare; they might have been spared Santayana's curse.

This is the unfortunate answer to the perplexing question of why those closest to our urban problems are unwilling or unable to offer useful views about events unfolding in front of their very eyes. The fact that there are careers, ambitions, and egos tangled in the web only adds to the difficulty.

Examining some of the specific issues confronting contemporary American police executives should not only demonstrate the questions they are facing but, perhaps, offer insights into the difficulties involved in solving them.

Downsizing

Virtually every agency has too many supervisors, and they do precious little supervising. Reducing their number allows for increases in the number of workers, without increasing the budget. There is no inalienable right to promotion in any work setting. The worker can derive satisfaction from a paycheck and from the psychic income that comes from public service. The cronyism that attends most police agencies doesn't really allow for much effective supervision or control in any case. Supervisors who came up through the ranks with their buddies are not going to discipline them or cramp their style, especially when their supervisory status is owed not to the police administration but to civil service testing.

Incidents such as the 1988 Tompkins Square Park disorder in New York City, where the police clashed with squatters in the park and their supporters while the yuppie residents, who'd complained of squatters and derelicts in the park, wrung their hands in self-righteous agony, resulted in over 120 complaints of police brutality. Films and testimony clearly indicated that the cops had run amok. They illustrate, very dramatically, how undisciplined the world of policing really is. There were hosts of supervisors at the scene, but there was not a single recorded instance of any of them trying to bring their furious charges under control or of disciplining anyone for what were clearly egregious and numerous acts of wrongdoing by the cops. Supervisors cannot be counted on to quell, or even discourage, police riots.

Discipline

Police agencies are mainly controlled through terror, and this terror is mostly aimed at the 1 or 2 percent who, if left to their own devices, would set a negative tone. I know that armies are similarly controlled and suspect that athletic teams may be as well. We, the audience, do not want to be reminded of such painful truths. On our screens, we love the images of justice-loving knights errant who happen to be organizational iconoclasts. We refuse to believe that real-life people don't always operate that way.

Wrongdoing will rarely be reported or acted on by supervisors in daily contact with their subordinates. Propinquity begets commonality of interests. The worker has a deep and permanent interest in gaining the affection of the overseer. The supervisor will be brought to intervene only if he or she believes the risks of failing to do so to be unacceptably high. In order to bring this about, harsh action needs to be taken against those who fail to report infractions. That same tough police commissioner, Pat Murphy, held commanders accountable for the failings of their underlings and demoted many high-ranking officers to prove the point. His administration was the only one in memory in which supervisors felt really pressed to control their underlings.

The key to control is the development of tough, effective central units, whose commander and members have been carefully selected, and whose objectives and policies have been clearly enunciated by the chief. This unit becomes the tool through which general compliance will be obtained. If the internal affairs unit does its work well, it will not only uncover wrongdoing but energize field supervisors into participating in the program.

It ought to be added that police agencies have never properly understood the psychological chasm that must be bridged when a worker is promoted to supervisory status. An order taker must be suddenly and miraculously transformed into an order giver. The military turned out ninety-day wonders (lieutenants) by getting them out on the drill field, where, by barking out endless orders in a process of conditioning and reinforcement, the lieutenants finally spanned the divide. I can remember never being comfortable, as a young sergeant, issuing orders. Because I hadn't been trained and conditioned to become an order giver, I was always secretly expecting defiant refusals to comply, which never came. It wasn't until well into my lieutenancy, five years and countless orders later, that I grew comfortable with the notion that I was there to give orders and they were there to carry them out.

Once the objectives have been set and have been communicated to the troops, a way has to be found to determine how well they're doing.

Measuring Results

The activities and success rate of police organizations can be measured, but it is a tricky process. If the three key priorities are fighting street crime, providing better emergency service, and promoting traffic safety, there ought to be a way of expressing the success or failure rate in ways the public can understand.

The first requisite in street crime is that it be accurately recorded and reported. It is not unheard of that police agencies fudge the crime figures, as we've seen, in order to look good. Besides the manipulations, crime is not invariably, or uniformly, reported, so there will be a significant percentage that is not represented in the figures. An additional irony lies in the fact that citizens report crime more faithfully when confidence in the police is highest, so efficient police agencies are penalized by having a higher percentage of the crimes that are occurring reported than cities where the citizens have lost faith and given up on their police departments. Because of this anomaly, a crime-ridden, totally unsafe city may produce a lower per capita criminalization rate than one that is generally safe. In such circumstances, it pays to compare the crimes most likely to be reported accurately: murder and car theft. The variables, however, are so many and so great that everyone agrees that a city should be compared only with itself. That is why reports of crime reflect this year's experience versus last year's, in the same town.

Random sampling and polling techniques are good but not perfect ways of verifying the integrity of crime figures. Once solid statistics are established, the agency can concentrate on arrests. *Clearance rate* is a term that can be deceiving because one arrested criminal may confess to twenty crimes (which will then be recorded as solved, or cleared) but may well be charged (arrested) for only one of them. It has always seemed to be more useful to concentrate on arrests for Part I crimes, the so-called street crimes, as an index of effectiveness.

Service simply requires the development of an efficient response system. Then the results can be easily measured and analyzed. Such questions as how many calls are received, what types, and how rapidly are they answered can be represented in numbers gleaned from the 911 system. As we noted, analyses reveal that many calls are of a chronic, repetitive nature and best handled through individual diagnosis and specific prescription—the system called Repeat Call Analysis Program (RECAP).

Because everything in the 911 system is recorded and timed, it is easy to obtain enormous amounts of management information that enables staff to analyze and plan, as well as to evaluate the system's virtues and flaws.

Traffic safety requires an answer to the question of how best to promote traffic safety and speedy flow. Hazardous intersections can be targeted for enforcement. Drunk drivers have to be arrested. The enforcement focus has to be on aiming at the events that cause deaths, injuries, and accidents.

Both traffic operations and police service can be expressed in facts and figures. The preparation of an annual report forces the agency to review its operations and examine its performance. Monthly management reports force chiefs to think in terms of the agency's direction, inform their bosses of the issues claiming attention, and the progress, or lack of progress, on the more important projects and programs.

Answers

There is a temptation in the bureaucracy to fashion answers for any question. However, integrity—and the communication of its message to the organization and the citizens served—demands more.

As a young police student, I attended a private cramming school that prepared us for police exams. An important part of the instruction was the preparation of answers to any problem, in essay form, always containing a clutch of pro and contra points and a conclusion. This act of sophistry became hallowed in police lore. A commander who was unhappy with a subordinate's response when the real issues were clearly being fudged would often say, "Don't give me a Delehanty answer." We had all sat next to each other on the hard, flat benches of the Delehanty Institute.

When crime rates go down, chiefs modestly point to programs that just might be doing the trick. When they rise, social and economic theories get a serious play.

As teenagers are the principal actors in street crime, I was relieved that, in the early 1980s, high schools in Minneapolis were closed and consolidated because the teenage population had plummeted. Crime, conveniently, declined in 1982, 1983, and 1984. All seemed to be following the script.

Then, in December 1984, an uptick occurred. Was it a glitch? The next thirty-six months confirmed that it wasn't, as Part I crimes rose in thirty-three of those months. By 1987 they had reached record levels. I didn't know why and said so, believing that citizens and cops ought to be aware of some of the agonizing and confusion that chiefs suffer in attempting to have all the answers to do the job. Then a state report came out that reflected explosive growth in the "at-risk" teenage population of poor males. So, although the overall cohort was declining, a critically important figure was going through the roof.

Such frankness with the public is healthy for a democracy because it illustrates, for the citizen, the central importance of being informed and participating in the life of the city. Big Daddy doesn't have all the answers.

Strategic Planning

A strategic plan can easily be adopted from such documents as the annual and monthly management reports because these documents force the executive and the staff to focus on the agency's direction. A strategic plan focuses managerial attention on the agency's objectives and encourages the development of a scheme for the foreseeable future. The plan should be a rough road map for the next three to five years and should be updated every year. The full participation of executive staff is important because the plan needs their insights, participation, and support, and their participation orients the staff to thinking about the future of the agency and its mission. Their commitment to the plan is essential to its success. Indifference to a program within the police bureaucracy is as deadly as outright opposition. Whatever is not vigorously pursued tends to disintegrate.

Deploying Cops

Cops are easily the costliest commodity in the police budget. One cop, with salary and benefits, will probably cost $50,000 to $60,000 per year, or more. Having a cop cover a spot (such as a seat in a radio car) twenty-four hours a day, seven days a week, usually, with days off, vacation, sick time, and so on requires the hiring of five officers. This comes to almost a third of a million dollars for the presence of one cop, in one place, all year long. Such other costs as cars and buildings pale by comparison. About 90 percent of police budgets are used for personnel costs. It is only too obvious that how cops are used becomes the key to whether an agency is well or poorly managed.

Most calls can be responded to by one cop. Studies in San Diego and my experience in Minneapolis have shown that cops tend to be more cautious, alert, and careful when riding alone. They can also answer more calls. Using two-officer patrols is a peculiar form of police featherbedding, yet large police agencies like New York's and, before 1980, Minneapolis, have continued to waste tens of millions of dollars on the practice, while usually asking for more cops. However, reform means tangling with the union. It should also be added that cops are fervid about backing each other up, and calls requiring response in strength always result in large numbers arriving at the scene. Using one-officer patrols requires additional training and the encouragement of the backup practices cops love to undertake, in any case.

Citizens want a cop, on foot, on their beat, but the imperatives of modern policing dictate the use of cops in cars equipped with phones, radios, and computers that enable them to handle the swelling volume of calls ever more efficiently. This is an area where public pressure works against the interest of making the bureaucracy more efficient. It calls for educating the public about what is reasonable and what isn't.

The usual debate centers on whether there ought to be more cops or not, yet no one can say what the right number is for a city. A very rough, seemingly sensible ratio is about two per thousand population, yet the NYPD has about twice that total and Washington, D.C., has even more.

The number of cops has to take into account not only the agency's need but the impact of any increase on the system. As I said before, if the current number of cops is overwhelming the criminal justice system with arrests and citations, then it makes little sense to strengthen that one link and leave the rest of the overburdened chain untouched. If the jails overflow and the courts are not able to handle the volume, it ought to be clear that an imbalance has been created. It isn't very sexy to hire new prosecutors, judges, probation or parole officers, public defenders, or jailers to handle the surges in the volume.

Random patrol by a cop rarely results in important arrests. Studies are revealing that crackdowns in target areas may help in reducing crime and that their effects may outlast the presence of the cops by a considerable margin. This is a kind of spillover effect on street conditions. It takes the criminals a while to reestablish interrupted patterns of behavior, and the reduction in police coverage also takes a while to be perceived. The problem with these saturation tactics is that they only displace street crime, they don't prevent it. We have seen, however, that even the most effective of crime-fighting measures bring political baggage that makes their adoption riskier than the average observer might suspect.

Wherever one looks, the problem looks the same: The crisis in American policing is not a money or resource scarcity but a management problem, and one that has not been recognized, much less addressed.

A *New York Times* report in July 1989 on the heating mayoral race had the candidates vying with one another over how many additional cops they'd hire. It was clear that the aspirant with the highest believable number would gain the favor of a panicked people.

There was no talk of management, of accountability, of measuring results, or of planning and certainly none on a question that hadn't occurred to any of them: the selection of the executive who'd lead the enterprise. Lost was any appreciation of the management challenge facing anyone trying to whip a demoralized, inefficient department into shape.

This unseemly auction showed just how far the most important players in law enforcement in America—mayors—are from appreciating the daunting management tasks facing the urban generals they appoint.

CHAPTER 10

Controversies within the Police Agency

The role of corporate managers is relatively straightforward. They are there to make money for the firm's owners. The task may be hard to achieve but it is easy to describe. Feedback rolls in very rapidly. It is a painfully direct process.

A public manager's job is not only much more complicated but it almost always involves the more important questions facing governments: defense of the nation, the economy, the environment, and the public's safety. Various, and sometimes unexpected, constituencies are affected by every act. Special interests vie for an edge. The official is there to serve the people, but the person requesting the favor is also one of the people.

It is difficult to distinguish between the narrow desires of the pleader and the broad interests of the people, but it is absolutely central that the distinction be made if public service is to have any meaning.

Internally and externally, the chief faces a wide and confusing array of issues. The decisions are never easy because of the pressures and interests involved. Even when the correct act is clearly evident, difficulties arise in relation to the affected interests that come forward.

Examining a few of the many issues, groups, and police units that get tangled in controversy or difficulty will aid in understanding the complexity behind seemingly simple problems.

The difficulties permeate the chief's official life and range all over the lot, from the hiring of recruits to external relations with such internally unpopular groups as the Guardian Angels.

Recruitment

It seems fairly obvious that a rewarding career that provides a useful service and pays well ought to be able to attract superior candidates. There is no reason that college graduates cannot be attracted to the police force. It is rewarding work, psychically and monetarily, and not nearly as risky as television would have us think. Statistically, many other callings—such as farming or construction—are much more dangerous. Among municipal employees, sanitation workers have a higher incidence of injuries.

Such states as Minnesota have proved the feasibility of the notion of higher standards by requiring two-year degrees. They get as many job applicants as the state's law enforcement agencies need. Yet practically all of the other states have markedly lower requirements. The police job is something of a property right of its practitioners, and they seem anxious to preserve it for the historic owners, the upper levels of the lower class. Minorities sometimes play into the interests of the group controlling the police job by protesting that lifting the standards would tend to exclude them and, of course, that many tests are culturally biased, a more persuasive position.

Because police executives, notably including chiefs, are up-from-the-ranks cops, it makes little practical sense to attempt educational qualification distinctions. Uniform standards extend the egalitarian nature of the profession so that, for example, women receive the same salaries and occupy the same ranks as men.

Even something as obviously and universally desirable as raising entrance standards will not receive unanimous support. Every attempt at reform will generate opposition, and tough, educated, experienced managers are needed to take on such difficult tasks as trimming the fat off a police agency or taking cops away from an overstaffed, vocal neighborhood and assigning them to an unknowing, short-changed ghetto.

Minority communities have latched onto residency requirements by way of increasing minority representation in the ranks. Courts have held that restricting employment opportunities in this way is perfectly legal, and such cities as Chicago use the practice with apparent success. The police union, representing the interests of its suburban-dwelling white members, resists this approach and fights such restrictions. There is a question of what might be called freedom of residency for the employee.

Women, Blacks, and Other Minorities

Police departments began in America around 1830, in Philadelphia and New York. They were, for the first 130 years of their existence, completely comprised of white males. This prejudicial attitude toward sex and race mirrored that of the larger society.

The pressures of the civil rights and feminist movements, the riots of the 1960s, and the grudging, growing awareness that the police would need black representatives, especially, to cope with the problems in the ghetto gradually moved the agencies to make some progress. Court decisions compelled further advancement for minorities. Since the late 1950s, blacks have begun to take political control of the cities. By 1989, most of America's ten largest cities had either a black mayor or a black police chief, or both. Yet the integration of minorities has tended to lag far behind the entrance of women into the profession.

In the 1960s and 1970s, I served as the federal government's expert witness to demolish such obstacles as height and strength requirements that barred women from the department and that were ultimately irrelevant in forces frequently peopled with obese and out-of-shape cops. In fact, even today, only a tiny handful of police departments have compulsory physical-fitness programs or any continuing requirements to stay in condition. Unions would be sure to oppose vigorously any requirement of periodic examinations or continuing surveys of physical capability. In Minneapolis, cops grieved over a rule that mandated their appearance for one hour a week at the local YM or YWCA, on company time. It is characteristic of the profession that cops enter in great shape and go rapidly downhill over the ensuing years because of a combination of such factors as an unhealthy life rhythm of rotating shifts, poor eating and drinking habits, and a lack of emphasis on fitness in the profession, curiously enough. That is not to say that they don't need to be in shape; they do, but the tough physical strength and agility requirements I'd been asked to attack were almost totally irrelevant to on-the-job performance, featuring characteristics and events that didn't relate to the cop's daily tasks.

Just as blacks can be relied upon to deal more sympathetically and sensibly with other blacks, women can be expected to bring negotiating and conflict-resolving skills that may defuse many altercations. Women are different from men and will therefore succeed or fail in different situations than men. They tend to be less violent and less reliant on force, including the use of the gun. In some cases, where authoritarian male types would try for physical domination, a woman's approach may succeed. However, in cases requiring physical strength, they may fail. It must be remembered that no one called for eliminating men from the ranks over their occasional failures. Women have demonstrated, especially since the mid-1970s, that they can do the job.

In the case of women joining the police force, as in so many other cases, heated controversy exists. However, controversy doesn't always reveal the true sentiments of the combatants. For example, many cops' wives object to women in the ranks for the ostensible reason of safety. The truth probably lies in their apprehension that cops may fall in love with their partners, and the introduction of sex into the equation is bound to prove intolerable. What was labeled safety might have been concealing well-founded reasons for jealousy.

With all of the progress made on behalf of women and minorities, police departments continue to remain racist and sexist institutions. The depth and extent are determined, first, by the real attitude (everyone pays lip service to truth, beauty, and justice) of the administration and, second, by the numbers of minorities and women in the ranks.

In one of those delicious ironies of history, the NYPD has been rather tolerant of minority issues because the struggle for control within the department was between Italians and Irish, with the latter usually in the driver's seat. In power struggle situations, other small groups, like minority parties in coalition governments, can become important allies. As a result Jews, blacks, Hispanics, and women haven't had all that much trouble reaching the upper ranks, as long as there weren't too many of them and they had talent. This delicate balance in the NYPD was struck a formidable blow on July 1, 1975, when the most recently hired, mostly minorities and women, had to be laid off because of the budget crisis. This cost the department a large cadre of women and minority males among the 5,000 laid off that day. They had been laboriously recruited in a special effort to increase their representation in the ranks. Most were ultimately rehired, but a devastating punch had been landed on the stability, security, and permanence of the job. Another irony followed in 1984, when a black chief, the city's first, was asked to preside over all of this complexity. Still, the department remains mostly male and mostly white.

Assignment of Cops

Communities rarely ask how the department decides how many cops their area ought to have, yet the answer is important to the community's safety. Here, as in so many other places, politics intrudes.

Minneapolis has a good, simple formula: assignment on the basis of Part I crimes and calls for service. This means that the trouble spots get the most cops. Even such a tautology carries political ramifications because the overclass resents the concentration of public services on the underclass. The resentment in Minneapolis was expressed in the general, gradual abandonment of the formula, as the more politically powerful areas received more than their correct share of cops.

In 1980, the assignment of more cops to poorer sections was preceded by public discussions and numerous community meetings, before the adjustments were adopted. Yet, the implementation of the reform sparked a controversy that never really subsided. Nine years later, the richer community and its representative, who never lost sight of the political capital behind the issue, continued to rail over the adjustments. The minority community benefiting never got involved in the issue, nor did they participate in the siting of a new precinct station house in their midst when it was first proposed. This siting was implemented over the protests of surrounding council members and without the help of the politicos whose community gained this desirable facility.

The controversy illustrated the enormous complexity of such public issues as the site of a precinct station. In this case, the white community wanted it and the black citizens were wary of "Greeks bearing gifts." There had been, here, an unseen need for the chief to educate the black community on the issues. The residual effects spilled over into the 1989 city council race as one of the black candidates complained of a "fortress" having been sited in the midst of the black community.

New York's police use an incredibly complex assignment-of-cops formula with many factors, by way of obfuscating the issue and preventing the political fallout that occurred in Minneapolis. With a formula that takes in crime, calls for service, population, area, juvenile delinquency, traffic, and about four other factors, the agency can lose itself in a welter of excuses and evasions and blame it all on this straitjacket. The plan is all-encompassing and produces such unwieldy results as both to invite ignoring it and still to allow assertions that it is being followed faithfully.

The cop managers have learned that when you are responsible for a hundred things, it is hard to be held accountable for any specific failure.

An additional assignment wrinkle is the pressure that black communities apply to have black cops assigned to their neighborhoods. This pressure, too, must be resisted. The chief is not there to further ghettoize the police. The assignments should be made on a sex-blind, color-blind basis. The presence of blacks as role models is a powerful inducement for their assignment to black areas, as is their use in coping with ghetto problems, but on balance, it is better to have them visible throughout the agency.

It might be argued that none of the reforms or changes stemmed the exodus to the suburbs, nor did it discourage the overclass from securing their own protection, in the city, through the hiring of guards and doormen.

Privatizing the Police Function

The hiring of private security people in America is one of the most significant, and fastest growing, movements of recent years. It arose, first, from the desires of the rich to purchase their own security and, second, from a gradual loss of confidence in the ability of the police to protect life and property. We now see security personnel everywhere.

A quick look around reveals a ragtag army of uniformed security personnel minding property, affording serenity to high-rise dwellers, protecting private functions, body-guarding dignitaries, and generally affording tranquility, in an uncertain age, to those rich enough to buy their own police forces.

Private security guards now, for the first time, outnumber the half a million cops in America's towns, and the trends project still faster growth. In the main, these have been low-level, unskilled, untrained employees, who are paid minimally for what amounts to little more than their presence, in a slapped-on uniform. Efforts to upgrade the industry smack up against economic realities. More qualified employees cost more. Licensing requirements would drive the price up. It might even be held that, ironically, the industry has proved a source of jobs for unemployed blacks and other minorities who have, in a sense, sparked the very fears that brought the industry to this growing stage.

Such organizations as the American Society for Industrial Security, made up of security personnel from large companies, many of them retired from sworn police jobs or federal agencies, work hard at elevating standards with minimal success. Many of their members are better paid, higher caliber personnel who are slightly embarrassed by the lower standards observed in the lower reaches of the industry that provides guard and security services.

As crime, violence, and fear escalate, those who can afford it purchase their own safety.

There is a rapidly expanding use of off-duty officers for private security tasks, too. Moonlighting has become an important source of supplementary income for cops. One of the ironies of their lives is that they may, at one moment, be hired as bouncers for a fraction of their normal pay and, at another, be called in by their departments to earn time-and-a-half to enforce drug laws, overwhelm the courts still further with more arrests, and satisfy the federal government's mindless craze for "aiding local law enforcement" with such funds. Or they may be called in to adjudicate a dispute, while on-duty, at a bar where they'll be working, off-duty, in a few hours.

Police departments are having the greatest difficulty regulating the sensitive area of police moonlighting. In some cities, sworn personnel (cops) have actually got legal control over such plums as regulating traffic around construction sites by having legislation passed requiring the use of sworn officers in such tasks. Only licensed peace officers are permitted to regulate traffic around construction sites in Minnesota, for example, so that a lucrative job opportunity is reserved for cops alone. Some cities forbid the use of the uniform in off-duty employment. Others allow it. Some attempt to control it by becoming the hiring and assigning agents, taking a commission for the task, and assuming the burden of administering this complicated and thorny operation. Most attempt to limit the weekly total to twenty hours.

The privatization of America's police has not only spawned a burgeoning industry but sucked public employees into the private sector, a situation leading to very touchy issues of conflicts of interest and creating competition that doesn't make the private guards' unions very happy. The growth of the industry has been tremendously haphazard and disorganized, yet it has not behaved as a competitor to police departments, as perhaps it should. The corrections field has been privatized differently, as for-profit corporations placed themselves in direct competition with the state corrections agencies in running prisons more economically. All of the bureaucracy could stand being subjected to the rigors of such competition.

Precinct Consolidation

Nearly everyone loves the neighborhood station and harbors feelings about the safety it provides. Yet cops are assigned to calls from cars, rather than buildings, by a centrally located and remote dispatcher who receives the call from 911. The local station house is, save for the officers appearing there to change into uniform and receive roll call instruction at turnouts, out of the loop.

Station houses suck up desperately needed personnel to handle desk jobs, offices, phones, and other bureaucratic accoutrements. They provide no protection or immediate emergency services, nor are their functions connected with such valuable services as training, planning, personnel, internal affairs, and maintenance. Moreover, they frequently fail to follow sensible geographic lines. In New York, for example, there are about fifty-nine community planning boards that could make logical precinct boundaries, but they don't. Instead, rather than face the public storm certain to blow over any closings (which is why the Minneapolis issue of a precinct station took such confusing turns, as the issues were reversed from the expected), the department lives with about seventy-five precinct stations. Efficiency clearly dictates reducing the number to, at most, fifty-nine. Here, as in the foot patrol issue, it means taking on the people, rather than the union. Every reform means taking on someone, but politicians really hate to touch a community's sacred cows, even after they've stopped giving any milk.

Minneapolis had six precincts in 1980, which were quickly reduced to four and rearranged according to the city's topography. A highway, for example, effectively splits the south half of the city in two, yet one precinct had responsibilities on both sides of the highway, although it couldn't get to the other side most of the time. Another precinct had been artificially hacked out in the central city, to allay fears of race riots. Another accommodated downtown interests. Both of the latter were eliminated, and the highway straddler was reorganized to conform to the limitations. The police professional must sooner or later recognize that his or her function is to serve the people and that the task sometimes requires flying in the face of treasured public myths and fancies, such as the necessity of a local precinct station house or a foot cop on the beat. Police chiefs are not there to please, but to serve, and although they must work hard to educate the public on the issues by speaking out, they must also move forward with the reforms. We all find it easy to distinguish the difference between pleasing and serving when, for example, dealing with the Dr. Feel-goods of our society, who give us placebos or harmful pills to make us feel up, yet the public insists on telling chiefs how to run their agencies.

We are rarely tempted to make suggestions to our experts, assuming that they know a lot more about their business than we do, but the principle doesn't seem to extend to police chiefs.

Some police units, for widely different reasons, develop into centers of unexpected controversy.

K-9, Mounted, and SWAT Teams

Cops look great on horseback, but they are useless. They have to look after their animals, and they lack the mobility and freedom to do much more than direct a little traffic, work in crowd control situations, and look terrific. Horses, however, have a mystical appeal to some powerful citizens.

K-9's, however, have many uses. The cops can patrol on foot or by car and maneuver easily. Searches and pursuits are much more efficient with dogs. Dogs can follow traces and locate lost or hiding persons. They provide a measure of safety and protection for the officer, and they are useful—despite their being discredited through their highly visible use during the civil rights demonstrations of the 1960s—in controlling unruly crowds or peaceful protesters. Dogs have been use to detect drugs, follow trails, find missing children, and search warehouses and other large areas.

Modern challenges such as hostage takings, barricaded suspects, and fortified drug houses have caused the police to develop new tactics. It's hard to say why these have become the peculiar phenomena of our age, but they have. The answer may lie in the growth of the mediational, conflict-managing approach to urban problems, which dictates negotiations and tends to eschew massive force. These riot-avoiding, nonconfrontational approaches by the police may also be emboldening angry guys to lash out.

Disciplined, coordinated actions have become essential. Failure to act effectively leads to such tragic results as the NYPD's attempt to capture Larry Davis, which resulted in a confused shoot-out, where the police suffered many casualties and the suspect escaped. Larry Davis was later to teach the cops another lesson, this time in their credibility, when a jury took his word over that of the cops and acquitted him. The history and performance of the NYPD had damaged the cops' credibility with the citizens on the jury. The Philadelphia MOVE fiasco was another, but not by any means the only, example of the need for a plan, preparation, training, and a sensible perspective.

Training under simulated crisis conditions that replicate the anticipated event is the key to developing the effective Special Weapons Assault Team (SWAT). Simulations can be tedious, but they will result in successful operations later. Storming a fortified crack house or a plane with hostages, or handling a plane crash or other disaster, requires expert preparation, discipline, timing, and lots of training. Everyone must know his or her role and have the skills to carry it out.

No agency should have standing, staffed SWAT units, as the events for which they are used will be rare. SWAT teams ought to be composed of specially selected and carefully trained officers who are normally assigned other duties and are brought together, *ad hoc*, to cope with these challenges. They absolutely must, however, train together—frequently and extensively. These operations require the closest coordination and the most delicate timing. They are truly team efforts.

Such aggressive approaches have to be guided by a clearly understood and widely disseminated policy directive that allows for consistent actions that are predicated on the law and on an explicit rationale.

Manuals

Virtually every agency has a procedural manual that contains descriptions of policies, with explanations, and prescriptions for action. If not constantly updated and edited, these manuals can become sources of serious problems, not only for what they contain, but for what is omitted.

Is there a written policy for handling domestic abuse or other cases that might be included under the rubric of family crime? What are the policies on pursuits? What about guidelines for questioning the victim of a rape? Any of these situations can result in serious problems for the agency. A police department I analyzed in 1989 had instructions for the questioning of a rape victim in its manual. There were both offensive and irrelevant sections containing such matters as probing the victim's sex life and prior experiences. When I asked why such offensive material was included, they said it really wasn't theirs; they'd taken it from an advisory from the county prosecutor and inserted it in their manual. They had been slow to realize that whatever was in their manual was theirs, not the county DA's.

Firearms discharge policies come into play whenever someone is shot by the police. In a litigious age, carefully thought-out and updated written policies become much more than the academic, *pro forma* exercises they once were. Today, the absence of a written reference to an approach or policy carries with it the presumption that you don't have one.

Accountability extends beyond the area of written policies and into the person of the cops doing the job on the street.

Name Tags

Cops today mostly wear name plates, identifying them by their apellations rather than the time-honored method of the badge number. The issues involved in this decision are accountability and humanity. As mentioned earlier, this seemingly innocuous reform produced pitched battles, in courts across the land, between administrators and rank-and-filers and their representatives. It may be hard to imagine the heat generated by the controversy, but the police union in Minneapolis spent $25,000, countless hours, and endless lobbying sessions to defeat name tags, unsuccessfully. The Boston police union, in a celebrated court case, beat back its commissioner's attempt to force them to wear name tags. The NYPD finally succumbed in 1975, after a vicious struggle. Cops hate to be stripped of the relative anonymity within which they function; they think it limits their freedom of action, and in connection with having their way with those who've failed the attitude test, it sometimes does.

Today, the appearance of the officer's name is mostly a commonplace. The seeming innocence of the event conceals one of the most important symbolic battles for control of the police. It was sort of the Pork Chop Hill of the cops' world as a furious battle raged over a seemingly valueless strategic objective, concealing the more serious struggle of wills that lay behind the action.

The unions fought to keep their members faceless, and the chiefs fought to promote accountability. As in so many of these struggles, the public arguments masked the real points of contention. The cops said they feared reprisals, against themselves or their families, from people they had arrested, but this concern could not be buttressed with any evidence of such danger. The central point was accountability. The cops wanted to go on exercising power in relative anonymity, and the chiefs were trying to humanize the force.

These behind-the-scenes struggles are continuous, and sometimes, as in the distribution of pension and overtime goodies, the chiefs jump into bed with the union.

Overtime and Disability Pensions

It is very difficult to spot a real concern about the waste of taxpayer dollars in the bureaucracy. No constituency exists for economies. The philosophy goes as follows: The money's there, spend it. At fiscal year's end, an unseemly rush to spend unspent monies results, lest—unthinkable prospect—any be returned to the general coffers. The concern about over-runs is real, but short of that, all the worry centers on spending what has been allocated. The fear may be "Use it or lose it for next year," a very real possibility. And the allocation process—in which the mayor and/or the council examines the proposed budget—is notably uninformed. The elected officials rarely pay close attention to the department's detailed budget documents, relying on budget staff to monitor the process. When, as chief, I went over my more than $40 million budget, typically in one two-hour session, the politicians would invariably snag on trivial, if sexy, points or projects. The session would turn into a debate in which support-ers defended my actions and detractors attacked, all without much concern about the budget items before them. The agenda tended to center on old battles and real or imagined grievances that had nothing to do with bud-gets. The sessions became a chance for the politicians to posture and rail at their captive staff members. They get away with this game playing simply because the public takes little interest in the government's oversight re-sponsibilities. These politicians are there to exact performance from the bureaucrats, but this duty is often forgotten.

In the political rush for votes, such profligate waste as putting scores of officers on overtime to promote visibility and give the semblance of action proves, especially around election time, irresistible. The millions wasted—and at time-and-a-half levels—don't seem to bother anyone in government very much. Some recipients, whose pensions are based on a percentage of their last year's wages, have learned how to parlay extra hours of meaningless hanging about into annuities for life. In the summer of 1989, it was revealed that some Stamford, Connecticut, police officers had, with overtime, grossed well over $100,000 the previous year.

The granting of disability pensions, frequently tax-free, when the injured officers might easily be given a productive inside job is another fiscal scandal waiting to be unearthed. But police agencies, as we've noted, are not institutions that reward whistle-blowers.

Finding a suitable inside job for ill or injured officers affords them the dignity of work and inclusion, saves taxpayer dollars on disability pensions, and sends a message to the troops that the agency is being administered on a humane, cost-effective basis.

This is another area of controversy where the union pulls all levers to get its members settled for life without much regard to the cost. As we examine the question of pensioning off the members versus finding something for them to do within the agency, among other issues, it becomes clearer that motherhood and apple pie also have their detractors in public life. Even the search for such truths as whether workers should be pensioned or employed somehow has its critics.

Experiments

The Minneapolis Police Department's experimental effort to cool off high-crime "hot spots" could mean slower responses to some citizen complaints this summer, says one City Council member.

Thus began an article in the May 17, 1989, issue of the *Tribune,* in which the politician went on to demand a curtailment of the program. A debate followed about the importance of the data to be gathered from an experiment that cost more than half a million dollars.

Experiments usually exact a high price. They involve playing with people's lives, whether one is dealing with medicine or policing. Even discovering a cancer cure would involve consigning a number of people to death in order to prove the efficacy of the treatment and save countless lives later. Few bureaucrats are eager to take the risks connected with experiments in policing. Chapter 13 illustrates the dangers of such high-minded pursuits as seeking new and better ways of dealing with family violence.

An agency's attitude toward innovation is reflected in its approach to experimentation. A department seeking funds and scholars to conduct searches for new methods looks quite different from the majority, which resist such initiatives. All will faithfully support the notion, in speeches and pronouncements, but few want to face the easily avoidable heat generated by politicians, as in the Minneapolis case cited. These same politicos will frequently call for new methods and innovative solutions at the same time that they're demanding more people on the streets and asking why time, effort, and money are wasted on such frills as this training or that experiment. They rarely spend much time making the needed connections between innovations and new and better ways of coping with police problems.

The innovator and pathfinder must expect resistance and opposition. An open and experimenting department sends waves of excitement crackling through the ranks. Cops feel their work is important when it's being studied, modified, or changed by prestigious scholars, even if they are instinctively opposed to most things intellectual. The Hawthorne effect, in which production rose simply because the ministrations of experimenters caused the workers to believe management cared about them, can be brought to policing. The true payoff, of course, is discovering new and better ways to protect or serve the people. Another challenge arrives when the police deal with those exercising constitutional rights.

Demonstrations

Most citizens think that a police agency is under the control of the chief and that it responds faithfully to the chief's will. This is only partially true, and it is critical to know which parts are true, and where.

Cops are largely autonomous workers who perform out of the sight of supervisors, exercising enormous independent discretion. It would not be farfetched to say that most of the police reforms that have sought greater accountability for the workings of the cops have centered on limiting this discretion.

Cops function mostly alone. They become used to independent action. They are, despite being in semimilitary bodies that ape the army way, not accustomed to working in coordination with others or as parts of larger groups, as soldiers do. Cops are taught to function not as team members, but as individualists.

Cops are assertive. They believe that challenges to their authority have to be met aggressively or they've lost their beat. There is something very like the Wyatt Earp model floating in their heads. They have been taught to use force because they have a monopoly over its legal employment.

Most experienced chiefs realize that in handling a disorderly demonstration, their only option is to decide when to go, or to decide to hold back. Once the order to go is given, however tight the controls or however numerous the supervisors present, the chief is essentially loosing one mob upon another. This is the lesson of Tompkins Square Park and the lesson in countless other places across the land. Cops don't do well with truculence.

The chief who wants to maintain control must orchestrate the handling of an event in a very tortuous fashion. It doesn't matter if it takes an inordinately long time to clear an area, as long as the work of the cops is carefully controlled and channeled. In arrest situations, for example, it is wisest to adopt a slow, mechanical, deliberate approach that processes demonstrators slowly, preventing the precipitate actions that result in clashes even if the slowness creates delays and inconveniences. This is usually the kind of case in which the chief has to be ready to take some heat from the enterprise being picketed. Sometimes it may even be wise to tolerate breaches of law.

For example, in Minneapolis in March 1988, demonstrators took over the street, burned garbage, and even threw some rocks at the police. I was driven to act, yet my hand was stayed by memories of similar events in other cities and the mistakes I and my colleagues had made in reacting speedily to the challenge posed by a disorderly demonstration. Once I gave the signal to go, my control over the troops was at an end. I tolerated the disorders for a couple of days. The cops seethed. The public's anguish mounted as the media bombarded them with provocative photos such as a front-page shot of a guy burning the American flag. That one got me letters from all over the country and a visit from a delegation of veterans. (We later arrested and prosecuted the flag burner after a longish investigation and going through a lot of trouble to get him. The U.S. Supreme Court's 5-4 decision in 1989, holding such acts to be constitutionally protected speech, invalidated the major effort we'd put into identifying and arresting this person. He was charged with and convicted of a felony. I wound up on television, a year later, defending the Court's ruling, to compound the irony and confusion.)

As the disorders continued, a general demand for action surfaced. On the third day, after a public warning that things had gone far enough and that there would now be arrests, I said, "Go," with the predictable consequences. Despite tight controls, much of the event became a hare-and-hounds chase. Charges of police brutality followed. By then, however, the public was exasperated with the demonstrators' antics and were likely to be pretty tolerant of aggressive police behavior. Waiting for the people's feet to pinch is an effective way of getting the public's support, but this support should not be considered a permanent investment. It is withdrawn at the first sign of real trouble. As any athlete can report, the public's adulation can be ephemeral.

Despite the mercurial nature of the public's mood, it is absolutely essential to engage them in a partnership if neighborhoods are to be made safer. The partnership has to be modeled on the relationship between the candid, open, and revealing professional dealing with a client who has a right to the truth.

Crime Prevention

Crime prevention means keeping criminal acts from happening. The police have learned the importance of the public's participation in crime prevention programs. After decades of such rhetoric as "Leave it to us; we're the professionals; don't get involved; you'll get sued by the burglar you shot," the police discovered that the Thin Blue Line just wasn't up to meeting the challenges of crime and violence all by itself. They needed help. The public, cops learned, mostly polices itself, and the forces supporting this approach had to be strengthened.

America is mostly policed by its citizens, not its cops. The levels of tolerated behavior are known and reinforced daily. The degree to which citizens are willing to intervene establishes the levels of safety and civility. The amount of social glue or neighborhood cohesion goes a long way toward determining an area's safety.

A stroller's dog poops on the path, and a guy on skates, being pulled by his huskie, stops to remonstrate: "That's a shame. You shouldn't just walk away from that, sir. It's wrong."

The stroller smiles sheepishly and sneaks a glance at his companion. Nothing happens, but a rule has just been strongly reinforced. I'd seen it a thousand times before in the Midwest, and I knew it had its effect.

This was another example of the self-policing that an orderly society imposes on itself. It is based on citizen concern and involvement, and it relies on a social contract that assures the intervener that she or he will be supported. The interest and concern expressed by the citizen exists in the New York subway system, too. However, in the subways, interveners suspect that any effort to enforce the rules is going to get them into trouble and that their trouble will be met with the averted glances of their fellow passengers. That is the real reason the subways are unsafe—because citizens have suspended self-policing operations there, and not without sound reasons.

Criminals are opportunists. They set out to exploit a good situation. If it isn't there, they go home. Alert neighbors, looking out for each other, will discourage them. Marked property is harder to sell and easier to trace. A locked and secure home is a bigger challenge to the burglar than an open or vulnerable one. Alert and aware citizens are harder to mug than careless or unwary ones. If mugged, they are probably more likely to assist the police, meaningfully, in tracing the suspect, than less interested and unprepared citizens.

The importance of the fear factor cannot be overestimated. Citizens alter their behavior on the basis of fear. Downtowns are abandoned if the populace feels them to be unsafe. Fear does not proceed in lockstep with the crime rate, although they are, of course, related. Fear may be fed by sensationalized accounts of horrible crimes, but we should not be tempted to such censorship as many city officials support in their stonewalling of the press. There is no right that doesn't carry some burden or disability, but the overall effect has to be weighed.

Organizing citizens into groups that help to protect themselves against crime is the essence of crime prevention. Covering an area with cops ("papering it blue" in the parlance of the trade) will very likely only displace crime.

Government has discovered, in recent years, the wisdom of working with, and listening to, the people. In the Midwest, this translates into block clubs, neighborhood watches, Operation ID (the serial marking of property to facilitate its identification and recovery), premise security surveys, personal security workshops, and such community-oriented policing programs as canvassing a neighborhood to see what problems the residents perceive and how they may be attacked, no matter which city department has jurisdiction over the issue. The point is to build a police–community partnership and to use the public's willingness to help and get them more involved in their own defense.

One self-defense issue is troublesome: the purchase of guns for the protection of home and family. Despite the assertions of the gun lobby, all statistics show that the likeliest thing to happen when a gun is bought for the protection of home and hearth is that it will be taken in a burglary and used in crimes, or that a tragedy will befall the family, often the children, because of the availability of the weapon. Precious few burglars, robbers, or other home-invaders get shot or arrested by honest citizens defending their homes. Despite statistics that demonstrate how very few citizens successfully defend themselves against criminal attacks, the police need to continue to press for citizen participation in the struggle against crime.

The question of whether to jump in and get involved or stay on the sidelines is bedeviling Americans. The proof of the obsession with the issue is the remarkable and disproportionate popularity of a small band of volunteers.

Citizen Volunteers

The importance of the Guardian Angels and other volunteer groups is symbolic more than substantive. Their numbers are not great enough to make a demonstrable difference, but they do represent the extent of how responsible we are for our own, and our neighbor's, safety. The answer is "Very."

The bureaucracy's attitude toward the Angels reveals their real thinking about citizen involvement in the struggle against violence and crime, whatever rhetoric they may be using. Mostly the Angels engender resentment. Cops exhorting city leaders for raises because the job is "so difficult and dangerous" are certain to resent the intrusion of unarmed volunteers willing to do it for nothing. This also accounts for the tremendous police antipathy toward police reservists or auxiliaries—volunteers contributing their time to wear uniforms, patrol the streets, and help the cops. They, too, are cordially resented by the rank and file, and it is a daunting task for the chief to make these groups succeed and to keep the volunteers motivated and involved, considering the institutional resistance. Any faltering of the enthusiasm of the CEO spells defeat for this program.

Summary

We have seen the complexities behind the headlines and the difficulties confronting the implementation of eminently reasonable ideas. Each problem and area represents a challenge as special interests, advocates, opponents, and demagogues emerge to exploit controversies or protect their turf.

Public life involves promoting the people's interests. This is an amorphous idea—and ideal—that is easy to lose in the heat and sweat of the daily battles. There are careers, private interests, profit, and ambition tangled with the need to Do the Right Thing. But as the movie of that title reminded us, it is a damnably difficult thing to manage. The issues, units, and groups listed here mostly represent useful and correct programs and policies, yet even they get mired in the swamp of controversy. The chief's task is to see to the people's interests and to keep working to promote them.

CHAPTER 11

Cops and the Constitution

Cops deal with the United States Constitution every day, in countless ways. The behavior of cops on the street really decides how well or badly that document fares in relation to the police. The Constitution has two main purposes: (1) It protects the freedom to act, as in the freedoms of speech, worship, assembly, petition, and so on, and (2) it restricts the power of the state over the individual, as in protection against illegal searches and seizures, *habeas corpus,* self-incrimination, arrest, and so on. The Constitution is the set of rules by which cops play their game. When the rules are enforced strictly, the players' freedom to act is restricted. Because the rules get changed through Supreme Court interpretations, the police must be ready to shift tactics, on the street, to conform to the new rules.

The role of cops is to enforce the rules. Their interest is in preserving existing conditions and institutions and in adapting to the gradual changes imposed by legislatures and courts. This role assignment necessarily leads to a conservative cast of mind, as it is cops' role to preserve the status quo.

The constitutional debate tends to center on the question of the power and efficiency of the state versus the freedom of the individual. Characteristically, cries of "handcuffing the police" and "coddling of criminals" attend decisions, such as those of the Earl Warren Court in the 1960s and 1970s, that restrict and define police powers more closely. Cries of "fascist" and "oppressor" usually accompany decisions described as conservative, which favor the power of the police over the rights of the individual.

For approximately the first 130 years of their existence, the police didn't worry much about the Constitution. The state courts, where cops mainly functioned, weren't too finicky about such arcane matters. Cops learned to "hit the flat" when a suspicion arose, without troubling about a search warrant. Third-degree methods were not uncommon. Not having access to a lawyer was a fact of life for the defendant. No warnings were issued, and confessions (direct acknowledgments of guilt) and admissions (incriminating statements) were regularly extracted by questionable methods.

The behavior of the police toward blacks in the South provided the more egregious examples of abuse. But although the police agencies of the North were less racist, they were just as guilty in their abuse of criminals. Police officers simply didn't have to get involved in such delicate questions as individual rights. Theirs was an action-oriented profession that delineated its role as getting things done without much regard for the rules of the Constitution.

We saw a good example earlier of the consequences of this "crime-fighter," "we're here to make the people safe at any cost" approach in the study of Philadelphia's Police Department, where they assumed their role to be to make the citizens safe at any cost, without regard for legal niceties. Sister agencies, probably pursuing cleaner policies, weren't having much better luck.

Interestingly enough, the Supreme Court's successive decisions did not make the police less efficient but actually produced the opposite effect. Over the years following such decisions, arrest rates soared and the prison population more than tripled, despite a relatively moderate increase in crime, nationally, from 1970 to 1989. There were, for example, 11.2 million Part I crimes reported in 1978 and 13.5 million in 1987, at a time when the population was going from 218 million to 243 million.

So, despite the agonized squeals of the police practitioners, it can easily be argued that the Warren Court decisions worked to enhance police effectiveness, not to decrease it.

Searches and the Exclusionary Rule

Of all the many questions troubling constitutional scholars and practitioners in the field, none is thornier than the question of searches. When are they reasonable and when are they intrusive? What constitutes a search? How far can one go? Each case seems to furnish a new set of possibilities. There is no knottier area of constitutional law because each search tends to be quite different from the one before. The problem has been exacerbated by the question of drug testing and urine tests, which actually require an intrusive search of the body.

The Fourth Amendment holds that "The right of the people to be secure in their persons, houses, papers and effects, against unreasonable searches and seizures, shall not be violated, and no warrants shall issue but upon probable cause, supported by oath or affirmation, and particularly describing the place to be searched, and the persons or things to be seized."

Immediately, one strikes those favored phrases "unreasonable" and "probable cause" about which a plethora of thick tomes have been written, without exhausting the lode.

A car is stopped for a traffic violation. The cop becomes suspicious of a nervous driver. May the cop search the car? The glove compartment? The trunk? At what point does the search become unreasonable? Does the cop have articulable grounds for the search? The courts have mainly held that the officer can take cognizance of items in plain view and, following an arrest (the taking of a person into custody, to answer for a crime), may search areas under the prisoner's immediate control. The principle is that the officer, to ensure his or her own safety, can look into the areas within the suspect's reach. These would include the glove compartment, but not the trunk.

What expectations of privacy does a student have over her or his locker? Does an intrusion into the body for a drug, using urine or breath tests, require a search warrant?

Up until 1961, America's cops didn't trouble much about searches. Yes, the feds had been stuck with the exclusionary rule since 1914, when it was held that they must, in federal cases, observe the Fourth Amendment and obtain evidence through legal means only, but it applied only to federal courts. Indeed, under something hallowed by the title of the "silver platter doctrine," federal agents could turn over evidence they had seized, illegally, to city cops, who wouldn't be asked how they had obtained it when they introduced it against a suspect in their state courts. Thus a two-track system of justice operated for almost half a century, ensuring those arrested by the feds of at least some of the protections of the Fourth Amendment, whereas those arrested by local cops couldn't even raise the question. The feds, jealous of their turf, made sparing use of this doctrine and simply worked within the rules. They were not then under the incredible public pressures that would flow from the crack epidemic in the late 1980s.

Then in 1961, the Supreme Court held, in *Mapp* v. *Ohio*, that the exclusionary rule applied to the states. Judges in local courts now had to be satisfied that the evidence before them had been secured legally. If not, it would be excluded. And that's how local cops came to find out about search warrants.

Over the ensuing decades, cops learned to obtain warrants, secure evidence, and prepare cases. Arrests that had been clouded by sloppiness, illegality, and recklessness were now much tidier. Training and preparation had to be provided. Kicking and screaming, the police were dragged into the far more professional and skillful tactics employed by federal agents, as they now moved to prepare their cases far more meticulously.

The first major effort to bring the police under the rule of law had been successful, and by happy coincidence, it came just as levels of crime and violence began to escalate dramatically. A frightened public demanded action, and the rapidly professionalized police were able to develop techniques that proved responsive. The cops greatly increased their arrest rate without losing the confidence of the people, as they would have if they'd stuck to their prior practices.

Today, a debate rages over creating good-faith exceptions to the exclusionary rule, but the discussion is clouded by definitions. The courts have held that evidence secured by cops under a warrant, when the judge has erred in issuing it because of a lack of sufficient probable cause, can still be introduced. The cops' reliance on the judge's order constitutes good faith. Zealots, however, have pressed—thus far, unsuccessfully— for a much broader interpretation. They hold that any evidence, however obtained, can be introduced if the cops aver they have secured it in good faith.

There was a long-standing reliance on unworkable systems of control before *Mapp*. The prevailing theory held that cops could be disciplined by their bosses, censured by judges, or even prosecuted by DAs for having secured evidence illegally. The evidence could be admitted against the miscreant, and the system would deal with the officer later. The only problem was that it didn't work. None of these bodies had the slightest appetite for embarrassing the cops they had to work with every day. It was only through the medium of *Mapp* that cops bestirred themselves to the needed reforms, unless they really did want to see cases thrown out on the "technicality" that the evidence had been illegally seized.

Mapp set the stage for a wave of Supreme Court–inspired reforms of the police. Although led by Chief Justice Earl Warren, the thrust was generated by the activist and fundamentally suspicious Associate Justice William O. Douglas, an ardent champion of individual liberties and a baleful observer of police practices. He took Lord Acton's dictum about power and its ability to corrupt seriously.

Decisions on Suspects' Rights

Over the 1960s and 1970s, an activist Court addressed such questions as a suspect's right to an attorney, not just at trial but in the more crucial beginning stages of the proceedings; the suspect's right to remain silent; the need to prove the voluntariness of a confession; and a train of related matters—all of which created strict guidelines for the police. The result was the development of a much more legal, professional, inventive, and effective cadre of law enforcers in America.

In the mid-1980s, a much more conservative Court held, in *Gardner* v. *Tennessee,* that it is unconstitutional for the police to shoot an unarmed, nonviolent, nondangerous fleeing felon. This surprising decision had the *post hoc* effect of rendering about half of the police shootings over the past 150 years unconstitutional.

Despite the alarums raised by advocates, succeeding Courts have only chipped away, inconsequentially, at the great decisions, such as *Escobedo* v. *Illinois* (having access to a lawyer early), *Miranda* v. *Arizona* (voluntariness of confessions), *Gideon* v. *Wainwright* (making a lawyer available to an indigent defendant), and the principles they established. The result of these decisions was to revolutionize the police in America. Even *Mapp* v. *Ohio,* the most tempting target, has successfully withstood repeated attempts at its evisceration.

The Supreme Court has tended to shy away from too activist a role in criminal justice matters because of their complexity and slipperiness. The Warren Court proved a dramatic exception, but even it had the greatest difficulty with the touchiest question of all: deciding what citizens can read, see, or hear.

Defining Obscenity

The average police agency spends only a tiny fraction of its time and energy on issues of sex, pornography, and the related items usually cited under the title of vice, yet there is an inordinate public interest in such matters.

Sex is inherently fascinating. Besides the interest of the general public, sex inspires equally fervid emotions among the supreme moralists railing against sin. It is a subject that attracts powerful interests—those of the numberless clients prowling the streets and those of the figurative ax-wielders who would undertake the strictest prohibitions against it.

The courts have struggled to define *indecency, obscenity, lewdness, immoral conduct,* and other slippery ideas. The landscape has evolved, from forbidding the entrance of James Joyce's *Ulysses* as obscene in 1930, to today's far more permissive approach to books, films, and other forms of creative expression. The law shifts with evolving mores.

After a tortured series of decisions in this century, the Supreme Court finally opted to dump the problem back on the localities by defining obscenity as an act that (1) appeals to prurient interest; (2) is utterly lacking in any redeeming social, artistic, or cultural value; and (3) fails to conform to prevailing community standards. This decision represents a significant withdrawal of the federal presence from the debate of what constitutes obscenity.

The problem was best characterized by an experienced student of the issue who, when asked to define obscenity, said, "I can't say what it is, but I know it when I see it." Unfortunately, the eye-of-the-beholder doctrine doesn't get us very far in a court of law. This is not helpful to a statutory society that insists that prohibited conduct be explicitly, and narrowly, defined. Vague and generalized prohibitions that might also encompass innocent acts are invariably struck down as being "unconstitutionally vague."

Although it is still possible to prosecute successfully under obscenity statutes, it's considerably more difficult than it used to be. Today, the police must basically secure the agreement of a judge that an act or a work is obscene before taking any action. Frequently, this means bringing a judge to watch an "obscene" performance or film.

Curiously, part of the feminist movement, sensing a connection between pornography and sexual violence against women, has inspired some ill-starred attempts to legislate responsibility, for a rape, on the publisher of a work. The theory rests on the tenuous possibility that the work inspired or influenced the act, and there have been a few studies that attempt to establish the connection. In the one jurisdiction that adopted this approach, Indianapolis, the courts threw out the ordinance tying publishers of material to the behavior of its readers. In this fashion it would be possible to hold the publisher of a pornographic tract responsible if a reader went out and, inspired by the contents, committed a rape. It was a tortured extension of the "dram shop" law, by which an innkeeper was responsible for the consequences if he or she continued to serve an intoxicated patron or allowed a patron to become drunk. The courts held that this law was unconstitutionally vague.

Entrapment

Sex is an area where the little-used notion of entrapment may come into play. Entrapment simply means getting someone who hasn't contemplated committing a crime to commit one. It is a seduction of the innocent mind. It is not facilitating the progress of one determined to break the law. It is one of the least frequently understood notions, among laypeople, in the law.

If, for example, a cop comes up to a prostitute and engages in vague generalities or responses to her leads, this is not entrapment.

The scenario might go something like this:

HE: Hi.
SHE: Hi, wanna party?
HE: Sure. What's the tariff, and what do you do?
SHE: Fifty dollars for a blow job.

This is a perfectly legitimate vignette for a legal arrest.
The twist on this exchange would be

HE: Hi.
SHE: Hi.
HE: I'm willing to give you $50 for a blow job, how about it?
SHE: Sure.

Because the officer initiated the action, the guilt of the target is not established. This arrest, if made, would be illegal. The defense of entrapment would succeed. In the latter case, the cop could not prove that he didn't entice an innocent person into committing an uncontemplated crime, overborne by temptation or perhaps even succumbing to unspecified enticements, in which money proved an incidental consideration. The law mostly wants to be sure that the committer of a crime actually intended to commit that crime.

Sending an aged-looking, bearded twenty-year-old into a bar to buy a drink, when the age limit is twenty-one, would constitute entrapment if it appears that no reasonable person would have asked to see this young man's identification and the operators are otherwise reasonably prudent in checking ages.

The issue of entrapment surfaced most dramatically in decoy operations in which the cops feigned a drunken stupor and had cash protruding ostentatiously out of their pockets, as they lay sprawled on subway steps or platforms. The aggressive tactics of an activist police administration brought the issue to a head in New York City during the late 1970s, and a chief's inability to answer the questions effectively cost him his job. An arrest would be made when a passerby plucked the money out. This was held to be too gross a temptation and the creation of a criminal act that the perpetrator hadn't contemplated. Decoy operations should be replications of the victimization experience of the citizens. The issue is arguable but the courts believe that the state should not create criminals by burdening citizens with unreasonable temptations.

Entrapment, like insanity, is one of those little-understood, but often invoked, legal concepts that seldom carry their users very far in courts of law. The police, up to their eyes in crime, violence, responses to calls, and other labors, have little interest in provoking the innocent into criminal behavior. They have quite enough on their plates already.

Impersonations

Real-life police work demands telling lies on the street and the truth in court. We don't expect an undercover operator to say yes when the drug dealer selling him cocaine asks if he's a cop. We cannot ask cops in sting operations to tell the burglars that they're not really fences. Chiefs will even order the police to lie in a wide variety of circumstances calling for deception, such as any investigation where subterfuge is used, for example, traps or undercover operations.

Cops may have to assume many roles. It would not be unprecedented for them to pose as reporters, doctors, lawyers, or ministers in order to achieve a legitimate law-enforcement objective.

What are the limits?

The law, of course, is the foremost and surest guide. Even here, though, the distinctions may be as subtle as the difference between practicing medicine, or law, without a license (a breach of law) and pretending to be a doctor without practicing anything (not a breach). The press is particularly sensitive to the issue because so much of their work involves trust. They get very upset when cops pose as reporters. Cops, unfortunately, have discovered that a press pass enables them to observe a lot of things they'd not be allowed to see if the targets knew they were being watched by cops. A crew of cops, posing as reporters, filmed kids smoking marijuana in a school yard and set off a spirited discussion following the kids' arrest. It looked like dirty pool to the viewers, and the press was furious, but the cops were responding to the very emotional charge of drug dealing and use in a school yard, and they broke no laws in enforcing them.

When the law becomes an uncertain guide, as in the areas described here, the police must adopt specific written policies. These will serve as orders to the troops, as guidance and reassurance for the people, and as important documents in resolving disputes or litigation. The profession being poached on by the police has the right to be informed of the nature and extent of this intrusion, but it must be kept in mind that police posing as reporters are breaking no laws.

Intelligence Operations

Intelligence is knowledge. No large organization can operate in the dark. Police agencies must have information about the forces in their environment in order to respond to challenges effectively. A series of well-publicized abuses have cast intelligence operations into public disrepute. The issue received a reprise in 1989 when WLIB, a black-centered New York City radio station, objected to the NYPD's taping of its broadcasts in order to use the information to monitor some of its listeners and their activities. Wasting police resources on such dangerous nonsense as infiltrating or monitoring totally legitimate groups had thrown intelligence into the dust heap of public obloquy. Yet we will see that a certain measure of involvement with even innocent groups is essential, both to use them as conduits to more serious enterprises and to establish the very fact of their innocence.

A police department's thirst for information is total and constant. It must allocate its resources, on a daily basis, to cope with the crisis of the moment. Absence of data leads to mistakes, and in policing, these can have tragic consequences. Simply relying, as many do, on overpolicing strikes, demonstrations, and such is both ruinously expensive and costly in the coverage it deprives other areas of for that period of time. Police administrators are forever robbing Peter to pay Paul.

In order to ensure punctilious adherence to the law in the *sub rosa* operations that easily lend themselves to breaches, such as infiltrating an organization for the purpose of gathering intelligence, the policies must be carefully thought out, put in writing, and monitored strictly. The focus must be on the prevention or interdiction of criminal acts, and the purpose must be articulated in writing. Bureaucrats are more careful than is generally supposed about what they sign their names to.

The methods must be appropriate to the circumstances. The area is made even more complicated because the infiltration, for example, may not amount to a breach of law, yet it might be considered disproportionate or unreasonable under the existing circumstances. Relying on the rule of whichever law may happen to apply is usually a solid guide, but it may be perfectly legal to infiltrate a totally innocent group and spend time spying on its members, as has happened in the past. This, though, may prove both a waste of resources and an unwarranted intrusion, casting a chill over the exercise of legitimate rights.

For this reason, groups have petitioned the courts, following a successful lawsuit, for a civil remedy—an order barring the police from undertaking infiltrations unless they are investigating a specific breach of law and have received clearance from a review panel set up to evaluate and monitor intelligence operations.

Today, it is simply not fashionable to infiltrate. The abuses uncovered as a result of the operations of federal agencies in investigating the activities of the Reverend Martin Luther King, Jr., for example, and the criminal actions of some urban departments in the 1960s and 1970s, not to mention Watergate and the sensational revelations of extensive files that amounted to little more than negative gossip, discredited the practice. It has reached the point where today's law enforcement executives are boasting of how they've restricted their agency's intelligence initiatives.

The NYPD had, in the 1960s especially, a crackerjack operation led by the Bureau of Special Services and Investigations (BOSSI). When Malcolm X was assassinated, the close associate next to him was an undercover cop whose identity was nearly blown when he was shown ministering to the fallen leader on *Life* magazine's pages. When American Nazi Party leader George Lincoln Rockwell came to New York, one of his closest aides was another undercover New York cop. When revolutionaries plotted the destruction of the Statue of Liberty, BOSSI interdicted the plot and arrested the would-be dynamiters. The key role was played by an undercover cop who'd been assigned to hang around such innocent organizations as the Congress of Racial Equality (CORE), picketing, distributing leaflets, and making himself useful. It used to be a theory at BOSSI that you could tell the undercover spies by how faithfully they attended meetings and events.

BOSSI's undercover cop finally spun off with a splinter group that was disgusted with the pacific ways of CORE and decided to take more determined action. This was a path many investigative groups followed. The unit would start by infiltrating an innocent group and would eventually drift into more adventurous waters with the passage of time.

This activity by the NYPD probably produced one of the most aggressive and successful intelligence operations any police agency ever had, but it had to be dismantled under the pressure of lawsuits brought in a climate of hostility toward such unpopular approaches. The surprising result has been that it didn't matter very much because America, for lucky reasons, was largely spared the terrorist acts that petrified much of Europe and the Middle East in the 1970s and 1980s.

Had terrorism existed here on any scale, the debate over these intelligence operations would not have been as one-sidedly against the police as it turned out to be. Intrusion into the activities of groups or the personal lives or affairs of citizens in a privacy-loving nation such as ours becomes an incredibly sensitive issue. This is true whether the invasion is human or technological.

National Identity Cards and a Central Data Bank

Were it not for fingerprints and photos, ours would be a confusing society indeed, with many people shifting identities to suit their convenience. Our love of privacy and mobility works to confuse the identity issues further. Cops tend to believe that their attempts to maintain order get hampered by restrictions on their ability to secure information.

DNA experiments hold the promise of extending our ability to identify people through such personal substances as semen, blood, follicles of hair, bits of body tissue, and fluids that contain genetic codes. But even a breakthrough in this area will probably result only in further enhancing the main source of information: fingerprint and photo files. There will still remain the problem of securing these traces of the suspect, who will, as the technology progresses, undoubtedly become more careful. Present court decisions have thrown the use of DNA codes into confusion as judges have begun to hold that they can be used to exclude a suspect, but not as a way of positively establishing the guilt of an accused until the reliability of the process has been scientifically and more conclusively proved. In a real sense, DNA has been relegated to the status of blood tests.

Yet our mobility and our reliance on checks, credit cards, and other debt instruments of faith virtually mandate the existence of a document the police might use, universally, in America to establish a person's bona fides. A hard-to-duplicate identity card, with a photograph, fingerprint, or other unique identifier, would certainly make it easier to handle the complex, impersonal transactions of the modern age, where so much relies on trust. Other nations use identity cards without causing any seeming harm to civil liberties. European countries regularly require foreigners to surrender their passports for a day, to allow the police to check on any warrants or other problems. Passports also help the hotels, which constantly extend credit.

A national identity card would probably facilitate the growth of the cashless society while reducing losses through mistake or fraud. It would make it easier to monitor the movements of criminals and to arrest them, in remote jurisdictions, while in flight. It would surely result in more accurate centralized criminal files and would probably, by making the local police departments more efficient, have the serendipitous effect of forestalling the movement toward a national police force. Ceding a bit of freedom, after reflection and debate, is invariably better than ceding a great deal of it under panic and goading by demagogues.

Opposition to such a proposal would be strident and extensive. Ours is not so much a liberty-loving society as a libertine one, where such disparate elements as bikers, religious zealots, activists and militants, the

NRA, and hosts of others vie for the retention of the freedom to do what suits them, without too much regard for the common good. Everyone wants to go his or her untrammeled way.

Such a radical notion as an ID card would require the development of a central data bank of criminal records and of information on missing persons. One of the important impediments to the refinement of such a file, as one already exists at the National Crime Information Center (NCIC), has been the notorious unreliability of police criminal records. The Federal Bureau of Investigation, which operates the NCIC, has been very reluctant to establish high standards of quality for the information entered. The result has been arrest and disposition statistics that can be used only as a guide, at best. The data are not updated in a timely fashion. Disposition information is garbled, when it is included, and names tend to get confused. The heavy use of aliases adds to the confusion. No one relies on the existing system to any serious extent, yet the feds, anxious to stave off the encroachments of competing federal bureaucracies, go to some lengths to mollify the careless providers of the data, the nation's police chiefs.

None of this, of course, even touches on the really sensitive question of the freedom of the individual versus the intrusive power of the state. There is no doubt that making the state more efficient usually means making it more powerful. Americans are very suspicious of their government and usually resolve power questions against the state. The problem is that this attitude tends to hobble the government yet doesn't diminish its responsibilities. The deprivation of the power to act is a classical violation of the managerial principle that authority must be commensurate with responsibility.

A national identity card and a central data bank conjure up Orwellian visions that have a lot of validity. The state has demonstrated its predilection for abusing power. Yet we expect the government to do certain things and we demand that they be done well. The push-pull of individual freedoms and the power of the state form the central dilemma of political life in society. It's never more dramatically illustrated than in the questions surrounding the operation of police departments. Striking the proper equation, between freedom and protection, is the delicate balancing act that forms the most important and intense debate of a democracy.

In periods of high crime and violence, Americans produce a rather supine willingness to give up some rights in exchange for increased protection. Experience has taught us that decisions taken in such climates, usually fueled by the exhortations of the ambitious, rarely produce additional safety.

The Social Security card and its life-assigned identifying number has sometimes crept into the status of a *de facto* national ID card, as its use expands and contracts, by fits and starts, in ways not envisioned by its creators. The fact is that there is constant pressure to tap into that system as the one reliable identifier. The Internal Revenue Service, for one, has made good use of that discovery, yet even that powerful agency has not been above succumbing to the temptations of abusing its power.

There is little doubt that a national ID card would, in an age of mounting tension over crime and rioting, enhance police effectiveness in identifying criminals who now slip in and out of various identities, would probably reduce instances of frauds and bad checks tremendously, and would facilitate the locating of criminals in flight, but there is equally little doubt that abuses and mistakes would occur. The question, inevitably, is how to strike the proper balance.

Confidential Relationships

The function of the law is to make living in a complex society possible and orderly, without limiting freedoms too severely. In establishing the rules of life, society has recognized that some relationships so clearly require trust, intimacy, confidence, and secrecy that the state has to be kept out. A decision has been made to preserve some relationships over the intrusive interests of the state, for example, to compel unwilling witnesses to testify in court or grand jury proceedings. The revelations made in such confidential relationships are protected against legal intrusion, but because of the overriding interests of the state in securing truthful testimony, the number of such exemptions is strictly limited and carefully defined.

Penitent and confessor, husband and wife, attorney and client, and doctor and patient form the core of such exemptions. The police have mostly stayed away from these delicate areas—and that is why there are so few controversies surrounding them—but it is not at all clear that feigning to be any of these in order to gain a confession would constitute a breach of law. Wrestling with these questions has resulted in the evolution of a concept known now as the *expectation of privacy*. This is the law's attempt to cope with such unforeseeable invasions as bugs, wiretaps, and other technical interceptors, and it has been extended to more easily understood human relationships. In a constitutional society, how do we deal with such issues as abortion, which are not explicitly referenced in the Constitution? The only logical possibility would appear to be to take an expansive view of the Fourth Amendment's suggestion that citizens ought to be secure in their persons, and thereby to infer a measure of control and the placing of limits on the state's power to intrude into such areas. The Fourth Amendment permits intrusion into the citizen's privacy, by the state, but it places strict limits on such actions.

These confidential relationships embody the sacred values of our society, and the police have been very wary of intruding into these areas. In any case, they're not especially eager to test these issues in the courts because they know that bad cases make bad law and would saddle them with strictures they can live without. The cops are not looking for court decisions that will make their lives more difficult.

The ACLU and Cops

The Constitution's most ardent champion might be held to be the American Civil Liberties Union, but its foes had, by the presidential election of 1988, managed to pigeonhole it into a political cubicle reserved for radical sects and causes. When a candidate referred to his opponent as a "card-carrying member of the ACLU," the meaning to anyone who had the slightest knowledge of the McCarthy era was crystal clear. The connection to the Communist Party was stark and unmistakable.

A lot of the trouble has come not just from the ACLU's adoption of unpopular causes—surely its most urgent priority—but also from the accompanying rhetoric, a lot of which has alienated the law enforcement establishment. Criticisms of the police following Supreme Court decisions, gratuitous charges about police actions or policies, and the cops' utter failure to see the law-and-order value of the Warren Court's decisions in enhancing the professionalism of the police, while extending constitutional rights to defendants—all have contributed to the hostility.

Where the National Rifle Association has regularly paid fervent lip service to its support of cops (however that might play in connection with the programs being pursued by the NRA), the ACLU has seemed to engage in deliberately provocative exchanges with the forces that the people look to for their safety, with its almost reflexive criticisms of police actions and its espousal of causes unpopular with the police. The rhetoric is often as harmful to better relations as the actual positions taken.

The NRA, as a consequence, retained the fealty of police chiefs and cops long after any logical assessment would have dictated abandonment. It wasn't until the NRA badly overplayed its hand, on such issues as cop-killer bullets, plastic guns, machine guns, waiting periods, constitutional amendments, preemption bills, Saturday-night-specials legislation, and resistance to a ban on semiautomatic assault weapons, that the police began to abandon the NRA standard. The NRA lost the cops, but over real issues, not over failure to say the right things. It's a lesson the ACLU still has to learn.

In a nation of marketers, the ACLU has forgotten the importance of packaging its product. Instead of encompassing its stands in what is broadly taken to be anticop rhetoric, it should be championing tough law-and-order postures, while insisting that aggressive tactics be pursued with strict regard for the law. The ACLU's failure to enfold itself in the mantle of the language of the law-and-order set has cost it any possible support from law enforcers and has thereby lost it the assistance of the people who love their cops as well. This has proved to be a classical case of attending to the substance while ignoring the form.

Much of the opposition of law enforcement to Warren Court decisions such as *Miranda, Escobedo,* and *Mapp* may be reflexive and associational hostility to the champion of the causes in those briefs: the ACLU.

The NRA, Cops, and the Constitution

Where the ACLU's rhetoric *vis-a-vis* the police might be fairly characterized as inflammatory, that of the NRA has been conciliatory and affectionate, even when coping with such subversive anomalies as advertising that Americans needed to arm themselves for self-defense because cops don't show up when they're called.

The NRA and the cops enjoyed, for most of this century, a symbiotic relationship in which cops were trained by and encouraged to participate in shooting meets sponsored by the NRA, which always described itself as the cops' buddy.

A funny thing happened when a now-discredited member of Congress, Mario Biaggi of the Bronx, himself a former NYPD lieutenant who later went to prison, introduced an innocuous bill to ban armor-piercing ammunition commonly referred to as *cop-killer bullets*. He and many who had every reason to expect the support of the NRA were shocked at the vituperation hurled at him by the powerful progun lobby. Police chiefs looked on nervously and, as a few took some tentative steps toward support for the bill, winced at the NRA's attacks.

As the volume and scale of gun–drug violence rose, police chiefs increasingly inveighed against the armaments race that Americans, uniquely, were engaged in with themselves. Approximately seventy million handguns were killing over twenty thousand Americans every year, through murder, suicide, and accident. Police executives, under intense pressure to do something, increased the pressure for arrests, concentrated on the drug connection, and inevitably began to comment on the availability of machine guns, pistols, and all manner of deadly weaponry. As they did so, they came under the NRA's withering fire, and a once-solid marriage began to disintegrate.

The escalating debate was played out against a backdrop of issues that had nothing to do with rifles, long guns, hunting, or sport. It had little to do even with self-defense.

A law banning machine guns was fought vigorously by the NRA, as was an attempt to forbid the purchase of plastic guns that would escape metal detection at airports. A bill to ban Saturday night specials (cheap handguns whose only purpose is to kill humans) plunged Maryland politicians into a vicious fray with the NRA in 1988. Esoteric legal battles, such as preemption bills that made state laws controlling over more restrictive city statutes, thereby liberalizing gun ownership, and state constitutional amendments guaranteeing the "right to bear arms" plunged state legislatures into unwelcome and unsought battles with the NRA.

Slowly, police chiefs got sucked into the struggle, reluctantly taking on the NRA and suffering scathing attacks from that powerful group. The NRA has not hesitated to wrap itself in the Second Amendment to the U.S. Constitution, which holds that a "well regulated militia" being essential to a free people's security, "the right to bear arms shall not be infringed." Blithely ignored, in all this, is the courts' holding that the reference centers on a militia and that the state has the power to restrict the traffic in arms.

The International Association of Chiefs of Police, the Major Cities Chiefs of Police, and other groups who'd long been the NRA's pals were horrified at that organization's assaults on their colleagues and its stances against commonsense measures to protect society from all these guns. Gradually, they drifted into postures of opposition and prepared critical resolutions. The chasm widened. Chiefs participated in full-page anti-NRA ads, and the NRA suggested that one of them, San Jose's Joseph McNamara, would allow sales of drugs to children. This was only the most egregious example of that group's bully-boy tactics. In other cases, they waged bitter campaigns to get chiefs fired or to keep mayors from hiring police executives they didn't like. It wasn't much for the NRA to have massive write-in or call-in campaigns against their targets. The gun issue, like abortion, has resulted in single-issue politics at its most virulent.

The big news today in the gun debate is that the NRA and the nation's police have divorced. This divorce holds the promise of turning the tide against an organization that has had its own way for decades and that has caused a proliferation of weaponry tolerated by no other society labeling itself as advanced.

Rights of the Least

The true test of a democracy is how it responds to the thoughts it hates, as Justice Oliver Wendell Holmes reminded us. If it protects the despised and the dissenters, then freedom lives. If it tramples the contemptible, repression soon spreads to less unpopular areas.

The police are hired to keep order. This usually means keeping the poor, the homeless, and the street people in their place. It is a role assigned by the overclass. The cops may often be a sort of army of occupation in the ghetto.

The role of charnel house cleaner for society's ills can be exasperating. Understandably, cops get restive and cynical in dealing with obstreperous drunks and truculent psychos, while listening to the pious mouthings of those who silently sent them to do just that. The temptation to strike out at the "assholes" must be made resistible. There is an instinct in society to be tolerant of actions taken against these unpopular elements, and it is hard for the overclass to see how their interests and freedom might be affected when cops are allowed to abuse the underclass. What they fail to realize is that the abuse of power feeds on itself and grows. Excesses must be attacked at their roots, and attitudes must be shaped by a concern for punctilious observance of the law. If a police department comes to believe that its mission is to fight crime, whatever the cost or methods used, then the tragedy of Philadelphia's MOVE incident becomes inevitable.

The cops on the street are the upholders of the United States Constitution in living, breathing form. They have the power to detain, question, arrest, subdue, shoot, and even kill. If they can be made to be servants of the law, the Constitution thrives. If they succumb to the temptation to be masters of the law and are not stopped, the Constitution will perish. What the Warren Court decisions most eloquently illustrate is the degree to which the constitutional rights of citizens had been violated, over the decades, by police departments that had not been brought under the rule of law.

CHAPTER 12

Controlling the Criminal

Everybody wants to get tough on crime. Even presidential campaigns have become spitting contests in which the more draconian approach carries the day. More cops, tougher judges, longer sentences, bigger jails, and more macho prosecutors are demanded.

Ignored is the enormously high per capita incarceration the nation already "enjoys" and the long sentences our judges mete out. There is a curious irony in the country's collective ignoring of the bulging prisons and the executions, as the myth that liberals are letting bums get away with murder gains wider credence, against all the available evidence. We are not as easygoing as we'd like to think. The myth's power is a solid testimonial to the levels of fear and to the temptations of self-hypnosis.

The popular thing is to call for stiffer penalties. If one Willie Horton is furloughed and commits a crime, cancel all furloughs. No one asks whether the program, in the main, works; the only real concern is whether it is perfect. Given this aversion to painful facts, is it any wonder that how Willie Horton got to be that way isn't even considered?

It soon becomes obvious, to anyone with more than a passing acquaintance with the criminal justice system, that crime and criminals are complex and that thoughtful answers are needed to the challenges they represent.

Various systems of control have been attempted, and two—incarceration and death—have really captured the public's fancy. In systems that work reasonably well a more sophisticated array of approaches is used, tailored to the specifics surrounding the crime and the criminal.

By looking at some of the inside issues that touch on the success or failure of attempting to control the criminal, we might gain an additional perspective on the complexity of the problem. The police are part of and caught up in the workings of a system over which they exercise virtually no control, except over their own operations, which are admittedly important. Yet their effectiveness depends on how well other players in the system handle their roles. The criminal justice system may be anything but systematic, but it desperately needs to be just that.

The Criminal Justice System

Criminal justice system is a label that connotes interaction (of which there is plenty), coordination (of which there is almost none), and cooperation (which proceeds fitfully, depending on the egos or altruism of the players). Although intended to be a system—and it cannot really function unless it operates as one—our criminal justice system really functions as separate fiefdoms, which is why it falters so badly.

No one is paid to think for the criminal justice system. It is an operation that is ruled by negatives. Tragedies occur and resources are assigned to plug the hole in the dike. No one is charged with distributing resources equitably in order to keep the operation running smoothly. Instead, the system grows and shrinks according to the vagaries of public alarums and fevered hopes. This means that the most strident voice or the sexiest proposals get the money. In this struggle for resources, the cops have an incalculable advantage. This is why most contemporary debates relating to public safety center on how many more cops we need to hire to reduce crime. An awful crime occurs, and the inevitable cry is to "hire more cops," without regard to need, consequences, or rationality.

The defendant is the sausage, proceeding through the processor. He or she is arrested by a cop, brought before a judge, represented by what is usually a Legal Aid Society–type public defender, accused by a district attorney, jailed by a sheriff, evaluated by a probation officer, imprisoned in a state facility, perhaps monitored, for freedom, by a parole board, and then perhaps released not into freedom but into a halfway house that allows for a transitional reentry into society.

Simply considering the sources of funds and power for these disparate players will convey the confusion and competition that attend so much of the system. Some players are appointed and some are elected; some work for the city, some for the county, and others for the state. They all have to go to some body of elected officials for their funds, and the battles that often take place over the allocation of money rarely afford the luxury of reflecting on the other fellow's needs. Incredible anomalies result. More cops are hired at times when the system is being crushed by a heavy volume of arrests. No one asks what effect more cops will have on the system. The result may well be the wrecking of any hopes of controlling the criminal population as court dockets are overwhelmed, prisons bulge, and harried prosecutors give up and strike hurried, bad bargains.

It would probably make more sense to have fewer cops, who would concentrate on the serious criminals and build tight cases against them, which would enable the city's leaders to check the adequacy of the resources assigned to the other elements in the system. Unthinkable as it may appear, one of the answers might be to strengthen the system by having fewer cops.

Even developing a computer system for tracking a prisoner from arrest to disposition and allowing all players to use the same basic document throughout the lengthy process require so many different approvals that few even attempt to adopt such efficiencies. Turf is sacred, and coordination among cops, prosecutors, judges, jailers, and lawyers is usually reserved for the big cases that have terrified the public.

So the system functions with unbelievable unevenness as the politicians (presidents, governors, mayors, and their legislative bodies) allocating the funds target them where they'll do the most political, rather than practical, good. That is why presidents love to sign drug bills that "aid local law enforcement," without considering systemic effects. The answer might well lie in strengthening the other, weaker, links in the chain, rather than getting the good public relations that comes from pandering to the public's fears and the baser instincts that favor harsh treatments.

There are many reasons why the battle against crime, drugs, and violence in America is being lost. High among them is our love of action and contempt for thought. Another is our willingness to embrace popular solutions to complex problems. Our politicians pander to these instincts both unconscionably and, to some extent, unconsciously.

Although there is a strong predilection to say, "The thing has been studied to death, let's get some action going," the fact is that precious little discussion, thought, or analysis has been devoted to crime, whereas the action waxes hot.

Looking at some of the issues that periodically surface may help in understanding what factors are at work, why there are so many failures represented by the crime figures, and how things might be improved.

Strengthening the police merely results in the development of a super-strong link in an otherwise weak chain.

Bail, Preventive Detention, and the Constitution

The question of control arises immediately upon the suspect's arrest, when conflicting forces—namely, the rights of the accused versus the need to protect society—come swiftly into play.

The specific question is raised in terms of bail. The accused is entitled to a presumption of innocence. The purpose of setting bail is to secure the presence of the accused at trial. The Eighth Amendment forbids excessive bail or cruel or unusual punishments. Very high bail, or denying a bond, would have to be justified on the basis of risk of flight.

In notorious cases the courts have been tempted to safeguard society by holding the prisoner without bail. This is perhaps understandable, given the public pressures aroused by rising levels of violence, but it confuses the purposes of the bail bond and, arguably, stands in opposition to the concept of presumed innocence.

A *habeas corpus* proceeding (meaning, literally, "you should have the body") is intended to establish the legality of the incarceration of the accused. It is one of the key ingredients of a strategy intended to check the abuse of state power. In such a hearing, the court must decide whether a suspect's detention is based on a rule of law or whether he or she is being held illegally and must therefore be released.

Preventive detention—or the jailing of an accused before the final disposition of the case, on the basis of the possible threat posed to society while the accused is at large—undermines the presumption of innocence and contradicts the Eighth Amendment. This is true even when the guilt of the accused is evident; the principle must be applied if it is to be safe-guarded. Preventive detention is one of those dangerous legal concepts adopted in the midst of public hysteria over rising levels of crime. Since the Supreme Court has not yet ruled on the practice, it is possible to continue it, notwithstanding its unconstitutionality. It must be remembered that even presumably unconstitutional practices and laws may be con-tinued until the issue is decided by the Court. Asked to reveal how he knew a pitched baseball was a ball or a strike, Bill Klem, a great old umpire, used to say, "They ain't nothing till I calls them."

Desk Appearance Ticket

It is easy to forget that the issuing of a citation, in lieu of jailing the accused, in misdemeanors and lesser cases constitutes a revolution in the thinking of the criminal justice system. Until the Vera Institute of Justice, an organization devoted to reforming the criminal justice system, pioneered the experiment in the mid-1960s, every person arrested had to wait—usually at least overnight, in a precinct lockup—to see a judge in the morning. Vera created criteria for release that basically held that it is reasonable to issue a ticket to, instead of jailing, a suspect who has been identified, is sober, and is not likely to continue breaking the law. The result has been virtually to empty the police lockups, reduce in-cell suicides, and make room for the serious offenders in the system.

The ubiquitous presence of today's desk appearance tickets (virtually identical to the speeding citation many of us are only too painfully familiar with) tends to cloud our view of the days before this simple reform was adopted. It isn't perfect. Some criminals fail to appear in court, and others commit crimes while out, but since its introduction in 1967, the overwhelming evidence is that it works and that it relieves the system of a load that would, in the current congested circumstances, crush it altogether.

Plea Bargaining

Plea bargaining, or the acceptance of a plea of guilty to a lesser charge in order to avoid the trouble, risk, and expense of a trial, is a concept often misunderstood. It has become one of the favored whipping boys of politicians. Opposition to plea bargaining is one of the favored ploys of hard-nosed, law-and-order types running for office.

In fact, the system could not survive without it. The overwhelming majority of criminal cases must be resolved without trials. The best systems can probably accommodate trials for no more than 10 percent of their cases, if that many. More judges are in the settlement business than are in the trial business. Settlement includes throw-outs, as well as bargaining for a plea of guilty. Trials are incredibly costly, lengthy, and troublesome. It would not be hard to conclude, after a perfunctory examination of the system, that much of its energy is spent in finding ways to avoid trials.

Why, then, the furor about plea bargaining? Why do so many electoral contests for the DA's job get tangled in debates over such matters? Why do some run on the promise that they'll not plea-bargain when they know that's a practical impossibility? The answers lie in the expectations we impose on our public figures and in their perceived need to accommodate us, rather than to lead or educate us.

The problem with plea bargains is that too many DAs, in their haste to clear their dockets and to improve their conviction batting average, have made bad bargains. Too many soft deals have been made with too much haste.

Prosecutors' most vulnerable point is conviction statistics. Since they must face election, they are not eager to defend a record reflecting a low conviction rate. Thus they are anxious to prosecute only winnable cases and then to settle as many of those cases as rapidly as possible. The trouble with this approach is that many hardened criminals are allowed to get away with a lot, simply because the DA doesn't want to chance losing, and that those that are caught have the chance to "skate" through plea bargaining and get soft or suspended sentences.

Sentencing Guidelines

The public loves to read "Robber Faces 30 Years in Bank Holdup." Every newspaper carries references to how X faces twenty years for this, and Y ten years for that, yet the system's insiders know that this is nonsense. The prisoners actually face only a fraction of that time since the figure cited is invariably the maximum and doesn't take into account any realistic prospect of the time likely to be served. The range of possible sentences may be from five to thirty years; a conviction will probably lead to the lower number, which will be reduced by time already served and good behavior. The end result is frequently that the fellow "facing thirty years" serves eighteen months.

Sentencing guidelines, which establish uniform penalties for like crimes, grew out of experiments that revealed wide sentencing disparities among judges asked to rule on identical circumstances. Another factor contributing to sentencing guidelines was the public's unhappiness with the disparities between official sentences and the prison time actually served. Uniformity has been the missing link in our sentencing practices.

Of course, prisoners who had committed similar crimes and who compared notes on their sentences saw the inequity. More than that, they felt it. It led to great unhappiness and serious problems of morale and discipline among prison inmates. Corrections officials, not needing gratuitous misery in places already necessarily harboring disaffected souls, began to bring the disparities to light, calling for reforms.

Gradually a move toward uniformity took shape and gained momentum. It finally evolved into the adoption of sentencing guidelines, through state law, which are nothing more than a grid that advises a judge what the sentence will be following a conviction.

Sentencing guidelines take prior record, the severity of the current offense, the capacity of the prison system, and the possibility of incarceration for a brief period in a local jail into account. They tend to focus on the personal violence offender more intently than on the property offender. Judges may not deviate from the suggested limits without good cause and must express their reasoning in writing. Review becomes possible under such circumstances.

These guidelines really constitute truth-in-sentencing in that they reveal what actually happens, while applying uniform standards. Therefore they are regularly seen as softheaded, liberal schemes and tend to get embroiled in law-and-order rhetoric. The public much prefers to believe our criminals really do "face 30 years." Guidelines also take sensible cognizance of prison capacity and create limits that work against the pressures that cause overcrowding. Factored into the guidelines is a statistical formula that encompasses prison capacity. Any adjustment to the guidelines, usually to make penalties harsher, must take this into account and must call for either expanding the capacity or reducing other penalties by an equivalent amount.

The guidelines, though, have failed to furnish the mechanism by which future menaces might be identified and interdicted. Although that was not their goal, guidelines might have helped in developing a matrix. Despite the public's devotion to the idea, incarceration for long periods has not proved to be an important influence on the crime rate. Swiftness of detection and certainty of punishment have increasingly been seen as the only effective crime deterrents. This means some consequence following the crime, but not necessarily confining it to incarceration.

Our per capita incarceration rate is one of the highest in the world, as is, of course, our crime rate. Since the late 1960s, we have tripled the prison population. This has occurred at a time when Part I crime, up to the crack pandemic of the late 1980s, was rising only moderately. We are not the easygoing, tolerant, readily gulled folks we believe ourselves to be.

Street crime is enmeshed in the drug culture, with guns adding to the violence. Career criminals commit an enormous number of crimes over a typical period of fifteen years. They are alcoholics or drug addicts who strike, opportunistically, at vulnerable targets. If there is no chance to strike, they return home to await a better day. Most criminals are casually involved while a minority of about 10 percent constitute the real menaces. Identifying them has so far proved impossibly difficult.

Our knowledge of crime and criminals is very uneven, our determination to learn more is notably lacking, and our willingness to act on what we do know not only falters but too frequently succumbs to the jingoist logic of those irresistibly drawn to grandstanding the issue. We need to build into our sentencing guidelines insights that identify the serious recidivist.

Much of the public, and many of their officials, see crime and criminals simplistically. This gets in the way of any hope of discovering solutions. Complex problems do not give way to the shallow descriptions of demagogues, who sense the eagerness of the people for quick, easy answers and who have no compunctions about pimping the issues.

Sentencing guidelines ought to serve to identify the really dangerous offenders, who constitute a small but menacing minority of the criminal population, and to deal with them consistently and uniformly. Successfully targeting these individuals and selectively incapacitating them hold out the promise of reducing the incidence of future crimes substantially.

Mandated Sentences

Legislators love to press for laws calling for "a mandatory sentence of *x* years for everyone convicted of drug selling or using a weapon while committing a crime." The latter is an NRA favorite. Who can vote against such a proposal? Yet the proposal makes no practical sense. Mandatory sentences move that criminal to the head of the line, past rapists, robbers, child molesters, and murderers. By the time the mandatory sentences have been handed out, there may not be any room at the inn for the other criminals. Some flexibility has to be maintained. Mandated sentences impose a counterproductive rigidity on the system. In the area of crime and criminals every time you press down here you get an unexpected something popping up there. This effect has come to be called the *law of unintended consequence.*

Imprisonment should serve as a punishment for the criminal, a lesson to others, and a protection for society. Thus it should be obvious that we ought to imprison personal violence offenders, rather than property crimes offenders, who might be better addressed through restitution, fines, community service, or other forms of punishment. The point is to identify those who pose the biggest future menace to society. The dangerous repeaters must be identified and isolated. One of the problems, though, is that white-collar criminals, frequently white males, would mostly escape prison, an outcome that would exacerbate the race problem in our institutions.

Identifying the future risks means developing a point system that focuses attention on those criminals likeliest to strike again. Compulsive behavior is hard for the police to control. If we insist on treating the date rapist in exactly the same fashion as we treat the male who rapes strangers, serially, then we will have small chance of preventing future rapes. Both are rapists, but they represent a different order of magnitude of risk for society. The date rapist is easier to identify, arrest, and deter than the menace who strikes at strangers. Date rape is a felony and should be treated as a serious crime, but the distinction is real and has to be made. The serial rapist is driven by internal forces that make him a menace to all women, and he strikes at strangers. The date rapist is a criminal, too, but his menace status, to women generally, is simply not as great.

Sentencing guidelines have to be adjusted for such factors. The nature of the crime, a statement from the victim, the prisoner's prior record, and an investigation into the prisoner's background and character will yield many of the points on which a sensible assessment of future-risk status might be made. The criminal justice system is singularly inept at identifying future menaces. The state has rarely taken its responsibilities to future potential victims very seriously. Politicians are much fonder of calling for mandatory sentences or hiring more cops.

Mandatory sentences are straitjackets that impose mindless solutions on complex or variegated problems. Adopting them invariably produces dysfunctions in other parts of the system. Mandatory sentences, and schemes like them, actually produce additional stresses on the plea-bargaining system because they tempt those affected to plea-bargain down to areas where the mandatory sentences don't apply, creating admissions of guilt to crimes that never occurred and other subversive stratagems. Mandatory sentences force all the players to work around the system. This breeds cynicism and contempt among all the players since a person may go to prison for having admitted to a crime he or she didn't commit, even though it involves a lesser penalty, and all those involved in the case become accomplices to this deception.

Determinate Sentences

Escalating crime levels in the early 1970s launched a search for sentencing reforms that would eliminate inequities and inefficiencies. This was the Holy Grail of Criminology. Inability to stem the rising tide of crime forced everyone to scurry about, looking for new answers.

One of the fads embraced was "determinate sentencing," where a particular crime, like robbery, carried a fixed, single sentence, such as five years. This eliminated the judge's discretion and the parole board's power to release the offender.

Determinate sentences carried a single, uniform penalty for every crime, with no deviations. Mandated sentences required the judge to impose a fixed prison sentence for a given crime, having no option to suspend or otherwise mitigate the punishment. This reform had a brief, inglorious life, foundering on the painful shoals of real-life experience. The crimes and the criminals varied too dramatically, from event to event, to allow identical treatment for all. Like so many egalitarian ideas this one sounded great but didn't work in practice.

Incarceration and Its Alternatives

The human animal is basically conditionable through two kinds of forces: negative and positive. People can be shaped by rewards, strokes, encouragement, affection, honors, and so on, and they can be similarly influenced by such negatives as imprisonment, fines, restitution, community service, and other punishments. It has always been hard to know which works best, but we've roughly agreed that if we use punishment, for example, it must be swift, it must be certain, and it must be relevant and proportionate to the circumstances.

If this is true then it follows that depriving someone of freedom ought to influence his or her behavior, as well as reduce the number of crimes avoided during the period of sequestration. But jailing everyone cannot be the only answer because it simply isn't feasible. Other alternatives need to be sought. The point is to control criminals through the use of effective and efficient measures. The only way to accomplish this goal successfully is through careful supervision and monitoring.

If punishment affects behavior then it follows that it should also work as a deterrent. Humans are unique in that they don't have to experience every event in order to learn a lesson. We learn by experience, yes, but we also learn by watching the experiences of others, and we alter our behavior accordingly. If we see others punished we find out the reasons and make our own calculations as to whether the thing is worth the risk. Not all lessons will affect all persons in the same way, but there are certain universal factors that affect the vast majority in approximately the same way. This is one of the powerful arguments for the deterrence theory of capital punishment. The importance of negative consequences can't be overstressed. A crime, followed by punishment, will be perceived differently than if no punishment follows. The human animal is sufficiently perverse to see encouragement in an act not followed by sanctions. The key deterrent is swift and certain punishment and the ultimate penalty is surely a part of this process.

It makes eminent sense to develop alternatives to incarceration because of costs and because of the benefits of tailoring the response to the act. Sometimes restitution to the victim makes the best sense. Some recent innovations have included the victim's confronting the criminal and discussing feelings and reactions. This brings the perpetrator face-to-face with the consequences of the crime. States that employ a panoply of alternative strategies, as well as incarceration, have had a happier statistical experience on recidivism than the more draconian jurisdictions.

More and more victims are either asking or being asked to make a statement at the time of sentencing. A good argument could be made that the manipulators of the system have, historically, frozen both victims and, ironically, defendants out of a process in which their interests are engaged very directly. The statement needn't be controlling but it seems wise to give victims a greater sense of participation in the process.

Fines can be a way of making reparation, yet a $100 fine will have a different impact on a rich person than on a poor one. There have been recent experiments with day fines, where the accused pays one day's wages, thereby equalizing the relative impact on everyone. There is roughly equal justice in being docked a day's pay.

Community work may be another way of forcing criminals to confront their actions, while producing a positive result for society. The work may involve cleaning graffiti, working in a shelter, cleaning debris off streets and highways, park work, or any similar task. The experience should be constructed in such a way that it carries its own lesson, as would, for example, having a convicted banker work with the poor or homeless. Such programs have to be monitored closely since nothing will breed contempt for the law faster than imposing a meaningless sanction.

Every community has chores to be done that don't conflict with union or jurisdictional boundaries, and community service is a good way of getting them done. It has the added benefit of channeling wrongdoers into what, for them, may well be a totally new experience. There is a lot of psychic income to be gained from simply serving.

House Arrest

Modern technology is making many new things possible in the way the police department deals with criminals. The courts can now, for example, tether a criminal to a transponder, using a wrist or ankle band that will send a signal if the person strays more than a hundred feet from the device. This makes house arrest a practical and cost-effective reality. It is very likely that many future offenders will be monitored through this system. One person, centrally located, could supervise literally scores of detainees under this program, which can allow for reporting to work, attending court, or fulfilling other commitments on a rigid schedule which is supervised by the monitor.

Halfway Houses

Almost everybody in prison eventually comes out. Verbalizing this fact reminds us that it isn't safe to just open the prison door and let predators out without any preparation for their reentry into society. Releasing them to a halfway house, where they can reside and be supervised as they begin to participate in society again, helps to bridge the chasm between confinement and freedom by keeping offenders from returning to the environment that spawned and prodded their behavior in the first place.

Providing counseling programs, including private groups who are interested in helping ex-convicts one-on-one, will improve their chances of success. Literacy training, for example, something almost anyone can do, might be the answer for many frustrated, defeated offenders, most of whom have serious educational deficiencies. Going from prison to the streets is tough enough without adding the shock of sudden release. The situation the offender returns to is generally regarded as the most important determinant of future prospects. Convicts suffer from low self-esteem, which probably flows from a realistic appreciation of their situational talents. Strengthening skills will help promote a sense of self-worth.

Probation and Parole

The volume of cases assigned to parole and probation officers has escalated so dramatically in recent years that it has not only ensured the defeat of the enterprise but has wound up discrediting these approaches as a result of the inevitable failures. George Bush had a good time with this issue as he excoriated Michael Dukakis over the Willie Horton furlough during the presidential campaign of 1988. No one seems inclined to trot out the parole successes or to speak of new possibilities and the necessity of taking risks. Too many promising approaches have had to be discarded because of the unrealistic burdens we imposed on them.

Students of criminology quickly learn that no single solution works. Any program or approach can be criticized because, in a slippery world trying to monitor and control the human animal, lapses are bound to occur. Perhaps only executions are definitive, if fallible. A panoply of strategies is essential in order to allow for the choice of the likeliest approach in an individual case. What works with one will produce an opposite effect with another. No two cases are identical. Risks must be taken. Failures have to be anticipated. The point is to keep the success rate at an acceptably high level.

Probation, or submitting convicted criminals to supervision and counseling rather than sending them to jail, eliminates the expense of incarceration, helps preserve the job and family status of the offenders, and holds out the hope of reformation. But the supervision must be real if it is to work. The probation officer is a caseworker and no meaningful checking or evaluation can take place if the work load is overwhelming. The tempting and foolish economies that took place in the 1960s, 1970s, and 1980s, which reduced the money and increased the case load, not only ensured the defeat of the system but deprived supervisors of any opportunity to exact performance from probation officers, while providing the bureaucrats with an easy excuse for failure. Making people responsible for everything is a good way to permit them to be held accountable for nothing. They can always point elsewhere when a failure is cited.

In order for probation to be meaningful the consequences of the criminal's failure to observe the rules have to be applied. Those who don't conform to the program must be sent to prison, with probation revoked. It is easy to make a mockery of this system when accountability is removed.

A probation report probably offers the best hope of identifying the serious recidivist since the probation officer must strive to understand the accused fully and be in a position to make meaningful assessments about the prospects for reform. No one else in the system is charged with the responsibility to master the background and history of the offender. It might be said that the probation officer is the only member of the system who is charged with understanding the accused and making some predictions for the future. This role has not been sufficiently appreciated or exploited.

Parole constitutes conditional release from prison, contingent on good behavior, while probation is release, without prison, conditioned on good behavior. The appointment of political hacks to parole boards has helped to discredit and defeat this approach. Budget constraints also make it easy to keep overloading parole officers until their case loads became unmanageably swollen.

The result has been a virtual abandonment of parole and a deemphasis on probation. Incarceration and draconian measures are the rage as the century draws to a close.

Reliance on any single approach will burden the strategy with responsibilities it cannot handle. There is no magic formula. Some must be imprisoned, some executed, some placed on conditional release, and some treated in other ways. No matter which punishment is chosen there must be consequences for lawbreakers. Punishment does work. The offender's return to freedom has to be seen as a bridge that must be negotiated. Risks must be run and failures have to be expected.

Probation and parole have been mangled by the tough law-and-order rhetoric of demagogues responding to public fears of crime and violence, which have escalated enormously since the late 1950s. Anytime the public succumbs to such simple appeals a door closes on a possible approach and strident voices are raised for ever harsher tactics.

Rehabilitation

Rehabilitation, like Christianity, is a wonderful idea that's never really been tried. Chesterton would have understood.

Rehabilitation relies, first, on a belief in the redemptive possibility. It involves helping, training, and educating offenders in order to make them contributing members of society once they're released. But will a society that isn't concerned about helping, training, or educating its noncriminal underclass be eager to spend its resources on criminals? The question answers itself.

The prison population is, with very rare and highly publicized exceptions, the underclass. It consists of the children of sexually exploited teenage mothers on welfare. They are illiterate, undereducated, and unemployable. Drugs and alcohol are their methods of escape. They are unskilled and unpromising. Their self-esteem is at rock bottom after a lifetime of being told that failure is their fate. They are victims of racism and are very likely to have been abused as children. Finally, they've been shaped into muggers, thieves, and vandals, and society insists they be destroyed. Rehabilitation doesn't become a high-priority item in the midst of strident cries for blood.

Rehabilitation, the positive pole, has as much going for it, in terms of reshaping the criminal, as punishment, the negative pole. A panicked people won't spend time on long-term, indirect, costly solutions such as jobs, education, inclusion, and social welfare schemes. Their failure to do so simply ensures the creation of more monsters.

Until those in the overclass learn that they are creating the muggers, rapists, druggies, and murderers that terrify them, nothing much will be done, beyond the palliatives of the criminal justice system, to stem the tide of violence.

Capital Punishment

Everything has been said about capital punishment, at least twice. Everyone knows which side he or she is on.

There's never been a bad argument on the subject, but we wait to hear one that is flawlessly persuasive, pro or contra. I favor capital punishment, having met a lot of people the world would be safer without. Yet I cannot deny that it is dangerous to allow the state to kill, that errors can occur, and that states without capital punishment haven't had materially different crime experiences than those that kill. Thirty-seven states allow capital punishment, but some of these haven't executed anyone in many years. New York, for example, which doesn't allow it but where the issue waxes hot, between a willing legislature and an abolitionist governor, hasn't executed anyone since 1963.

Does capital punishment deter crime?

Why did all those early movies contain the line "You'll get the chair for this"? Probably because there was an instinctive sense that punishment did, indeed, deter, especially those afforded the luxury of prior planning.

Most studies compare homicide rates in different cities or states to demonstrate capital punishment's lack of effect. One state may have capital punishment and a high murder rate, and the next may not have it and may still have a low murder rate.

Is this, then, a conclusive argument that capital punishment doesn't work, or does the disparity really suggest the complexity masked by the murder rates? Lots of killings occur between people who know each other, often involve drunken rages, and could probably not have been prevented. We might, parenthetically, argue that arresting wife beaters constitutes murder prevention because of the escalating nature of the crime, the frequency with which it ends up in a fatality, and the deterrent effects of arrest.

The integrity of a community—its cohesive nature—is a decisive factor; rural and suburban areas will have fewer murders than cities; blacks will have higher rates than whites (the leading cause of death among black males aged twenty to forty-five is murder) because of racism and poverty. The availability of handguns will be a determinant (states with lax gun laws have higher shooting rates than those with stiff controls).

It is most likely that only a fraction of murders—those that are planned and calculated—can be affected by weighing the risks and possible consequences. We must look deep within the homicide rates to find areas where the threat of execution might stay a killer's hand.

Minnesota has gone over three-quarters of a century without executing anyone and hasn't been swept away by violence. It has had, by American standards, a pretty pacific experience in fact. This might suggest that the stability of the value system might be a more critical factor.

People are fond of trotting out arguments that pretend to resolve the issue one way or the other. Learned studies are cited but we "evermore go out the same door wherein we went." Perhaps, to add a bit of gallows humor, we can assert that the only thing scientifically proven is that executed persons never recidivate.

Ted Bundy symbolized the issues perfectly. The publicity that attended his fight to avoid execution ensured an enormous amount of public attention to his case. How could that battle have failed to communicate, to all onlookers, the awfulness of the fate he was trying so desperately to avoid? Finally, on January 24, 1989, he was put to death, in Florida. Before he died he confessed to scores of murders of innocent young women, many of whom had tried to help him as he, on crutches (one of his stratagems), asked for aid. He'd bludgeon, mutilate, rape, and kill them and then abandon them to foraging animals. The highly public nature of his case ensured the widest dissemination of the facts. How could such an educational campaign have failed to serve as a deterrent to others? In fact, it could not.

Ted Bundy's case, though, illustrated other points as well. Foremost among them was the fallacy that, through incarceration, society would be protected. Why turn the state into a killer? Bundy escaped jail twice and committed horrible crimes while free. Those victims would be alive if the state had acted effectively, in almost any sense. Certainly most criminals are released, but this should be done discriminately and with monitoring and supervisory controls in place to reduce the risks to society. Some can never be released. Bundy's execution—an undeniably cruel act—at least ensured the safety of possible future victims.

The Framers clearly intended to allow capital punishment, else why did they hold, in the Fifth Amendment, that no one shall be deprived "of life, liberty or property, without due process of law"? It is clear they envisioned the taking of life.

When asked whether he'd witness Bundy's execution, or, indeed, whether he'd ever witnessed any at all, the hard-line governor of Florida said, "No, but I didn't witness the murders either, nor did I see the victims." He struck an impressive balance.

That Bundy was white, handsome, educated, literate, and charming made it easier to conduct a debate on issues that didn't get tangled with race or poverty. That he admitted his crimes spared everyone the hand-wringing that so frequently attends these events.

Bundy, who'd shown early promise of a successful political career, had led a privileged life. His crimes were calculated and awful. He stalked his victims like a hunter after prey. One observer called him a "killing machine." Ted Bundy was the ultimate litmus test. Anyone looking into his case and deciding he ought not be executed purely and simply opposes capital punishment, and there is no more to be said. Those who approved his electrocution favor it.

A 1988 poll showed that 71 percent of Americans favored capital punishment. Clearly a commanding majority feels that punishment deters and that it conditions behavior.

The circumstances would have to be carefully circumscribed. Death should be reserved for calculating, cold-blooded killers, such as those who murder for hire, who slaughter children, or who mug and kill innocent strangers. The racist factor has to be addressed. Black lives have to count for as much as white lives. Death row cannot be made, or kept, a black ghetto. In the end there are no finally persuasive arguments, pro or contra. Ted Bundy probably symbolized the issue best.

The state has a responsibility to take reasonable measures to safeguard potential future victims. This is what assessing public safety is really all about.

Crime and violence have increased dramatically in America over the past thirty-five years. In the early 1950s, for example, New York City had averages of one murder a day, with a population of eight million. In 1988 there were about five killings a day, among a population that was certified at seven million, but that probably contained a million uncounted aliens. Drugs were obviously playing a big part in the rise, but so were changing values and guns.

In the end you "pays your money and you takes your choice." Studies haven't helped to resolve the question.

Maybe Ted Bundy did.

Separating those who, like Bundy, have to be executed or sequestered, from the majority of criminals—who will be released—is a daunting task. Identifying the real menaces, and targeting them for special treatment, has proved an elusive goal.

Selective Incapacitation

The problems surrounding street crime and violence center on such words as *guns, drugs,* and *recidivists*. Recidivists contribute disproportionately to the crime rates because of the enormous numbers of crimes they produce as well as because of the nature of these crimes. It takes only one atrocious crime, such as the Kitty Genovese murder, to spook an entire community, and television now raises this communicative factor to geometric proportions. The airwaves are full of body bags. The recidivists don't have to be very numerous to constitute a menace to society.

If this tiny minority of serious repeaters could be identified with some degree of statistical reliability their incapacitation would make the people measurably safer. It is easy to see that the criminal who commits a hundred crimes a year (not, judging from recent studies, a ridiculously high figure) would, if imprisoned for a decade, be prevented from doing a thousand crimes. That's a thousand fewer victims. There is an exponential quality to this equation that should not tempt us into mindlessly repressive measures. What needs to be sought in this, as in all other human enterprises, is a tolerable risk factor.

The issue is perhaps best illustrated by the problem of serial rape, a compulsive act that is fueled by powerful psychological forces and that is committed repeatedly, on strangers.

There are good reasons to hope that criminologists might, following experimentation, analysis, study, and evaluation, develop a matrix that would identify the serious recidivist. This appears to be an area that will, following the growing debate on sentencing guidelines and their limitations, receive growing attention. The theory, at least, holds the promise of making the people safer while actually reducing the prison population as we become more discriminating about whom we send to jail and whom we control in different ways.

Privatization of Corrections

Governmental bureaucracies have functioned as monopolies that are untrammeled by considerations of profit or sources of funds. When they are freed of such constraints, the waste and inefficiency accrue. In recent years, following the scandals and pressures occasioned by an exploding prison population, desperate governments have turned to the private sector for help. The movement seems to have taken greatest root in the corrections field, where some jails and prisons have come to be operated by private, for-profit corporations. The attractions are economy and efficiency, not innovations or reform.

Such competition forms a healthy challenge to bodies that have grown fat and lazy because of the absence of the pressures of the marketplace. Privatization fuels the competitive forces that drive the engine of capitalism. Our government bodies tend to function much like socialism and it seems clear that, however lofty their aspirations, the failure to take the human animal's nature fully into account has spelled doom. Incentives, greed, competition, and the pressures of the market energize the economy. The absence of incentives proves deadening. The governmental environment is normally lacking in the stimuli that form the ingenious core of our economy. Comfort, ease, certainty, and taxes prove fatal to enterprise and innovation.

With the recent successes of private corrections, it seems altogether possible that politicians might, in future years, consider the prospect of bidding out such services as garbage collection (we've seen some of this with the recycling movement); fire suppression; and park maintenance (New York's most successful park operation, the Bronx zoo, is not a government operation). Many of the countless other services might be included and, yes, even policing.

We have been looking at some of the issues of control that impinge on the effectiveness of the criminal justice system, over which the cops have little say. They are the family problems and concerns of the criminal justice system, which, as we have seen, is not a system at all but a series of variegated parts trying to work in sync, while jealously protecting their turf. That the latter concern often, in the heat of battle for resources and the public's favor, proves irresistible is one of the profound tragedies of the operation. The criminal justice system must learn to cope more efficiently with society's failures.

Preventing crime means creating a just, inclusive society. Making the criminal justice system more effective requires an appreciation, by politicians in power, of the complexity of the issues and of the need to adopt strategies and approaches that may, at first blush, be unpopular. Controlling America's criminals is a difficult task, which will demand the use of a range of programs and fresh ideas. Sentencing guidelines are unpopular, but they work. Locking everybody up is popular, but it doesn't work.

CHAPTER 13

Responding to Woman Battering

A man comes home, in a drunken, jealous rage, and batters his wife with a cast-iron frying pan until her head becomes a blob of matted hair, bits of brain and bone splinters, and grotesquely misshapen flesh. At the end of his fury her head is held to her body by a few shards of skin. In the next room their eight-year-old boy tries to escape in the blaring nonsense of his television set.

Three women are stalked, like animals on the run from hunters, until they are finally run down and slaughtered. In suburban Suffolk County, New York, officials feel the community's outrage over their sluggishness to respond to the warnings along the way. The women had repeatedly sought help but reluctant police officials had declined to interfere in "domestic squabbles," adopting the traditional indifference to "family matters." Three corpses became the monuments to this policy of nonintervention. The aversion to such "interferences" has also washed over into the related fields of child abuse and molestation, incest, abuse of elders, and other familial horrors.

In Torrington, Connecticut, another woman, fleeing from a murderously assaultive husband, pleads for protection from the police and doesn't get it. She is finally tracked down and hideously assaulted.

In Minneapolis a desperate wife shoots and kills her husband, as he smashes his way in and rushes at her. He is a cop.

This is the reality behind the sterile abstraction known as *woman battering*.

It begins with angry words and is followed by a shove or a slap. If it is not interrupted at its inception it escalates, frequently to murder. Alcohol or drugs usually accompany the tragedy. Both the batterers and the battered were often themselves victims of child abuse or family violence. It is a cyclical family tragedy. Sometimes it is connected to a mental illness and sometimes it flows from the paranoic disorders induced by drug abuse.

While some men's groups have argued to the contrary, the reality of battering in America is men beating up women. The occasional deviation is remarkable enough to constitute the exception that proves the rule. Too much energy has been spent on the smokescreen that this isn't a gender-specific crime. It is.

The family has always been a sort of sacred enclave. We have, historically, been reluctant to pry into its workings. It is the essential core of societal organization, yet it can encompass child abuse, incest, violence against parents, murder, and the epidemic of child thefts we seem determined to believe are occasioned by strangers. As we kick over the rock we are beginning to discover that the family can be a place of pure terror as well as the center of caring and nurturing.

How often have teachers, doctors, family friends, welfare and social workers, or cops ignored the telltale signs of familial abuse? It has been necessary to pass tough laws to bring official notice to bear on the burns, bruises, welts, broken bones, genital injuries or irritation, bloodied or soiled underwear, unkempt or out-of-place clothing, dramatic changes in behavior, lack of energy, extreme anxiety to please or even the suicide attempts of children caught up in awful home situations. How often have emergency rooms patched up and ignored injuries that should have raised the alarm that a crime may have been committed? The tales of the victims are frequently dotted with references to such official interventions as police responses to the home, medical treatment in hospital emergency rooms, complaints to a teacher, or the observations of a social worker. Yet most cases of abuse seem to creep past these people, undetected.

The statistics, understated abstractions in themselves, mask the terror that comes from seeing the stalker in his car looking up at your window, the sounds outside doors or windows late at night, or the stomach-thumping sight of a once-familiar face suddenly emerging from the shadows.

Family Violence

Family violence encompasses a wide range of behavior. Almost two million women are battered each year and some form of violence occurs in one fourth of all marriages. About one out of every five women seeking emergency medical aid is a victim of abuse. More than two million children were reported abused in 1986 and more than a hundred children a month die through abuse or neglect. Parents found to have been abused as children are six times more likely to abuse than those who haven't been, and at least four out of ten of all abuse cases involve alcohol or drugs.

Prostitution in America is virtually nothing more than fifteen-year-old girls fleeing these horrors in their homes. Their willingness to expose themselves to the tender mercies of the streets is eloquent testimony to the terrors they left behind.

The police, as the first responders to many abuse situations, are centrally important to the issue of domestic violence. Yet they, like the rest of the system, have been very slow, until recent years, to take up the cause of protecting women and children. Under pressure from the growing feminist movement, abetted by such whopping lawsuits as the one that almost broke Torrington, the police have finally bestirred themselves to reluctant action.

Why this reluctance?

Police chiefs have a lot of claims on their energies. They tend to let sleeping dogs lie, as they scurry from squeaking wheel to squeaking wheel, applying grease. That it is now domestic abuse and family violence that are squeaking should suggest to us the possibility that other urgent concerns are probably being neglected. This at least suggests one good reason why police chiefs need to be constant, Socratic examiners of their organizations, their operations, and their priorities.

Cops will not be able to handle woman battering intelligently if they don't have a sense of the internal dynamics operating in the relationships that frequently involve escalating levels of violence. This inability to attack the problem successfully is further complicated by the psychological ploys used by batterers, such as the visiting of guilt on the victim. "She asked for it." The victim may even come to accept the blame. Her resistance is overborne, her self-esteem is shattered, and she gradually becomes a captive, both physically and psychologically. She may even be brought to believe that she deserved such treatment or that it's normal.

One of the most celebrated cases in recent history, Joel Steinberg's abuse of Hedda Nussbaum and his murder of their "adopted" daughter Lisa, illustrates the complexity of the physical and psychological dynamics at work.

The case proved a textbook example of the sort of dark deeds concealed under the rubric of "family." Steinberg's Svengali-like control extended even into areas we might logically think Nussbaum could have escaped rather easily. When she was taken to a hospital following a beating and had to have her spleen removed, or when she lay paralyzed, watching her "daughter" slowly die, she was unable to break the spell and reach out for help. Steinberg's paranoic obsession at being stared at, and his striking out viciously at his wife and children for it, demonstrated the complicated effects of cocaine on his abusive personality.

Theirs is a story that encapsulates the issues of domestic violence and child abuse perfectly, among highly educated, upper-middle-class whites. Every study of these phenomena discloses a surprising incidence at the higher, as well as the lower, social strata. Practitioners in the field were not shocked by disclosures that a high-ranking official at the Securities and Exchange Commission was a wife beater.

Once brought to her senses, through the awful tragedy of the child's terrible death, Nussbaum managed to see the depths to which she had been taken, through drugs and conditioning, in the sickest relationship imaginable. The descent was inexorable and gradual, involving instinctively applied psychological ploys of rewards and punishments that ultimately gave her lover gurulike power over her life. Isolation was a key element in her domination.

Yet their circumstances often did come to the attention of various officials. Teachers should have raised questions about Lisa's telltale marks and behavior. Nussbaum was treated by doctors for beating injuries. Family members were exposed to evidence of abuse. Neighbors must have heard things. Cops had been called to prior incidents. The events did not, over a decade, play out in a vacuum.

The case is also illustrative of the complex dynamics surrounding intrafamily violence and abuse. Many suspected Nussbaum's behavior and vigorously criticized her complicity or failure to act. Some felt she should have been prosecuted, but prosecutors have to make such deals in order to secure damning testimony against the principal culprit.

The central lesson is the critical need to interrupt the cycles of domestic violence and child abuse. This is the one area of police work where homicide prevention might be made a reality.

Adopting an Approach

The adoption of a workable approach to domestic violence requires that a number of essential components be in place:

1. Usually a peace officer can make an arrest for a misdemeanor, without a warrant, only if it is committed in the officer's presence. Since most domestic assaults (e.g., punches, slaps, nonpermanent injuries) are misdemeanors, the cops' hands have been tied. States are now passing laws enabling the police to make an arrest for an assault misdemeanor even when it has not occurred in their presence. Usually it must have occurred during the preceding four hours. The definition of assault has also been expanded to include threats with dangerous weapons or placing the person "in fear of immediate bodily harm."

2. Having the legislation in place enables the creation of a policy that mandates an arrest, in the above circumstances, if there is (a) evidence that the crime of domestic assault took place and (b) probable cause to believe in the guilt of the accused.

3. The definition of a victim, in such cases, includes not only spouses but anyone with whom the batterer resides or who resided with him. The characteristics of a victim can include being members of the same sex, as well as being former lovers, couples, or roommates, or any factors that indicate a prior relationship. Narrowly defining the relationships that involve domestic abuse holds the threat of omitting a significant population of sufferers.

4. Arrests would be expected in situations where there are visible signs of injury, where a dangerous weapon is involved, where the officers believe that the violence will continue, where the officer has prior knowledge of an offender's predilection for violence, or where there has been a violation of an order or protection, or where an arrest is necessary to protect anyone from further acts of violence.

5. Even threats or a victim's warranted fear can result in the offender's arrest. The development of a response policy has to take all these factors into account.

Elements of a Model Policy

Source documents must enunciate the agency's policies clearly and in writing. Domestic violence is a crime and it must be treated as such. Arrest is the preferred approach. The victim requires services and supports such as shelters, counseling, protection, and the moral support of advocates and other allies.

There must be a comprehensive training program for the police.

Relationship must be defined and be sufficiently broad as not to exclude any significant participant or class of participants.

Domestic violence must be defined in the law and should include injury as well as the use of threats, weapons, or fear. A time frame, such as "having occurred during the preceding four hours," should be included to preclude frivolous accusations and to pressure the victims to come forward.

The basis for an arrest has to be spelled out. First, there must be the *corpus delicti* (literally "the body of the crime"; the factors that go into establishing that a crime occurred); then there must be evidence pointing to the guilt of the accused. Disciplinary consequences for failing to take such actions as arresting the batterer must be explicitly described.

The policy should describe the agency's attitude and approach to woman battering.

The relevant laws, allowing the officer to arrest for a misdemeanor not committed in his or her presence, and similar circumstances relating to threats, use of weapons, or inculcation of fear, should be cited. Orders of protection procedures should be enunciated and access to their existence facilitated. It won't suffice to have an officer respond, be told that an order of protection has been violated, and not be able to check on the order readily, such as through the use of the mobile digital terminal in the squad.

The police role, as part of a coordinated, systemic response by all the players in the criminal justice system, has to be described so that the workers can understand both what is needed and how their actions fit into the overall response of the system. There need to be audits of dispatches to domestic abuse calls, to verify compliance.

The problem of abuse is most frequently first encountered by responding cops. They must be especially sensitive to the importance of quick, effective action. If they fail, tragedy results. The adoption of a model written policy ensures that a mechanism exists for a uniform response that follows the organization's philosophy. There was a time when bureaucracies eschewed putting too much in writing, on the theory that comparisons between acts and requirements would render them vulnerable to suits and accusations. That situation has now been reversed, and failure to have written policies almost automatically renders an agency vulnerable to the charge that it is indifferent to the problem in question.

Police chiefs are discovering, as they did in Torrington, Connecticut, the difference between an insurer's and a steward's responsibilities. They know that it is unreasonable to expect themselves to anticipate or prevent a particular crime, and that they cannot be held liable for its occurring, but they are learning that they are expected to act, like good stewards in cases where they should have known, could have anticipated, and must have acted, because of repeated prior incidents that pointed to continuing breaches.

An insurer's responsibility is to account for every incident or breach. Every claim has to be addressed and every incident must be resolved. Insurers cannot claim a general concern about problems while professing innocence about the details of an event they've insured. Stewards are generally responsible for the orderly conduct of affairs, without necessarily being held accountable for aberrational single events.

Thus the victim of a robbery would probably lose if he or she sued the chief for failure to prevent it. The frequent victim of batterings, who reported them to the police, and who demanded action and failed to get it, will have a case when the next, anticipatable assault takes place.

Insurers assume responsibility for every single event and are required to restore the situation. Stewards manage the enterprise and are guided by such questions as what they should have known, when they should have known it, what they should have done about it.

Why Arrest?

Arresting the offender is a societal statement that the act is a crime, that it is wrong, that it must stop, that punishment will follow, and that it would be sensible to secure treatment that will help in changing this behavior.

A lot of human acts that produce long-term benefits carry short-term anguish. The assaulted woman can readily see the immediate problems. The long-term possibilities of a safe, tranquil, "normal" life are dimly perceived, if at all. She can see that he might lose his job, go to jail, get angrier and more dangerous, actually mean it when he promises he'll never hit her again, or cease to care for her or love her. Her mind is a confused mix of emotions and fears, which are further complicated by her being mired in a relationship that is bound to transcend this moment. She will find it difficult to bite the bullet and insist on an arrest. The process is not without risk. Many women enter the bleak fields of poverty by leaving their male providers.

The cop, still reluctant to interfere, is not much help. The introduction of another strong advocate in the very first stages holds the best hope of getting the victim to follow through with the prosecution that brings the full weight of officialdom behind the effort to stop the battering. Someone who's been in her situation before can offer credible advice. The existence of a refuge—a women's shelter—is essential. The victim has to have somewhere to go immediately and she frequently has children who must be safeguarded and sheltered. The shelters are a stopgap haven, serving for the days or few weeks it takes the woman to find more suitable and permanent quarters. Yet this brief respite is crucial, both for the protection it offers and for the advice and emotional support extended by those working or staying there.

The threat of jail coerces the batterer into treatment, frequently of the sort offered by Alcoholics Anonymous. Recent court decisions have, however, called this approach into question because of the strong religious component of AA.

It is amazing how many batterers testify that they never thought of themselves as abusers. Over and over one hears the refrain, "I never considered myself a wife beater. Sure we fought, but everybody has their little tiffs." No one ever stopped them. The system never seemed to say, unequivocally, "This is wrong and it must stop." That is the prime function of an arrest policy.

Batterers report violent scenes in public places like restaurants, where a slap or a blow may have been struck, with others averting their glances and saying and doing nothing. Although the dangers are obvious the reality is that involvement is crucially needed. Citizens do police each other. Acceptable levels of conduct are dictated by what those present will tolerate. Silence is acquiescence.

It is bad enough for citizens to do nothing but unfortunately it is understandable. We are all frightened. The risks are clear. We don't get paid to interfere. It requires a deal of moral and physical courage—and they are different—to intervene in a violent incident of female battering.

It is not understandable, however, nor should it be permissible, that cops do nothing in such circumstances. This is an area where their discretion must be limited and be directed to act. They must be punished if they fail to do so.

Police Attitudes and the Minneapolis Domestic Violence Experiment

The police culture, still largely male and white, has traditionally been uncomfortable with the notion of intruding into the family: "A man's home is his castle"; "Don't come between a man and his woman"; "She probably had it coming"; "They'll kiss and make up by morning, and then I'll be the villain"; "She's not going to sign the complaint in court." These are the attitudes that have helped shape policy. In order to reshape behavior the attitudes of both the police and the victim must be attacked. Failing to do this results in the police paying lip service to new approaches while clever circumventions are devised, and in the victim continuing to suffer violence while hoping against hope that it will disappear without her having to come forward.

The human animal understands consequences. People act and something happens. If that something is bad or painful, they alter their actions. If it is pleasurable they extend the action. If nothing happens, they are likely to continue as long as it pleases them. We can, instinctively, see the logic of this construction, yet for some reason it is not enough for the police to base the official approaches of the state on what they logically know to be true. The police must learn not only to use the data produced by the few scientifically tested and verified approaches but also to encourage scholars to look deeper at more and more social problems that ultimately explode into police work.

In order to establish a workable policy for domestic violence, the Minneapolis Police Department, in 1981 and 1982, conducted an experiment. They had responding cops either mediate a domestic violence dispute, exclude the male from the home for at least eight hours, or arrest him. The cops were given no choices. The approach was dictated by an instruction booklet that assigned the response randomly. The police checked their sheets and either arrested, excluded, or mediated, depending on the instructions on the color-coded pad they'd been issued.

The follow-up study revealed that arrest held the best hope of reducing violence for the six-month period following the intervention. The results are being checked, through replication studies in six other cities.

Was this playing with people's lives? Was it sensible police procedure to eliminate officer discretion? Was it even legal?

The press can have a very good time with such questions. Few chiefs are willing to take that kind of heat. This goes a long way toward explaining why most police departments are loath to undertake something as universally admired as scientific experimentation. Even though it holds the promise of revealing new and better ways of doing things, the risks involved look pretty daunting.

Doing things by the seat of the pants and doing nothing at all are responses too. This obvious fact is too frequently forgotten. Police departments have been following time-honored, but not tested or verified, approaches. Neglect is a form of treatment too. Its consequences are being paid for in a series of lawsuits alleging police inaction.

The police cannot, of course, break the law in any of their operations, so the question of the legality of the experiment had to be resolved. Where circumstances mandated an arrest—such as in a felony assault—it had, of course, to be effected. But the police, like everyone else in the system, are allowed enormous latitude. What happened here is that I assumed this power to my own use, while mostly depriving my charges of the right to employ discretion. This is not a popular act among the rank and file. In the main the cops followed instructions faithfully. The exceptions were amply justified by the circumstances of the cases.

In medicine we have been conditioned to accept the painful reality of experimentation. We know that a cure for cancer would involve giving it to some patients while giving others a placebo. A number would have to die to prove its efficacy. Millions more would benefit later. If this isn't playing with people's lives, what is?

The search for truth can take some very tortured twists and turns.

Getting the Cops to Arrest Abusers

Cops may fail to record a domestic assault, listing it in their logs as a "dispute, gone on arrival" or "unfounded" or anything else that gets them out of recording a crime on an official form. It's just more paperwork, and they frequently don't take such events very seriously.

Merely exhorting the cops to follow the written policies will not be enough, nor will perfunctory training sessions work. The administration needs to put teeth into both the compliance and the educational programs. Officers will have to be disciplined for failures to respond; the training programs must be serious and deviations from the practices taught have to be punished.

What will be needed and does work is a system of verification that plainly advises the cops that they risk being discovered if they fail to comply. Randomly checking dispatches to domestic violence locations offers the best hope for correcting the problem. A woman or a neighbor calling 911 and alleging a domestic incident will have the call dispatched in just that manner. The calls can be checked and investigators can be assigned: "Was there an incident here the other night? What happened? Did the police respond? What did they do?" The answers are then matched with the reports the cops submitted or failed to submit, and follow-up action is taken. Cops respond energetically to such proddings, and the tasks can be assigned to existing personnel.

There is a struggle for power between the cops on the street and the chief. The cops want maximum latitude and want to handle calls their own way. Each case is different, and cops guard their discretionary power jealously.

Discretion does not need to be eliminated, but it must be limited and channeled. This is a push–pull struggle between the chief and the troops that is ultimately resolved through the imposition of disciplinary measures. In the world of the police, where the greatest power is centered on the lowest rank level, the only practicable method of control is to convince the cops that they'll be disciplined for failing to conform to the policies. If the cops don't fear the chief then they're going to handle the calls according to their prejudices, convenience, or personal perspective. Curiously, not many actions against cops have to be taken. A few cops being brought up on charges is usually more than enough to capture everyone's attention.

Domestic violence calls pose dangers for the responding police too, because of the violence and drugs usually involved. They are highly unpredictable situations. Responding cops are being thrust into scenes of historically escalating violence, frequently involving heavy drinking and mindless, reflexive actions, often including weapons. Interrupting these events early in the violence cycle, before they escalate to murderous assaults, holds out the best hope for everyone's safety. Although cops know all of this, their affection for their discretionary power is so great that they'd rather risk the dangers than be restricted.

One of the ways to protect cops from the unpredictable scenes of domestic violence they're being dispatched to is to cite chronic trouble spots in a "dangerous location" file, which indicates the dangers and the nature of the previous problems at that site on the cop's computer screen.

The Minneapolis Domestic Violence Experiment had worked. Following the adoption of what we all felt was a workable and enlightened policy of requiring arrests in domestic abuse cases, prosecutions soared. Other departments quickly adopted the methods and approach.

The cold water of reality intruded, months later, when an audit revealed that many of the cases the cops were responding to hadn't even been recorded. Disciplinary action followed swiftly, which was itself followed by more general compliance with requirements.

The development illustrated the importance of verification and the folly of accepting anything on face value in the police bureaucracy.

It is a bromide to add that training will be needed in order to produce success in any program. There is hardly a study that doesn't exhort the necessity for further training. Yet, in domestic violence cases, training is not only needed to teach the cops how to deal with this challenge but, perhaps even more important, to change their prevailing attitudes as well. Training is usually geared toward improving operational techniques. Training is normally content to leave the attitudes alone, and, usually, that's a wise decision. Attitudes usually take too long to change. It's a lot easier to change behavior than thought. But this is a case where attitudes drive actions and, unless the one is changed, the performance will be pro forma and fail, making domestic abuse one of the few areas where the training must strongly emphasize the need for the proper philosophical approach.

In order to bring verisimilitude to the process, advocates, victims, and former batterers ought to be used. Theirs is the credible testimony which holds the greatest promise for convincing skeptical cops that the problem is real, serious, and in need of attack. It would not be an exaggeration to say that domestic violence is one area of police operations where a significant change in approach will never be possible until the underlying prejudices are overcome.

Remembering the Minneapolis murder and other tragedies like it, the painful fact is that cops are part of the general population too, and a training program ought to include the probability that some of the students may themselves be batterers.

The best training reinforcement is success. If an arrest takes place, and the woman follows through and the prosecutor and judge take it seriously, and the batterer is coerced into treatment and the violence stops, then the program will work. It is a lot easier to sell the idea at that point than it would be if the horizon were littered with obvious failures.

Overnight Jailings

When a batterer is jailed overnight following his arrest, the message conveyed is dramatic and clear. Society considers the event both important and wrong. Jailing also offers the victim a temporary respite and some measure of protection from immediate wrath. It may also allow a cooling-off period.

Jailing will also strengthen the judge's hand in coercing the batterer into treatment. The actual experience of even a brief period of incarceration "concentrates the mind wonderfully," to paraphrase Samuel Johnson.

Orders of Protection

Battered, stalked women can apply to the courts for an order barring their tormentors from visiting their home or harassing them at the workplace or any other locations, under pain of being held in contempt of court.

This is one of the few areas of American law where an injury may be anticipated, and prevented, through the intervention of the court. Usually our system does not, in criminal law (there are, in civil law, injunctive orders that require or forbid some action), anticipate or even try to interdict acts. We normally require some evidence of moving toward a purpose before we can arrest. Such initial steps will result in charges of "conspiring to . . ." or "the crime of attempted . . . ." but even they require hard evidence of overt actions.

Orders of protection are just that: instruments intended to protect potential victims. Their effect is vitiated when exceptions are made. If the male returns, contrite and affectionate, the practical value of the order is nullified if the female doesn't insist on the order's being enforced.

The police must be trained in executing such orders. Systems must be devised for being able to check on their existence (e.g., through the computer-assisted dispatch screen in the squad car) so that time will not be lost. The process is currently attended by too much confusion and delay, which endanger the potential victim.

The victim must insist on recording every breach of the order, and whether the offender is caught or not, the police must make a record of the incident. Subsequent events, often tragedies, make the need for a history of the incidents critical. The police are also far more likely to respond effectively if the victim demonstrates her seriousness and that possibly damning records are being kept regarding their response.

Other Elements and Other Players

The cooperation of the other elements of the criminal justice system must be secured or the program will fail. District attorneys, worried about conviction rates, will not be anxious to prosecute such chancy cases as domestic assaults. Judges eager to clear their calendars will resist having them clogged with domestics. Jailers will not be pleased to see their crowded domains jammed further with assaultive males.

An arrest policy—a seemingly logical, sensible, and correct approach—is not an automatic winner. It might even be necessary to secure pressures from activist groups on the other elements of the system.

Prosecutors should consider establishing special units to prosecute family violence cases. The victims' protection is essential in these cases. Continuances and repeated exposures to testifying need to be kept to an absolute minimum. The use of videotaped statements ought to be considered, to spare the woman the ordeal of repeated cross-examinations. Such strategies are especially important in cases of incest, child abuse, rape, and other ordeals that victims ought not be forced to relive, except when absolutely essential.

Judges are in the best position to control the offender's behavior through the coercive power of incarceration. They need to use this power to protect the victims and to secure a cessation of the abuse. Compelling treatment, such as Alcoholics Anonymous or drug programs, issuing orders, and ensuring an orderly court process will help to communicate the seriousness of the process to the offender. Above all, judges need to understand the issues and to take these cases seriously. They and the prosecutors will also have to pursue cases where the victim is reluctant to participate, through the use of photos, taped calls to 911, witness testimony, or other evidence. This is a particularly thorny area.

Defense attorneys also have obligations that go beyond their obsession with winning. They need to bring a sense of duty to truth and to the diminution of the violence of these events. They must, of course, represent the interests of their clients, but the construction put upon these interests must be broad (such as the preservation of the family's peace and stability) rather than narrow (focusing on getting the client off the hook). Certainly a good deal of the problem of eroding public confidence in the legal profession today can be blamed on the lawyer's concern for victory as opposed to the search for a just solution to a problem.

Follow-up monitoring is especially critical in cases of chronic and escalating violence. The behavior may have been occurring for years. A system of verification is needed for the protection of the victim. Probation officers are the eyes and ears of the court in such circumstances. Making impromptu visits, verifying employment, checking medical records for injuries that might indicate abuse, watching for compliance with treatment programs, encouraging charges to further their education, and generally overseeing the activities of those they are assigned to supervise are the functions that give the monitoring process the teeth it needs in order to work effectively. Excessive caseloads subvert this process.

Prosecutions can proceed absent the direct involvement of the victim, but they are rarely successful. Direct testimony is the most powerful evidence, and it allows the jury to evaluate the principals.

Treatment Programs

Treatment programs have to be available. The point of the arrest process is to stop the violence, by either jailing the batterer or forcing him into treatment. This makes the existence of useful, relevant programs essential, in these and other issues such as drug cases, where efforts are frequently defeated because of the absence of follow-up treatment facilities. The range of programs has to be broad because the problems driving abusive behavior can range, in variety and complexity, from alcoholism to drug addiction, and from mental disturbance to any of the other scores of ills that attend the human condition.

It is in these largely invisible follow-up areas that the system fails so often, mostly because elected officials find it difficult to get excited over programs that don't play well on television or on the front pages of the newspapers. They are much more comfortable pointing at the Willie Hortons than they are at the thousands of successes behind those occasional failures. Maybe the essential problem of the criminal justice system in the domestic-abuse, drug, gun, and related areas is that we're sending people of poor quality into public life, and they are the ones who decide all these questions. It is an old saying that, in a democracy, the people get the government they deserve. If we insist on sending feckless caretakers and survivalists to city halls, we will continue to receive the sort of deplorable "service" or outright betrayal of trust that today dots the pages of our newspapers.

The Woman's Responsibility

Advocates of tough policies on domestic abuse have silently but persistently searched for the magic bullet that will extricate the victim from the dilemma of coming forward. The most recent wrinkle is the move to secure evidence, independent of her testimony, to prosecute the batterer. Such evidence might be photographs, recorded calls to 911, the testimony of witnesses, visible injuries, or statements of the offender. And, in fact, there is no actual legal impediment to proceeding in this fashion, except that, in the real world, these tactics encounter a lot of resistance.

Ours is an adversarial system of confrontation. The accused faces the accuser. A search for the truth follows. The absence of an accuser, in all cases except the clearly understood case of murder, where the state stands in for the victim, is usually fatal to the prosecution. Judges and prosecutors are very reluctant to proceed without the determined presence of the complainant. Juries expect the accuser to confront the abuser.

But women are not likely to find an alternative solution. They have to face the economic, emotional, and physical risks of coming forward and pointing the finger at their tormentors if they want justice to prevail. The system, nevertheless, must still do its best, even when she fails to cooperate, and this may mean proceeding with an unpromising case for the prosecution. This is where feminist consciousness raising groups could be coordinated with the police.

The system's need for, and insistence on, confrontation may well be characterized as the great unspoken debate attending the domestic abuse issue and the system's response. It has to be faced.

A police chief trying to do something about domestic violence will fail unless the cooperation of the other elements in the system is secured. The judges, prosecutors, jailers, and so on won't cooperate unless they see some prospects of a successful prosecution. At the moment, the discussion has centered on arrests, because of the police reluctance to make them and because of their necessity for the entire process to begin. An arrest is the way a case is introduced into the system.

As the police resistance to arrest is overcome, and it is happening rapidly, the failures will come downstream, to the DA's offices or the judge's chambers. A failure, anywhere, will still produce the same tragic results. The batterer must be arrested and must then learn, through his experience with the process, that he must either change his behavior or face the painful consequences.

The victim must escape from the psychic thrall of abuse before she can hope to deal with its reality. She must learn that it is not only abnormal but unacceptable. She must find the courage to confront it and must insist on stopping it. As progress mounts the central importance of the woman will inevitably become clearer. The feminists who hope to spare the victim the additional pain of having to come forward and point the finger at her batterer are wasting energy on a well-intentioned search for a legal remedy they won't find. They'd be better off ensuring that the system will be sensitive to the victim's needs, that it won't subject her to ordeals that might be avoided through the use of videotaped testimony, for example, and that it will offer her the necessary support and protection.

Conclusion

A lot of progress has been made in recent years. Research, experimentation, litigation, interest-group pressures, and the simple desire to promote the public's safety have all contributed to the forward movement now underway. But a lot remains to be done.

Domestic abuse is complex human behavior. Its cure will require complex solutions. The determination to attack the problem is a key step forward but it has to be accompanied by concerted action.

Hanging over the issue is the specter of ruinous litigation. The police chief cannot be held responsible for every failure, but each of those failures can be examined for responses to such hard questions as how much the police knew and what they did about it. If the record is dotted with evidence of indifference, the city, and the chief, are going to be in trouble. It's too bad that such negatives drive so much of our public policy, but it is far better to be driven to do some good by a negative force than none at all.

The traditional police approaches of ignoring the problem, trying to mediate or massage the dispute into a nonevent, excluding the male, or doing nothing have plainly not worked. Arrest seems to offer the best hope for reducing domestic violence, and there is the additional instinctive sense that direct action offers the best hope for success. Ignored problems tend to fester; they rarely dissolve. The chief's responsibility is to take whatever legal measures he believes wisest, based on something more real than seat-of-the-pants feelings, to promote the safety of his community. Abuse is not confined to the poor and ill-educated. It cuts across both the financial and educational strata. The two factors that appear to consistently surface in studies of domestic abuse are its prevalence and its complexity.

The family is the foundation of our nation. All else is built upon this organizational core. Until a suitable substitute is found we are going to have to rely upon it to retain our national cohesion. Attacking the serious problems that beset it holds out the best hope for preserving and strengthening the family.

CHAPTER 14

External Challenges, Controversies, and Opportunities

How can a police chief be prepared for dealing with a bewildering array of groups and issues that often get tangled into unexpected controversies? There can be no school to prepare the executives for the myriad possibilities awaiting them. The bromides of management schools and the pointers given in case studies are only tangentially helpful.

Yet the chief must learn to swim skillfully in these waters, recognizing the risks, identifying the problems, and moving swiftly to resolve the difficulties before they develop into maelstroms. Any event can explode into banner headlines.

There are three approaches chiefs can use to prepare themselves for coping with the problems they are certain to encounter: (1) They can obtain the work experience and variety of assignments that will arm them with a grasp of the agency's strengths and weaknesses; (2) they can secure a formal education that will provide them with the intellectual skills needed to cope with complex questions; and (3) they can work on the development of a firm philosophical perspective that will serve as a touchstone and moral compass as they navigate the uncharted public waters of the police world.

"The good of the people is the chief law." Thus did Cicero enunciate the first priority of the state. The police chief's actions need to be guided by that simple idea. The forces at play will tempt and toss the leader's inner gaze in every direction. Counselors will offer conflicting views. The appealing short-term solution almost inevitably contains the seeds of long-term failure, and the long-range answers almost always involve short-term risks and pain.

In the confusing police world of shifting problems, chiefs have to rely on the adoption of programs and approaches that accord with the philosophical base they've constructed through reading, study, introspection, reflection, discussion, and the tortured search that characterizes the process of problem solving.

The name, issues, and facts will change for police chiefs but there is always a kind of sameness to the questions raised by the various surfacing crises, and to the discussions. In the heat of the moment the Rosetta stone of an ethical perspective, one we might call wisdom, becomes the best guide to action. An inner code, born of the crucible of thought and experience that inspires the development of principles that might be applied to varying situations, has to be formed. The following public groups and organizations perfectly illustrate both the problems of and the opportunities for service in all their complexity.

Guardian Angels

The scene stood out in my memory for many years. Curtis Sliwa was offering, to the chief of the subway cops of New York, the services of a group of mostly minority kids from the Bronx to help police the graffiti-daubed system. Back then they called themselves the Magnificent Thirteen.

I listened quietly as the charismatic young man enthusiastically made his pitch. At the end he received the fervent thanks that so often accompany the bureaucratic signal that there will be no commitment.

After he left I urged that we use these volunteers but my boss swept my entreaties aside with concerns about legal issues, lawsuits, training, and the inevitable problems with the police union. We didn't want meddlers crawling all over our system, did we?

Thus was the face of the bureaucracy set, in 1977, hard against the group that came to be called the Guardian Angels. The scene was to be repeated frequently as police executives verbally paid lip service to the notion of volunteerism and citizen involvement, while, in practice, they expressed their reservations with subtle resistance to the idea and outright hostility.

Almost everywhere they went, the Guardian Angels ran afoul of the constabulary. Yet, whenever I spoke to a community group, the first or second question would almost always be what my opinion was of them.

Why is there such interest in a group that is usually small and, except for the genius of their founder for securing publicity, not terribly consequential?

The answer, I suspect, lies in the symbolic question they represent: Am I my brother's keeper? In this age of noninvolvement citizens want to know what their responsibility and role really are. Should they get involved or leave it to the professionals? Will they suffer a ruinous lawsuit if they take action? What are the limits of self-defense?

Everyone has read the man-bites-dog stories of citizens who defended themselves, stoutly, and got arrested or sued. These myths grow and prosper. The reality is otherwise. Our system is still one where, if you enter with clean hands, you come out unscathed—and it is still pretty capable of distinguishing between clean and dirty.

The Guardian Angels symbolize the importance of citizen participation in providing community safety in a democracy. As I've mentioned before, the people largely police themselves.

The historical police message of "We'll take care of it, you stay out of it" has served to undermine the community's sense of its responsibility for its own protection, but there is an instinctive restiveness about leaving our safety in the hands of mercenaries. Nevertheless, these police messages get repeated so often they gradually come to be believed and accepted by the public.

Today cops are discovering how very much they need the involvement of citizens in promoting a community's safety. They now conduct much-ballyhooed programs in order to promote a partnership with the public. They've even invented a catch phrase for it—"community-oriented policing"—which carries a convenient acronym (COP). The effort tends, however, to founder on such specific sticking points as relations with such scorned volunteers as the auxiliary police. It positively deteriorates when it comes into contact with such groups as the Guardian Angels. Cops are not very respectful of outsiders but they are downright contemptuous of those who offer to do their job for free.

The inability of the police chief to reconcile the anomaly of lip service to the volunteers and the organization's actual response to such groups as the Angels and auxiliaries will ultimately poison the COP programs. The chiefs cannot verbally embrace the concept of partnership and allow hostility to volunteer groups to flourish in the police ranks.

Why do I favor the Angels?

They do useful things, involving minority kids who need structure, discipline, and something meaningful in their lives. And to me it doesn't look like a money hustle. They use donated space, pay no one, and keep expenses at rock bottom. No one has ever complained to me that they've been approached for funds.

The Angels do pursue confrontational, aggressive street tactics, such as questioning suspected drug dealers. They organize picketings and leafleting and openly challenge the "street bums" their colorful leader is so fond of pillorying. All, I might add, to the public's absolute delight.

What about vigilantism?

We are overconcerned about vigilantism in this country. The images in the movie *The Oxbow Incident* die hard, and rightly so. Vigilantism, however, means breaking the law in order to punish presumed wrongdoers. The answer to vigilantes is to treat them as straightforward lawbreakers. Allowing any organizations, like the Black Muslims, for example, to take over and patrol ghetto streets in order to keep junkies out, using dubious tactics of confrontation and intimidation, is not without its great risks. Holding that vigilantism is not a major threat is to say neither that it doesn't exist nor that it can't, but the fear of it, in practice, has been, with a few exceptions such as in that movie or the actions of the Black Muslims, overdone. A genuine partnership between cops and citizens cannot be endangered because of fears over vigilantism that are, in the main, unrealistic. If the Angels or the Muslims or the auxiliaries step over the line and break the law in their zealousness over order, they must be arrested, but this shouldn't destroy the programs of cooperation that are working. The police must channel such energies into legal avenues.

How Effective Are the Guardian Angels?

A National Institute of Justice study revealed that there is no current effective way to measure the impact of the Guardian Angels. In the same vein, we might say exactly the same thing about measuring the impact of hiring x number more cops. Yet the Angels appear to have a positive impact. Their presence seems to prove reassuring to everyone but the police. Citizens frequently report how comforted they were by the presence of the Angels' colorful patrols.

Cooperating with the Guardian Angels may create tensions between the chief and the rank-and-file cops. A lot of actions that favor the people will cause discomfort in the ranks, and the chief must do what is good for the people rather than what is popular with the troops. Police chiefs are going to discover that their response to the Guardian Angels will reflect their actual, if deep and hidden, feelings about citizen volunteers.

If chiefs share their officers' antipathy to these groups, then the community-oriented policing programs now so ardently extolled will amount to little more than latter-day Potemkin villages.

Gays

Gays, a significant minority in America, represent a number of civil rights questions, such as equal employment, privacy definitions, and even public health and safety matters. Should they have the right to be employed as teachers and cops? What police officer behavior—in enforcing sodomy laws, for example—constitutes invasion of privacy and what constitutes legitimate control of public actions? Should AIDS sufferers be forced to register or be subjected to other forms of state control in order for the general population to be safeguarded?

These are some of the general questions surrounding gays. Gays also get tangled in the thicket that envelops society's pariahs, again testing attitudes toward the hated thought and the targets of prejudice.

Many would argue that sodomists ought not to be hired as cops or teachers, yet this argument assumes facts not in evidence. Would those advocates intrude into the sexual practices of heterosexual candidates? Is there a prejudice about the cops' macho image behind the resistance? Gays have the same rights to employment, housing, and other freedoms as any other segment of our population. The deprivation, or limiting, of any right has to be predicated on articulable, legitimate grounds. It is permissible to deny employment to someone who is diseased or unable to do the job, and housing can be similarly denied to vandals or nonpayers of rent, but these deficiencies must be proved.

The family unit is bound up in myth and religion, because of its role as society's core. We instinctively sense its importance. Our survival depends on the family. Gays are frequently perceived as subverters of the family or, at best, as indifferent to the institution. As alarms over societal survival escalate, those seen as threats are responded to more harshly. Tolerance requires relaxed self-assurance. It doesn't do well amid panic.

Yet gays and lesbians have, in the manner of other minority groups, become unified, more powerful, and assertive of their rights. They have welded themselves into strong interest groups in many cities. They've demonstrated, established newspapers, held parades, and elected officials. State legislatures and city councils have openly gay members reflecting the interests of their constituencies.

Maneuvering the thin line between would-be moralists and gays has proved a difficult task for many police chiefs. Before the advent of AIDS, gay bathhouses and gay bars, where homosexuals met, were frequently the targets of police raids. Liaisons between strangers in gay meeting places were frequently the focus of police energies. Arrests for "lewd conduct" abounded. The argument tended to boil down to definitions of what was public and what was private behavior.

The gay community has flexed its muscles in recent years, even to the point of rioting over the anguish surrounding the murder of Harvey Milk, one of the first professed gays to be elected to public office, in San Francisco.

In an age of powerful and changing groups, the police executive is frequently called on to take decisive action, such as the enforcement of policies against illegal activities by gays or a legitimate response to a gay demonstration or the investigation of some atrocious crime against a gay person. If the chief's actions are not informed by a philosophical grasp of the issues, the possibility of a stumble that will produce tragic consequences is greatly enhanced.

As a result of mostly legal actions by gays, which have demonstrated gays' increasing power, the actions of the police have altered dramatically. Today more sensitivity and understanding are connected to the police department's responses to gay issues. The police chief must, nevertheless, have developed a philosophy that can be used as a guide through such roiling waters. This would typically consist of an ability to answer such questions as "What activities or behaviors would I act against?" "On what legal basis would I predicate my actions?" "Would such actions be just?" and "How would my agency's actions benefit or hurt the people's interests?"

These views must also be shaped to fit other unpopular groups and minorities.

The Homeless

Emblazoned deep in America's psyche is the vision of the staggering derelict wiping motorists' windshields with a greasy rag, cadging coins, while drivers anxiously wait for the green light at the Bowery and Houston in New York City and at many other corners. I grew up with that vision. The homeless tended to be alcoholics on a city's Skid Row.

By the mid-1980s, though, the homeless population swelled, as mental institutions had been emptied, the number of drug addicts grew, and housing costs drove the marginally housed to join the traditional alcoholics of the street. The federal government's abandonment of any responsibility to house the poor greatly exacerbated the problem. City streets became dotted with bag ladies, bearded wanderers with backpacks, disoriented spirits mumbling to themselves, and newly impoverished women and their children. Many stood lone vigils, with cups extended, begging coins. At night they emerged, zombielike, to wander the dark streets.

To this day severe winters make the Sunbelt cities more attractive sites for aimless wanderings and sleeping under bridges. There seems the prospect of a serious squatters' movement developing, whether north or south. The overall impression is of a society in decay, where norms no longer apply and consequences no longer matter. A way hasn't even been found to get the mentally ill to take their medicine. Hardly any facilities are made available to the homeless, such as shelters, detoxification centers, psychiatric wards, or residential facilities. Those that exist are often such terrifying places as to convince the displaced that they're better off sleeping in subway roadbeds (despite the obvious dangers) or stations, with "one eye open" rather than having to use shelters where they must sleep with "both eyes open," as one underground dweller put it.

The homeless are not a single group, but a polyglot mix of people in trouble, bound together by their common plight of having no home. They are both victims and victimizers. They suffer crimes and some commit them. By their very presence they communicate a disquieting premonition of social disintegration.

Controlling the homeless has mostly been left to the cops, and they haven't been afforded the facilities needed to do the job adequately. Meanwhile chambers of commerce scream that little old ladies are abandoning America's downtowns and insist that the cops act to remove drunk, panhandling, urinating, or unsightly "menaces." It is through such pressures that the police are assigned the tough task of controlling the underclass.

Just keeping these people moving from place to place will ensure a continuation of the problem and fill everyone with a sense of futility. Services and treatment must be made available. The police should have the power and the ability to pick up public drunks and take them to a detoxification center, where they can be held, involuntarily, up to seventy-two hours. During this period they are sobered up, cleaned up, medically evaluated, and offered treatment. Even chronic alcoholics would get a chance to save their lives. The lockup is essential to ensure some measure of consequence and to channel alcoholics and others to exposure to the possibility of treatment programs.

Additionally cops ought to have the power to take the obviously mentally disturbed to another involuntary lockup psychiatric facility, where they can be evaluated and either referred for treatment (which ought to include the possibility of institutionalization) or released. This may offer the best hope for coercing the obdurate into taking their medicine, thereby greatly easing the burden caused by treatable mental illness.

While this approach, of removing drunks to detox and the mentally disturbed to evaluative facilities, would surely not solve the problems, it would go a fair distance toward restoring some measure of structure and would provide cops with a viable, legal strategy for coping with these very tough urban problems. The existence of these threats would also be likely to influence the behavior of those on the street.

The police need the legal power to control and bring a sense of order to the street. This should include the authority to supervise street vendors and hawkers, who will, if left to their own devices, turn America's downtowns into Middle Eastern bazaars. Cops' legal authority ought to extend to the seizure and confiscation of the goods, following due process. Admittedly the legal challenge posed by such requirements is daunting but it appears indisputable that laws are needed to regulate behavior on public streets that take into account the needs of all users, not just the eccentrics and the exploiters.

The balancing of rights will prove difficult and fear has forced many to abandon hosts of public places, like urban downtowns, leaving them under the control of the homeless. There are issues of privacy versus public safety to be dealt with. The public's morale will be affected by the cops' response to these street conditions. The quality of the police response will be dictated by the quality of the referral programs available. Here, too, the chief has to take a systemic view and plump for the existence of the needed services, whether they are directly related to the chief's duties or not. Chiefs, in constructing a working system, have to ensure that all the parts are in place. They need to take an expansive view of their role even if it means being accused of interfering in matters that don't concern them or actually diverting resources from their agency to one whose services might be needed more desperately. Chiefs can be powerful advocates, and their agencies are going to get drawn into doing a lot of things that may or may not be directly related to their assigned mission. Chiefs might well strengthen their agencies' operations by eschewing the offers of more cops while insisting that the resources be spent for such ancillary purposes as detox centers, mental-health-care facilities, and shelters. Such selfless advocacy would carry enormous weight.

It's certainly a truism of public life that unattended problems get worse. The city's poor, homeless, spaced-out, and alienated might well become angrier and more militant with the passage of time. Will the police always be able to control the vandals within the gate? The police constitute a very thin blue line, created to handle the ordinary and expected daily problems, and not to cope with extraordinary challenges like riots, massive squattings, or large-scale, continuous demonstrations. However, if present conditions are allowed to continue the growing plight of the disaffected is bound to find expression in violence.

The problems in America's cities have been made much worse by the flight of stable families to the suburbs and the influx of unprepared, unstable families into urban cores. These movements ensure a concentration of the poor, the homeless, the needy, and the problem causers in the central cities. The police chief, as a public figure of some stature and experience, is in a good position to speak to the broad issues represented by these groups and trends, and to suggest possible remedies. There is no reason why a chief can't be an advocate for housing as well as for other needed services for the excluded, or against such awful urban problems as have been created by racism, yet they've been silent.

Class, Race, Economics, and Crime

In 1968 the National Advisory Commission on Civil Disorder issued a report which contained one basic conclusion: "Our nation is moving toward two societies, one black, one white—separate and unequal." In that same report President Johnson called for an attack on poverty, in language that today, after the pillagings of the Great Society's poverty pimps, sounds a little naive. The gloomy prophecies of its pages about blacks have, in the words of Malcolm X, "come home to roost."

Our ghettos are awash with drugs, guns, and murder, and they are fast spilling out into the other streets of our cities. Across the land we saw, in 1988, record numbers of killings in Washington, D.C., Minneapolis, and many other cities. A recent study concluded that almost 40 percent of New York's record number of murders in 1988 were related to illegal drugs. But drug dealers are not just shooting each other. The reported number of innocent-onlooker shootings has risen alarmingly. These hapless victims are contemptuously referred to as "mushrooms" by the gut-toting drug killers.

City streets are littered with the human graffiti that remind us of the accelerating decay. "No foundation, all the way down the line," a phrase borrowed from William Saroyan, fits. Eight years of Reaganomics and bootstrappism have given us a fat, prosperous overclass and a dangerous, excluded underclass.

The underclass is the unmentionable secret that dominates the hidden thoughts of our police chiefs. They assess each other's prospects with such cautiously whispered questions as "What's your minority population?" The specter of long, hot summers seldom strays far from their imaginations. Chiefs, of all backgrounds and races, discuss, in their private councils, the prospects of riots or escalating waves of violence.

Spike Lee's important 1989 film *Do the Right Thing* depicted the problems eloquently, even as it resisted the temptation to give facile prescriptions. It made a whole lot more sense to initiate a debate than to succumb to the demagogue's approach.

During the silence the plight of the underclass worsens markedly, whether measured in terms of income, education, or presence in jails and on death rows, or in their absences from board rooms or university halls.

The Urban League and other predictable and unlistened-to little bands sound the alarm, every year, in learned reports and studies, but no one is listening. The public's attention is not going to be given voluntarily, it has to be wrenched from it by a crisis. It's coming, in the form of escalating violence and crime, rioting, pillaging, looting, and killing— what every police chief I've talked to fears and expects. Virginia Beach in 1989, Miami earlier that year, and Shreveport in 1987 were only harbingers. The kindling is there, everywhere, awaiting only the spark of an incident. But even then we will be certain to focus on the spark and will ignore the combustibles our moral myopia has created.

Blacks are the principal perpetrators of street crime in our society and its principal victims. The leading cause of death of young black men is murder. They are rarely present at the birth of their children. Our jails are filled beyond capacity with blacks. We've more than tripled the prison population in recent years, and now we're starting to free them, pell-mell, because of court orders trying to curb overcrowding. Black males constitute 6 percent of our population and 40 percent of the prisoners. Our per capita incarceration rate is regularly described as being third, to the Soviet Union's first and South Africa's second. Europeans are appalled at the length of our sentences yet we like to believe ourselves a generous and easily abused people.

The criminal justice system is collapsing. In its confusion and tawdriness, it resembles nothing so much as an oriental bazaar. Yet the insistent call for more cops, tougher judges, bigger jails, and more macho prosecutors grows shriller. Our Praetorian Guards have never been bigger, stronger, or more efficient, but they're losing, in ways precisely analogous to the Vietnam war, and with the same official silences, body counts, and promises of victory.

Nobody wants to look at the upstream questions of family, education, income, jobs, teenage pregnancy, or any of the other numberless disabilities visited upon our underclass. We've lost our passion for the huddled masses and the tempest-tossed. In our myopia we focus on crack, the variable, and ignore the constant, the need for the underclass to escape the awful realities of their daily lives.

Interestingly enough, despite the law-and-order rhetoric and the swelling numbers of arrests, a subtle political shift has occurred in police operations. As black leaders take over the cities, aggressive tactics that fall most heavily on black robbers and muggers, such as stakeout units or decoy operations, are being abandoned as unpolitic, even when they perform most impressively. The debates that surround these, and related, issues are muted, if mentioned at all. A full discussion of the ramifications would require its own forum. This abandonment of aggressive tactics, in a tough-law-and order age, is precisely the sort of anomaly that attends our confused and confusing twistings. Civilizations stagger and stumble to their disasters, they don't seem to proceed to them with lockstep precision.

Black criminals are the product of two hundred years of slavery, one hundred years of dependence, and twenty-five years of exclusion, poverty, ignorance, unemployability, drug and alcohol addiction, abuse and abusing, and the brutal conditioning and neglect they've been subjected to since before birth.

It is no accident that a group in Chicago, called the Beethoven Project, anxious to do something about the plight of black youngsters, is now concentrating on improving the parenting skills of pregnant teenagers and the prenatal care of their babies. Treating blacks as if they were just another immigrant group that came here voluntarily, with family, culture, religion, and roots intact, is one of the great misconceptions of our age. It ignores the devastating effects of deracination.

Blacks have been abandoned by white America—literally, in the flight to the suburbs, and figuratively, in the corporate and government policies we have adopted. Even Jews, long in the vanguard of the social and economic struggles in America, have largely abandoned the black cause so many of them fought, and even died for, earlier in this century, to join the rest of us in an orgy of self-absorption.

I once begged President Ford to come to the Bronx, today's Vietnam, to bear witness to the desolation eating at the country's soul, but he wouldn't listen. By happenstance Jimmy Carter did come and he made a famous stop at Charlotte Street, now made into a milepost on the road to the presidency. Ronald Reagan followed suit and even engaged some colorful locals in a heated exchange that had the desired effect of getting it all on the evening news. Both made empty, hollow promises that had the cruel effect of falsely raising hopes. Instead of remedies the Bronx got Wedtech, a ghastly scandal involving politicos and the highest reaches of the federal establishment.

"My family was poor but they weren't criminals. Why should poverty be equated with crime?"

"Why don't the blacks pull themselves up by their bootstraps the way other immigrant groups did?"

These questions ignore the uniqueness of the experience of the blacks in America. Our racist instincts are fed, every night, by television images of manacled blacks being led away from a crime scene. Frequently there is a body bag in the picture. Our suspicions are confirmed.

The criminals we've created have to be punished and have to be understood. It is silly to argue that the criminal predator is the victim of horrible conditioning and, therefore, absolved of guilt. There have to be consequences for illegal actions, but there must also be an understanding of the causes and some concomitant determination to do something about them.

Similarly, even as we hold the recidivist strictly to account, we have to rethink the policies that have brought about such a high percentage of criminals in the underclass. It is not too hyperbolic to say that we are as responsible for the existence of our criminal class as the German people were for the existence of the Nazis.

We paid a fearful price for our silences and hypocrisies during the Vietnam war. It took us a long time to discover the moral imperatives at work there. Our generals should have warned us; instead, they asked for more time, more funding, and more of our children. Our urban generals, even as they bail furiously against an overwhelming tide, should be crying out an alarm warning of the holocaust they clearly see coming.

The results are there for all to see—guns, drugs, and murder—but we refuse to see the causes. As long as we pursue policies that exclude blacks from jobs, schools, housing, and hope and consign the black underclass to lives of violence, brutality, and criminality, we are going to reap an ever-increasing harvest of misery.

Solving the problems of crime, drugs, violence, guns, and urban terror will mean clearing the swamp of poverty and redirecting the funds to programs that ensure education, jobs, housing, income, social service programs, inclusion, and the prospect of making it for America's poor and desperate. It means redistributing income along juster, more equitable lines. It means offering help to our fellow citizens, even as we threaten the failures with imprisonment—for the failures have to be addressed, too. Solving the problem will mean thinking about the hard social, cultural, and economic questions that now widen the chasm between the overclass and the underclass. The legal issues were mostly resolved through the civil rights legislation of the late sixties.

Sooner or later we're going to ask where all these criminals are coming from and how we helped to create them. Then will come the harder question of what we are willing to do about them.

Who excludes the blacks? How are they kept down? Who shapes the policies that drive the underclass to drugs, guns, murder, and criminality?

The Overclass

Very, very few Americans will define themselves as members of the overclass. The term connotes a stupendous oligarchy of great wealth and power. What Pogo taught us—that we've met the enemy and he is us— never held truer than in defining the overclass.

The underclass might be defined as those thirty-five million or so living beneath the official poverty level of about $11,000 per year for a family of four. It is a membership club for the poor and it includes street people, ghetto blacks, impoverished whites, and all the others excluded from the American Dream. It is easy to define the term in generally acceptable concepts.

The ruling class, however, has greater difficulty identifying its votes, taxes, community meetings, contacts with politicians, and other exercises of power as making it the overclass. It is the middle class that controls America and that encompasses the millions who live in reasonable comfort, who have the skills of experience and education to protect their interests, and whose decisions—collective and individual—decide the fate of local and national questions.

The ruling class decides whether to arm or disarm, whether to listen to Jesse Jackson or George Bush, and whether to address the problems of the poor or those of the rich, in deciding between tax programs.

The overclass are the solid burghers most of us take ourselves to be, even as we resist the label with all our might.

In order for police chiefs to function effectively in a highly political role, it is necessary that these executives understand the complex forces at work around them. Failure to grasp the implications of sensitive issues, or to be aware of the ramifications of their actions and policies could, for example, cause them to step on one of those hidden land mines that are strewn over the urban landscape. Chiefs must be alert to these possibilities and provide leadership to help shape public attitudes on controversial questions.

Placing a halfway house for criminals in a residential area is going to result in controversy. Property rights are sacred. Establishing residencies for retarded people or for alcoholics or even trying to find the site for a new jail—one that everyone agrees is desperately needed—will pit the bureaucrats against the affected class. Every action, however noble, produces an injured group—or one whose freedom is being limited—and the possibility of a negative reaction. Chiefs, even if not directly affected, must, because of the indirect impact of all of these issues on their operation, participate in the debate.

Closing a porn shop may result in a lawsuit raising various constitutional issues. Aggressive traffic enforcement may produce resentment among the driving population, many of whom are members of the middle class. Somebody's ox will always be gored.

The overclass has hired the cops to keep the underclass under control and out of sight. Programs that strike at overclass prerogatives are going to spark problems. Anticipating these reactions will enable the chief to plan and to attempt to interdict unpleasant consequences.

The chief's best hope for success is to tie the program to the long-term interests of the overclass. Appeals to altruism will receive a lot of sympathy but little real help. An increasingly self-absorbed nation has to see its real concerns imperiled before it will be moved to protect them, especially if this requires reallocating resources.

Yet "the people," that amorphous mass of humanity joining to create a nation, possess enough strength and wisdom to create miraculous results once they have been persuaded of the wisdom of a policy. And it is in them that police chiefs must put their faith if they are to sail the boiling waters of controversy that appear to be awaiting today's urban police executives.

CHAPTER 15

Myths, Unions, Press, Weather, and Crime

Police chiefs have to be aware and wary of the myths in their communities because they can so often prove to be goads to inappropriate or dangerous actions.

In the late 1970s and early 1980s something called the "Minnesota Connection" absorbed and frightened residents. So-called God-fearing families were having their blond, young goddesses plucked from the hearth by evil pimps, to surface in Times Square in hot pants and halter tops, ready for action. The pimps would be black, giving the necessary racial dimension to the myth. There weren't many cases but the account appealed to the prejudices of an audience made more accepting by the fact that the myth was propounded by two cops who harbored a mixed set of motives, including religious fervor, ambition, celebrity status, greed, and, I supposed, a small measure of sincerity.

Negative things seemed to be happening to some families and people wanted to find some demon to blame.

Closer scrutiny revealed that fifteen-year-old girls fled to the streets in order to escape intolerable conditions in homes plagued with alcoholism, violence, and sexual abuse. The usual profile was of a child having a sexual experience forced upon her, by a trusted family friend or member, before the age of twelve. Additionally the girl would be tainted with guilt, one of the weapons of these abusers, by being made to feel she had somehow enticed the act. Finally finding the strength, at around fifteen, she fled to the streets and began the life of prostitution.

The myth began to disintegrate under the assault of reason, as cases

were investigated and explained. The handy label had to be abandoned
and the truth—that middle-class families, not black pimps, were the demons—had to be faced.

The same mythology surrounds missing children. Hucksters are busily marketing the notion that children are being kidnapped all over the
place, for ghastly purposes. Milk cartons and frequent mailings keep the
industry alive. The myth purveyors are driven by the complex sets of
motives that compel the zealous or the greedy or the ambitious to seek a
vehicle for their appetites.

Not one child was stolen, by a stranger, in my nine years as Minneapolis's chief of police. Plenty of kids were taken by natural parents, as
they made the progeny the weapons of their warfare with former lovers
and divorced spouses.

Then came the gang myth.

Outsiders, from Gary and Chicago, were polluting Minnesota's
youth with notions of violence and quick bucks. The press picked up the
theme with relish. Events came to be described as "possibly gang-
related."

School officials, juvenile workers, and even cops were not able to
report the presence of organization, colors (gang jackets or symbols),
rumbles, hierarchy, drive-by shootings, any sign of them in the school, or
any proof of their existence in the familiar forms of Chicago and Los
Angeles street gangs. Perversely the definition changed, to include those
dealing in drugs. Since drug operations require organization and permanence, this approach seemed to suit the myth concocters nicely.

What was masked behind this myth, though, was a very real youth
problem which, if personalized, may have burdened society with the need
to act. This would have meant summer jobs, dropout programs, recrea-
tional centers, and other costly projects. Most preferred to embrace the
myth and indulge their prejudices. Hustlers screamed "gangs" in order to
get funding for their "youth programs." The chief was held out to be an
ostrich in refusing to see the problem.

And what city is free of the myth that "out-of-towners" are scurrying
to the municipality to soak up overgenerous welfare benefits? The problem no one wants to see is that of kids getting pregnant, dropping out of
school, hanging out, and drifting into lives of defeat, despair, and
criminality.

The public embraces these myths with fierce devotion. They are tangled with prejudices, fears, and the need to find demons to blame, lest we discover our own complicity in societal problems.

The Minnesota Connection myth was an invitation to go after "black pimps" without much concern for rights or legalisms. A stereotype had been created which could not be attacked without much risk. The gang myth was another invitation to roust black kids without examining the conditions of their lives. Poverty pimps, with elaborate programs that promised a lot and delivered not much more than money for them and jobs for their cronies, kept the gang rhetoric at strident levels. The public demands action and it is easy for the chief to demagogue the issue or get panicked into overreactions.

Crime Waves

There are crime waves and there are crime waves. Some are manufactured and some are real. Crimes are aberrational, unpredictable acts. They rarely follow a discernible pattern. The public will be spooked by crimes they can't figure out how to avoid. Should an event trigger a "there-but-for-the-grace-of-God" reaction, citizens will be frightened. Reactions can be unpredictable, too, and chiefs understand that panicked citizens mean trouble.

In a sense the chief must constantly take the community's pulse and calmly lead the way. One of the strategies the chief must consider is how much information to release to the public and when to reveal it. If there is a serial rapist or killer on the loose the chief has an obligation to alert the people so they may take some precautions. Withholding information can be justified only on the basis that a trap has been set or that the investigation will be impeded, in an articulable way, if the information is released. Too many cover-ups have made citizens rightly suspicious of the police. The way to regain the public's confidence is to adopt an open and accessible style.

The media can have a substantial effect on the public's perception of crime. A chief's view of the press, for example, goes directly to the heart of the question of the public's right to be informed. An open relationship with the press produces very different responses from one shadowed in suspicion and hostility. The fact that the media have to push so hard to get "the facts" illustrates the difficulty of securing relevant information even in a free society.

An informed, alert, interested public is not only in the best position to defend itself and its loved ones but can be the chief's most powerful ally in the many battles to be waged.

Weather and Pressures

In Frostbelt cities the police activity graph hits a hump in the warm weather months in the classical bell curve. The summers tend to be long and hot. Politicians, who get bombarded with demands for action, simply transmit the pressure to the police administration. Few have the vision or patience for complex approaches that might hold out the hope of long-term solutions. All of us want a cop to solve our problems, and we want that cop now.

The winters produce notable easing of this pressure and provide the opportunity for training, experiments, refittings, planning, and other preparatory or reflective activities. The chief executive must attend to the daily crises in the summer in a productive, calm fashion and must exploit the opportunities inherent in the less busy periods. If the opportunities for training are not seized, the boredom of inactivity will lead the cops to mischief. Thus training provides the double benefit of a better prepared force and one that is tempted into fewer dysfunctional acts. It is certainly possible that cities that have horrible winters, like Minneapolis, will someday be viewed as having been blessed by their cold climates.

While America's march seemed, for a long time, to be headed inexorably in the direction of the Sunbelt, it seems at least possible that the prospect of escalating, year-round urban violence may slow or reverse this trend. It may prove safer, in the future, to live in places where the cold keeps the streets clear for some months of the year. Since nothing much is being done about worsening conditions in the ghetto, it seems safe to assume that things will be growing worse. Given the benign climate's cooperation, it seems a lot likelier that riots will occur in the warmer cities that have the greatest number of underclass residents. "General Winter" is probably worth five hundred cops to a city like Minneapolis.

Police chiefs have responded to the challenge of deteriorating urban conditions by upgrading service or by taking an expansive view of their urban responsibilities. Nowhere is this more eloquently illustrated than in the development of community-oriented policing (COP), which is nothing more than the recognition that something must be done about conditions that threaten the community's sense of order and well-being, whether the conditions are police problems or not.

COP represents the response of police executives to building urban pressures to attack the problems evident on the street. There is a chasm between the public's expectations and the ability of the police to deliver the needed relief but, as the most visible and permanently present arm of government in the neighborhood, the police have felt the pressure and moved to respond. It will probably facilitate other efforts at securing citizens' participation in promoting their own safety, such as block clubs, neighborhood watches, and other programs pushed under the rubric of community crime-prevention efforts.

The chiefs have had to learn to make a virtue of necessity and this has often meant making unlikely alliances. One of the least likely involves the need to exploit the opportunities inherent in the actions of an activist press.

Investigative Reporting

If the press is a fearful monster then its investigative reporting is often seen as its most malevolent activity. A chief's attitude toward this genre will prove a useful litmus test of both his philosophy and his prospects for securing the support of the people. The people will not invest in public servants who respond paranoically to probings, and they have little trouble sensing the importance of an enterprising press in their lives.

The explosive growth of the news industry and the fierce competition it engendered have prompted the adoption of innovative and aggressive news-collection techniques. Reporters have become investigators and independently unearth wrongdoing. Their discoveries have been announced in the most sensational fashion, over blaring TV sets or in blazing head-lines. Government becomes a favorite target. Bureaucrats wince as the flaws in their agencies are paraded in public view. Damaging disclosures are seen as justification for the hostility felt toward the press. The memoirs of the great are dotted with thinly veiled traces of this fear of and contempt for the Fourth Estate, witness the attitudes of even our presidents to the probings of the press.

The trouble with such attitudes is that they get in the way of effective functioning. Taking things personally, being thin-skinned, giving in to the ego, and wallowing in self-pity ultimately lead to behavior that will cause the executive to lose the confidence of the people.

Ensuring a clean and effective organization requires the existence of investigative, verifying mechanisms that identify problems and offer the hope of applying solutions. Whether these mechanisms are internal or external relates more to vanity than to the substance of reform. It is surely better that the agency cleanse itself, but any cleansing is to be welcomed, by insiders as well as outsiders. This is a lesson rarely learned by public executives.

The media are the conduit for the public's information. One cannot believe in the importance of an informed electorate and resent the proddings of an aggressive press. The connection between the media's snoopings and the public's right to know was best expressed by Jefferson, who held that, if forced to choose between a government and no press and a press and no government, he'd opt for the latter. Such beliefs inspire the actions of our heroes. Police chiefs would be well advised to thoroughly examine their attitude toward the press and their commitment to serving the people. They are one and the same.

The press is, figuratively, in the chief's face and, if not seen as the conduit for informing the public, might easily be mistaken for the enemy. Behind the chiefs, in their own back yard, is another institution that also represents both challenges and opportunities.

Police Unions

A laborer is worthy of his or her hire. Workers have a right to unite and organize. Their representatives should work to preserve their welfare. Unions have secured dignity and essential protections for American workers. Police unions are among the fastest growing sectors of the labor movement.

The underclass may riot over a police incident. Gays may march and burn to express their anguish. The overclass may prod and press to get its silent way. The homeless may sprawl over downtowns, causing havoc. Any of the hundred other ugly possibilities may confront a chief, on any given day, but the thorniest, most complex, and demanding relations, on a daily basis, are with the press and the police union.

The first and most important decision that police chiefs make is whether they are going to serve the people or throw themselves into bed with the union. When the issues of summer or weekend work, one-person patrols, name tags, precinct consolidation, brutality, corruption, or any of the countless reforms needed are explored, it will quickly be perceived that the people's interests and the union's desires are usually in conflict.

The most unfortunate omen, on the appointment of a police chief, is that the police union praise him or, heaven forbid, endorse his appointment. As one issue after another arose in the three police agencies where I served as a high executive, I could not help but be struck by the consistency with which the unions' interests diverged from my concept of the people's good—and there was never anyone present to thump the table and demand that the public's interests be placed first.

The historical development of police unions involved their emergence from a fraternal status to dues-paying, thoroughly organized, professional associations able to hire the best talent. As a result of dues checkoffs (the automatic collection of union dues from members' paychecks), unions have developed the fiscal wherewithal to hire the best professional talents, finance political campaigns, lobby effectively, or pay for the many needs of an organization protecting the rights and privileges of its members.

As budget crunches took their toll, and the police came to be respectably paid (most citizens would wildly underestimate the salaries of the cops they see on the street, who are probably costing about $50,000 to $60,000 a year each, with all benefits included), the dilemma of what goals to seek was resolved by going after management rights, which the cities' labor negotiators, not having to live with the results, happily surrendered.

Today the first question any outsider newly appointed as chief asks is "What's in the contract?" Frequently there are, for example, such oddities as a promotion scheme that requires elevations even in an agency bloated with a supervisory ratio of over 40 percent. Thus the chief must promote employees even when no more supervisors are needed. At other times there are seniority clauses relating to assignments or shift selection, resulting, for example, in some departments—which have permanent tours—having three different segments: one, very junior, works midnight to 8 A.M.; the next, mostly midlevel, works 4 P.M. to midnight; and the old-timers work 8 A.M. to 4 P.M., ensuring the presence of the least experienced when the greatest knowledge is needed, on the late tour. There are strictures about assignments or transfers. There are limits on the chief's disciplinary and appointing authority. Other contracts restrict the number of work days (New Yorkers would be surprised to discover that their cops show up for work, on average, less than two hundred times a year) or freeze in place featherbedding practices such as all two-person patrols. The point is to limit the managerial authority of the chief and to allow the workers to assume much greater control over their work life.

In the 1960s unions added to their strength by entering the political arena, with checkoff funds, campaign workers, votes for the candidates, newsletters, and such. They rapidly developed formidable lobbying skills at city halls and state legislatures. The absence of anything resembling a national union is what mostly spared the U.S. Congress from having to confront a powerful national lobby in its corridors. Police unions in America are locals, even when the affiliation is with the Teamsters, who once made a strong attempt to organize the police but who were mostly beaten back, leaving isolated pockets of affiliation with the Teamsters.

As the power of the unions grew they began to participate in peripheral, but important, operations, such as the selection of civil service commissioners, arbitrators, mediators, and other outsiders who would be likely to play important roles in resolving key police issues. Since the unions also took part in the elective process police chiefs frequently found themselves outflanked, even in the mayor's office down the hall. Today police unions frequently carry a lot of weight in the decision about who gets appointed chief.

The central, and often overlooked, point was that the union is there to look after the interests of its members and not of the public.

The battle for control of the police agency, and for the imposition of the reforms needed to maximize its effectiveness, is increasingly fought between the chief and the union. The most powerful ally that the CEO can bring to this struggle is the people, for it is their interests that are at stake and their strength that is needed if there is to be any hope of success.

Chiefs who choose to fight will be blasted in the newsletter, see full page ads taken out against them, suffer through union votes of "no confidence," be exposed to the stinging rebukes of the union's many allies in the political arena and elsewhere, get mired in lawsuits, and generally have to learn to live with the permanent enmity of colleagues in the ranks. Every opportunity for public criticism will be seized. The mayor will be importuned to get rid of the chief. Indeed, there is something of a "union watch" on a new chief's hiring. The organized-labor network gets the poop on the nominees, plumps for those it likes best, and works against those whose reforms it fears most. It becomes a wearing struggle. The reward for the chief comes from the affection and support of the people and the joy of service.

Unions are necessary and useful institutions. The worker has a right to organize and fight for protections, benefits, economic gains, and counterlevers to management's power. We've seen the abuses that untrammeled power can work on defenseless workers.

Management has a role to play: to guide and direct the enterprise. The union's role is to protect the rights of the workers. In the police world much of the struggle has involved role confusion, in which the union has, inappropriately, tried to manage the operation. This is where the conflict centers. The chief is necessarily thrust into an adversarial role with the union. The chief's task is to keep the struggle on a healthy and relevant plane and to understand the worth of an essential institution: the union.

Other Players

These are only a very few of the groups and problems facing police chiefs every day, pressuring them to respond in ways that may either accommodate a special interest or offer a stopgap solution at the expense of the greater good. In addition there are the other segments of the criminal justice system, a variety of public groups and *ad hoc* bodies that unite for a special purpose and may reappear in other alliances. It is a constantly shifting tableau.

Most chiefs have not been prepared for such a complex assignment. It requires more wisdom than knowledge, more understanding than intelligence, and more torture than certainty. Education and experience are essential to success, but the trap lies in failing to discover that the qualities and preparations that got the chief the job may not be the qualities needed to succeed in the role. What police executive would believe that Ibsen, Shakespeare, Mozart, Wright, Goya, and Melville hold the key to success in public office? Yet they provide the insights and understanding that lend wisdom to one's inner view and grant the philosophical grasp to guide executives among the difficult public issues that dot their life. Dealing with myths, powerful groups, and mercurial constituencies requires a firm view of the objectives and of the means to achieve them.

Choosing the people as the prime base of support, from which will flow the strength to take on the many issues the chief will face, is a practical and workable strategy. It requires close adherence to the principles of openness, accountability, and sense of purpose described earlier. It is easy to forget this idea since the temptations are there, palpable and visible, while the interests of the people may come in more undefinable, unseen, unrepresented forms. The people's interests may take on a very amorphous aspect. Sacrificing the people's interests is very much like removing small amounts of water from a large lake. Each dipping produces an unnoticeable, virtually unmeasurable result, making rationalization easy.

The chief's day is dotted with crises, pressures, importunings, and problems. The only real guide is an internal compass, and true north must be the people's good.

CHAPTER 16

Reforms: Setting the Stage

The need for reform is usually announced in blaring headlines:

- "Ring of Cops Accused of Drug Thefts, Murder"
- "10% of the Force Reportedly Involved in Corruption"
- "Black Citizens Decry Latest Police Shooting: Accuse Department of Brutality"
- "Investigation Reveals Wide Involvement of Police with Drugs"
- "Management Analysis Calls for Sweeping Reforms in the P.D."
- "Citizen Wins Huge Suit Alleging Police Inaction"
- "Union Assails Chief's Attempts at Changes"
- "Widening Police Scandal Said to Involve Political Figures"
- "FBI Entering Investigation into Police Wrongdoing"

We've all seen them. Every city has had its share. Insiders decry conditions and call for reforms. The agenda is full and busy. Despite the obvious need for change there are many obstacles and many inducements for inaction. The path of reform involves activism, risks, and costs.

It was reported that New York's Mayor Robert F. Wagner, who held office for a decade during the 1950s and early 1960s, said, "My last prayer, before going to bed, is that I don't awaken to a police scandal."

The police, as wielders of great power and as the targets of the great temptations of brutality and corruption, are in almost constant need of reform. The central player in such an effort is the chief. Chiefs must develop the political and tactical skills that enable them to function in their own world of the police, within the larger criminal justice system, and, beyond that, within a society that encompasses many publics, including the press, politicians, unions, civil service and other official bodies, lobbies of all shapes and sizes, and expected or surprising friends and adversaries.

If one had to conjure up the image that best illustrates the CEO's role, it might be that the chief is a balloon in a room full of other balloons, labeled "Police Union" and "Civil Service" and "Mayor" and "Council" and "Judge," all chaotically rubbing against each other in no discernible pattern, with occasional and sudden explosions.

The Public Sector

Practically everyone who moves from the private to the public sector is struck by the complexity of public processes, the number of players and their variety, and the need for understanding the forces at work and their possible effect on the project at hand. Parvenus to politics—and every act of government, and of the chief, is a political act—almost invariably remark on the complexity of the world they've entered. This intricate environment may well, when combined with the importance of the questions faced by the government, explain, at least partly, the fascination of public life.

Undertaking anything as dramatic as reform—which usually involves not only harsh measures, but also a radical change—requires a keen understanding of the environment as well as a recognition of the important issues, lest credit and energy be dissipated on frivolous pursuits. There is a finite amount of political currency, in terms of public attention and support, to be spent, and too many executives have used up their capital on irrelevancies or sure losers.

The players in the criminal justice system are traditionally thought of as partners, whose cooperation is essential to any reform. But the truth is that they can frequently become the obstacles to change when they represent entrenched, powerful interests whose profit lies in maintaining the status quo.

Machiavelli remarked on how reform inspires the fury of the interest endangered, while those who will benefit see, at best, a misty possibility of gain and cannot be relied upon to take great risks on behalf of what they view as an amorphous prospect.

Subtlety is required. Mindless, slavish adherence to a strategy that once worked will, in altering circumstances, come a cropper. Flexibility is needed. No single approach will be best in all circumstances and, some-times, the best possible approach may be beyond the practitioner's ken, forcing a rollback to the next best tactic. There is little point in asking executives to accomplish what they are incapable for performing. One has to focus on the executive's talents and limitations and marry these to the most suitable approaches. The only requirement is that strategies and tactics, though they may shift, reflect a recognition of what is the right thing to do, and get pointed in that direction.

Reform tactics might include the direct approach or a frontal assault; a gradual, evolutionary process; the conciliatory method, or a search for consensus; even retreat, compromise, or whatever other strategy may seem appropriate to the circumstances.

An essential guide to the tricky process of reform is that, whatever strategy is adopted, it must conform to the rule of law very strictly. When the adopted path doesn't seem to be leading anywhere, the executive must have the breadth of view to acknowledge the error and to stop and change direction.

Steering the Agenda for Reform

All police organizations are both alike and different. They are alike in their sense of mission and their structure, problems, approaches, and daily workings. They are unique in the sense that the police organization is a product of its peculiar urban culture, political history, and experience. Cities are, after all, very much alike, yet markedly different, because of the chemical mix of their citizens and changing circumstances over the decades.

The problems requiring reform in each police agency may be very different. One department may have serious problems with the black, gay, or Hispanic communities, while another may be seriously involved with the criminal element or youth gangs. Whatever the specific nature of the wrongdoing it is inevitably going to come under the rubric of brutality or corruption most of the time.

Some police organizations get mired in corruption problems involv-ing alcohol control issues, which can take many shapes, such as afterhours clubs, notorious bars, selling to minors, or even bootlegging, a not-quite-forgotten art, with payoffs to the cops in order to keep operating. Others might drift into the demimonde of vice, where sex becomes the temptation that twists the law. Others stumble over gambling issues, and, lately, all have been sucked into the drug problem and the sick, profligate culture it has spawned. Corruption usually centers on sex, money, or power.

Where the cops meet the poor is where the rubber of oppression meets the road of brutality. This is most clearly illustrated by incidents between cops and blacks, for example, that sparked riots. These incidents, seemingly isolated, were usually routine encounters that escalated beyond control, nevertheless reflecting an underlying racism. The explosion dramatized a routine reality.

The same might be said for any encounter between the police and those they regard as "assholes." In recent years the growing population of the homeless and the pressure to control them have forced increasingly sophisticated and sensitive police agencies to undertake actions, like sweeps and roundups, that frequently inspire charges of repression or worse.

Brutality and corruption relate directly to the interaction between cops and their clientele. In these areas we see the external relations of the police world at work, but these are frequently driven by internal problems that, for lack of reform, have festered and grown, giving a kind of internal impetus to external abuses.

Internal Problems

Organizations are shaped by the incidents that have dotted their pasts, and by the players who have directed their fortunes. Because these incidents differ from place to place, each organization develops its own unique culture. The age-old question arises of whether individuals shape events or whether historical forces shape the outcomes. Chances are it's both.

In the 1950s and 1960s, New York City had a police department that practiced widespread brutality and corruption. The mayor's commendable fervor about awakening to a police scandal was anything but misplaced. Brutality encompassed abuse of blacks, under the guise of controlling a "dangerous element," as well as heavy-handed responses to not-very-disorderly demonstrations and a frequent resort to third-degree methods. Until *Mapp* v. *Ohio* in 1961, search warrants concerned only the scholars and the feds. The investigators, on minimal provocation, invaded the homes of suspects without fear and without concern for constitutional niceties, and they questioned their targets roughly, without having to worry about supervisory disapproval. Rights were routinely injured. Complaints availed nothing.

At the time, corruption centered on bars and gambling—pads and scores. Drugs were frowned upon as dirty. There was a definite value hierarchy in play. The rituals were well known: If you wanted to keep your hands clean, you eschewed assignments in plainclothes units enforcing what were called "public morals." This meant alcohol, gambling, and prostitution. It was remarkable how those who spearheaded the bloody reforms of the early 1970s, under the leadership of a commissioner who had shared their climb, had managed to avoid plainclothes assignments, while spending their careers in such clean places as the police academy, planning, or similarly ivory-towerish units. They emerged from these warrens free of the taints of brutality and corruption that stained so many of their colleagues and that were so graphically illustrated by the revelations of the Knapp Commission investigation. An important part of the selection process was a review of the past commands in which the executive had served. Knowing that it was nearly impossible to have served in plainclothes enforcement, for example, and stay clean, those with such entries in their dossiers immediately became suspect.

In Minneapolis, for example, the citizens, alarmed by municipal unrest in 1968, embraced the offered solution and elected the police union head to the mayoralty. Those who had helped him prospered. Those who had opposed him suffered the fate of the losers: demotions, transfers, or unattractive assignments. As the two-year mayoral cycle played out, an unfortunate tandem rhythm was set in motion, and in's alternated with out's in controlling the city. A decade of this reduced the police to a national laughingstock of political musical-chairs gamesmanship that made the agency little more than a political party (several parties) in uniform.

Every election in the 1970s brought about enormous shifts of personnel, reflecting the spoils of victory and the realities of political defeat. The faithful were enlisted in the lawn-sign pounding, leaflet distributing, calling, and other organizational chores necessary to ensure the triumph of one's champion. In such a world merit and performance did not count as much as whose side one was on when the mayoral ballots were counted.

Perhaps never in America's history had a police agency been as nakedly, or as thoroughly, politicized. The upper ranks of captains and inspectors numbered twenty-three stalwarts. By 1985 the number had been pared to twelve. Comfort, privilege, and a public-be-damned obsession with spoils had guided the agency for a decade.

These awful excesses ushered in a period of reform, just as abuses had forced New Yorkers to confront their brutality problem in 1966, in the form of a debate on a civilian review board. While attending to one problem New York postponed efforts to promote accountability. Six years later, under the impetus of the Knapp Commission's disclosures of corruption, they'd take on this problem, too. In Minneapolis, civic disgust led to the election of a reform mayor, in 1979, and the launching of a decade of change.

As mentioned earlier, in 1980, for example, Minneapolis had a sworn force that was swollen with over 40 percent supervisors, creating the absurd ratio of almost one boss for every worker. There were six precincts where four, at most, were needed. Cops patrolled in all two-person cars which, in times of scarce resources, constituted expensive featherbedding. Women and minorities had been excluded from the police force. The thumpers—those ham-handed dispensers of instant justice—could expect to be protected, and they were. Six permanent chiefs and two acting chiefs guided the agency over the 1970s.

In the 1980s, the tremendous struggle to get cops to wear name tags became a symbol of the issue of accountability, as the union fought furiously to resist the notion of identifying public servants by their surnames. Other battles took other forms in other places, but the struggles contained remarkably similar outlines.

New York, in contrast, cannot be said to have had its department tainted by partisan political struggles. These were mostly left to the union. The agency itself, however, was shot through with abuses that came from the combination of wielding great power and not being held accountable for its use. The literature is full of references to the problems faced, periodically, in other jurisdictions.

In Kansas City and St. Louis, the municipal controls are still wielded at the state house level, rather than by city hall, because of corruption problems everyone has long since forgotten. Chicago, Philadelphia, and Boston have seen their own share of municipal difficulties, occasioned by cupidity or cruelty. American cities have been hosts to locally unique and specific abuses of power that have ultimately required heavy reforms. The daily press alights on these, as bees on flowers, but moves on rapidly, causing the public's attention to shift elsewhere.

In the 1980s, Miami became a paradigm for just how bad a police agency could become. Its problems of murders, thefts, assaults, drug dealings, and other crimes by cops could arguably have been said to arise from the large numbers hired to cope with racism after the serious riots of 1980. Too many had been hired, too uncritically, in too short a time span. They were put on the street without proper screening, training, or preparation.

A review panel set up by the city of Miami to seek underlying causes of the civil disturbances on January 16 and 17, 1989, in which one person was killed, seven wounded and twenty-two stores burned, found that the police needed greater citizen oversight, that there was a commonly held perception that the cops were abusive, and that there was bias against blacks, even in an agency led by a black chief, whose predecessor had also been black.

In the late 1980s the police in the nation's capital were threatened with a federal takeover as a result of charges of mismanagement.

These are good examples of how poorly conceived reforms can produce future crises. The need for reform was visible, to insiders, everywhere, but the appetite was often lacking. Reform meant a kind of civic bloodletting, often of colleagues, that few chiefs had the stomach to undertake.

Identifying Targets for Reform

There are many ways of establishing what reforms are most needed. In New York, for example, the need for better relations between police and minorities, or between police and students or demonstrators, could not have been more obvious than in the 1960s. Similarly the scandals erupting over pads (monthly payoffs), shakedowns (individual extortions), flakings (framing a suspect with planted evidence), burglaries, and scores (single events where cops take money) finally created a demand for reform. In Minneapolis the imperative need was to take the police out of partisan politics. In that city, a mayor, disgusted and frustrated over his inability to eradicate the abuses, refused to seek reelection despite being a very young man.

Frequently there have been reports, studies, or commissions to point the way. The 1987 Philadelphia report served not only as a guide to the reforms begun in the mid-1980s but also as a rallying point around which a consensus and a scale of priorities might be built for police agencies everywhere.

Sometimes it makes good sense to create or invite an outside investigative body to analyze the agency's problems and recommend reforms. This approach carries the added weight of objectivity and eliminates complications of personal interest. In order for such efforts to succeed the investigative body must identify real and serious problems and must suggest workable and clearly written solutions that secure the public's support and are embraced by the administrators responsible for following the mandates. This is a delicate process since failure in any area will cause the entire effort to collapse. The bureaucratic shelves are full of studies that were, for one reason or another, never harkened to, if they were ever read at all. It is easy to imagine the distress and confusion caused in the mind of any politician or chief by the specter of a congressional committee's investigation of police brutality. The point, though, is that both reports and inquiries can, and should, serve as road maps to needed changes.

The chief police administrator, functioning in a complex world of fiercely competing interests, must be careful to choose targets carefully. Too many defeats will lead to an unhealthy public odor that will cause public support to go elsewhere. Trivial or superficial issues, not perceived as contributing to providing higher levels of safety, will be viewed by the public as mere exertions of will that do not rise much above ego satisfactions.

Chances are that no more than two or three major issues can be tackled in any given year. If one assumes a reasonable tenure of half a decade, it becomes clearer that the chief will have ten to fifteen windmills at which to tilt. It is important that the right ones be chosen, and that these include proactive attempts to investigate and control the agency, as well as reactions to the problems that have been reported.

Sources of information may be the public's calls, letters of complaint, press inquiries or exposés, or official reports of investigations. The chief sifts and evaluates, gradually developing a sense of where the real problems lie. It is important for the record that the reasons for pursuing or ignoring a complaint be articulated in writing.

A police chief must choose the targets for reform with great care. A misstep or wrong assumption will lead not only to a dissipation of energy but to a questioning of the need for reform at all. Setting the stage for the needed reforms is as important as the actual conduct of the process of attacking police wrongdoing.

CHAPTER 17

Reforms: Doing It

Reform is the improvement, amendment, or correction of that which is wrong, corrupt, or unsatisfactory. It involves striking at an existing condition, which implies that there are a number of participants and allies interested in the activity's continuing. If reform is undertaken in a vacuum, the forces affected will work and coalesce to defeat the effort. Strategy, tactics, and planning are paramount. Available opportunities must be seized, timing must be considered, and a climate that is receptive to reform created.

A severe budget crisis, for example, might well become the vehicle for effective prunings, rather than a mechanical separation of the youngest and most energetic. Coupling such a crisis to a call for such managerial reforms as firing the unfit or the criminals within the ranks will have an almost instant appeal to a public eager for better service, but reluctant to fund it. A lot of reform is undertaken under the formula of making a virtue of necessity.

An investigation, an arrest, or an incident can also become the impetus for reforms. Such events possess dramatic properties that automatically focus public attention. If displayed as symbols of widespread, underlying problems, they might easily be the rallying points for generating public support for sweeping reforms. Obviously the cases must be chosen with care. If they are not true paradigms then a dead end will be struck and the public's energy will deflate, with painful consequences for future efforts. Success builds on success and failure promotes more of the same.

The efforts of other outside agencies, such as grand juries, the FBI, prosecutors, special investigative bodies, or boards of inquiry should be warmly embraced. Too many investigations by special boards are resisted and resented. The public's interest lies in cleansing the agency, thereby freeing it to operate more efficiently.

Civilian Review

The issue of civilian review is nothing more than a battle between the controlled and the controllers.

Cops make many shorthand judgments, based on myths and realities. They stereotype because it speeds up their processes. They react on the basis of their expectations and, although no one is going to say this publicly, their expectations are that blacks are more likely to be "wrong" than whites. This accounts for why so many blacks get pulled over. The odds are better for "getting" someone who has an outstanding warrant or obtaining evidence of a crime.

This doesn't get talked about because no one wants to be labeled a racist.

The overwhelming majority of blacks are solid, honest citizens who believe in law and order, but not as a code phrase for repression. Their victimization rates illustrate the reasons for their deep concerns about safety.

Blacks are disproportionately represented in the underclass and their situation gets worse daily. They represent almost half the U.S. prison population and occupy university seats at a fraction of the ratio of their presence in the general population. Every meaningful statistical measure records this decline, whether it's income, education, welfare, teenage pregnancy, cause of death, age expectancy, literacy, or birthweight. Blacks continue to be victims of racism, and the police, who are a key part of the institutional control mechanisms, tend to mirror the feelings of society. When the logic of the crime stats is factored into the equation, racist myths are reinforced. Blacks are more likely to be engaged in street crime or drugs than whites. The cops see the results, and deal with the symptoms of a deep social malaise.

Whites, of course, are more likely to be engaged in white-collar crime, and the differentials evident in the treatment the defendents receive fuels the resentment of blacks.

Cops have the tough assignment of controlling the underclass in the street. These are the homeless, the alcoholics, the addicted, the poor, and the mentally disturbed. They are frequently black. The cops make quick judgments and act on them. If they size a person up as a loudmouth they will be more likely to work off their exasperations, somehow. This might involve obscene language, brutal actions, or creative uses of the disorderly conduct statutes or traffic regulations.

Police chiefs know this and are torn between supporting colleagues, with whom they've invariably grown up in the agency, and dispensing justice. They are also caught in the dilemma that control of the agency comes through the power to hire and fire, promote and demote, assign and transfer, and discipline and reward. Each of these is central to a chief's ability to run the department. We can all understand the difficulty of having been given a tough assignment without the tools to carry it out.

Police chiefs know they will be held accountable by the mayor, who will be held to account by the people.

The civilian review controversy has nothing to do with review and everything to do with who controls the disciplinary process.

The argument is made that the police shouldn't investigate themselves, but this proves a hideous simplification when the grand juries, prosecutors, judges, the FBI, legislative bodies, investigative organizations, the press, and civil litigation become the vehicles for holding the police accountable for their actions, in addition to the internal inquiries undertaken by police agencies.

Some reviewing agencies are, of course, more active and effective than others. Local courts, for example, failed miserably to curb police abuses relating to arrests, searches, testimony, and so on, but the Supreme Court, in a series of dramatic decisions in the 1960s and 1970s, revolutionized and professionalized the police.

That the mechanisms of oversight perform unevenly and imperfectly is a simple fact of life. Cooptation has been refined to an art, and even civilian review boards are not immune to its charms.

Openness and review are the lifeblood of the democratic process, but the meaning of review has been transformed into control—a very different thing. Every police agency ought to welcome audits, examinations, and reviews.

No police executives can afford to surrender any of the key tools that enable them to govern their agency. The power to investigate and discipline is fundamental to effectiveness. Police chiefs are also probably the best qualified to judge the appropriateness of police actions and to distinguish, for example, between necessary force and brutality.

Can the police investigate themselves? Do they?

A close examination will probably result in the same answer to both questions: yes and no.

Yes, they can, and do, investigate themselves, but no, they do not have the exclusive power to do so. The death of two innocent seniors in a recent drug raid, for example, was investigated not only by the Minneapolis police, but also by the medical examiner, the grand jury, the FBI, the county attorney, and probably others. Civil and human rights agencies frequently get involved in such cases, too, as well as nonprofit groups such as the American Civil Liberties Union. And there are frequently civil suits, to boot, which promote a painful accountability of their own.

Police actions are subjected to a good deal of outside scrutiny, of mixed effectiveness, and having more outside scrutiny would probably be a very good thing.

The debate over civilian review really centers on whether the cops should be investigated and disciplined by the chief or by a board, appointed for that purpose, that functions independently of the chief. It is not an accident that, in the recent brouhaha in Minneapolis, one of the demands was that an independent board be appointed, and that at least four of the five members be chosen from the minority population. The proposal that gained the widest currency was to restore to the city's civil rights commission the power to investigate and adjudicate once held by that agency. It had been removed during the halcyon days of police primacy in city hall.

The city council later adopted a measure calling for a detailed, longer-term study of the problem and its possibilities. This is a lot more sensible than plunging into precipitous action in the fever of the moment.

There is nothing wrong with review. There is a lot wrong with divesting any executive of the power needed to function. There is a strong temptation to express our exasperation with fecklessness by paralyzing the government.

An outside agency would require a substantial staff. It would not be under the pressures to perform that now impinge on internal affairs units. The chief would be reduced to a cipher in the process.

The cops know that, in dealing with street people, they must sometimes use force. They possess a legal monopoly on violence, and even the best-intentioned cops are forced to use violence sometimes. They do not trust outsiders, even decent ones, to make judgments about their actions, although I've always believed that outsiders would be easier to fool, or coopt, than the chief.

Cops fear the decisions of cop-hating militants who might be drawn to seek posts on a review board. The militants see the cops as an army of occupation in the ghetto, whose feet must be removed from the necks of the oppressed. The chief knows that discipline is a key element of control over the agency. Striking the proper balance between an aggressive force and discipline in the ranks is a delicate, difficult business.

The disaffection of the underclass leads to riots, which are frequently sparked by a police incident, and the cops have to put them down. This draws very clear battle lines, figuratively and literally. The review board issue becomes an important symbolic battleground, with the overclass watching warily, but from a distance.

Civilian review boards can be vehicles for reform to the degree that they can provide a public window into the internal workings of a police agency and report to the people on their observations. They are also in a position to call for official investigations, such as by the FBI or the local prosecutor or a special state investigative body or even a grand jury. Review boards should not have the power to adjudicate disciplinary cases. This takes them out of the scope of review and plunges them into running the agency for the chief.

Court Decisions

Court decisions since *Mapp* v. *Ohio* in 1961, and moving forward with *Escobedo* v. *Illinois, Miranda* v. *Arizona,* and *Gardner* v. *Tennessee,* to name a few, have inspired the most vituperative reactions from police executives, when they should have been hailed as the inspirers of desperately needed, long-overdue reforms. It would be difficult to think of influencers of comparable worth in eliminating such police abuses as baseless searches and seizures, third-degree methods, and even the employment of unjustified deadly force. In this century, Supreme Court decisions have probably moved the police more rapidly along the road toward the Holy Grail of professionalization than any other single factor. This fact probably accounts for the hostility they have uniformly provoked among practitioners.

It seems clear that one of the great police reforms of this century, *Gardner* v. *Tennessee,* where the Supreme Court held that it is unconstitutional to use deadly force on an unarmed, nondangerous, nonviolent felon, was made possible by the intervention of police executives who joined in an *amicus curiae* brief that was certain to have had a powerful impact on the Supreme Court Justices.

This surprising development illustrates quite clearly the many divergent paths possible for the generation of police reforms, as well as the many different roles an activist chief can play.

Police chiefs have both the duty and the responsibility to move the police toward cleaner, more legal, and more effective levels of performance. By doing this, they can secure the public support so essential to effective functioning.

Techniques

Once the problems have been identified, sorted out, and prioritized, and a corrective strategy has been adopted, it is important that the public's support be enlisted. Citizen involvement, such as calls to radio shows, letters to the editor, and calls to political leaders, is central to the reform process. Without the public's participation, the reformer can be easily isolated and defeated by the array of forces inevitably stirred to opposition.

The press, as the conduit of the public's right to know, become the most important tool in any strategy of reform. They are not the only ones, however. Public bodies, such as citizens' leagues or the League of Women Voters, are natural allies in a struggle for reform. It is important for the police to enlist such partners. Their constituencies are frequently influential, intelligent, and interested.

Executives abhor intrusions yet it may be the soundest practice to invite an inquiry, examination, or audit. The first message such an invitation conveys is a lack of fear that one will be embarrassed or compromised. The second is that one has a genuine interest in reform and is willing to risk outsiders' examination to bring it about. The third is the implication of a commitment to carry out the needed reforms. All are useful messages.

Reforms consist of both form and substance, and they must be pursued in tandem. Symbols do matter. In an age of image bombardment, it is important to get through to the public and convey the message of the need for reform and to attack the problem. The chief must be able to distinguish between the issues that impact on police performance—hence, the public's welfare and safety—and those that constitute the mere trappings of office. Too many administrators have spent too much energy securing compliance with orders for the sake of ego satisfaction rather than worrying about how any given breach may affect the public interest. Command is not an ego trip. It is not an assertion of will to "show them who the boss is." Command is granted to facilitate the high tasks of public service. Martinets impose their will, inflate their personas, and feed their egos. The public servant focuses on the people's needs.

Reform is not just a program of action but a plan that must be preceded, and accompanied by, education. The public must understand the need for reform and clearly see how it ties in with improved service and protection.

The techniques employed must relate to the problems discovered. The public must recognize how its interests are bound up in the reform. The process must be invested with fairness. Reform-minded chiefs would be wise to start a sort of "day one" operation, where they announce that they will look back only to the degree to which they are forced, and that to the degree possible, the department will start afresh from that day forward. Even the "meat eaters" have to be given a chance to join the program.

The chief's character is critical to the reform effort. Chiefs' messages and actions should be consistent and reflect the value system they're trying to impose. Reform demands tough actions and chiefs have to be ready to live with the enmity these actions inspire. The selection of the chief, by the mayor, is critical to the fate of any reform efforts because such exertions require extraordinary determination, vision, and courage.

Administrative Reforms

Relying on outsiders, as many timid chiefs do, to wield the ax of reform blinds many agencies to the value of internal administrative approaches that would prove far more effective than the law or a court's ruling. The objective of reform is usually to narrow and define an officer's discretion and to channel the officer's acts toward organizational objectives.

Cops have been rather indiscriminate shooters for most of their existence. The "Dirty Harrys" adopted the Wyatt Earp model and used their guns without inhibition. As they shot young blacks or Hispanics, disorders or riots frequently followed. These events earned the attention of mayors and chiefs.

Through the simple expedient of an order by the NYPD's police commissioner, in 1972, the police were transformed into restrained, responsible shooters. Thereafter every shooting would be investigated by a supervisor. Every bullet would be accounted for. There would be no warning shots or shooting at moving vehicles. The agency's regulations would be more restrictive than the operative law.

Firearms-discharge review boards were established to decide the legitimacy of a cop's use of a gun. Overnight, police shootings declined dramatically. Curiously, since its nationwide adoption—the reform was widely embraced by the nation's chiefs—shootings and killings of cops have been declining sharply. As the police became less violent, the violence against them greatly subsided.

Orders covering such radical changes must be given in writing and must be written in clear and explicit language. Effective arguments could be made that such reforms, from within, permit the police to keep functioning effectively. Court-imposed or legislative reforms (such as court decisions or corrective laws) tend to be more restrictive because of an uninformed meat-ax approach, which is frequently inspired by an awful case to begin with.

Requiring cops to document every use of force, and to face discipline for failure to do so even where force was plainly legitimately employed, will force the cops to think twice before thumping the "dirtbag" before them.

Chases require direction and structure. Those pursuits, for example, that result in publicized tragedies will almost certainly inspire a legislator to introduce a bill to ban the practice or to place some hobbling restriction on the operation. The result can be disastrous. Chases are a vital element of police operations. Again, the adoption of a reform from within may well preclude its imposition from outside.

The use of written guidelines that call for radio dispatcher coordination of all chases, the involvement of supervisors, prohibitions on cowboying or caravanning, strict instructions about interceptions and roadblocks, and policies governing when to break off a chase (e.g., when the risks to the public are too great, when the offense is trivial, or where there is a good chance of a later apprehension) will not only forestall imposed restrictions but aid mightily in battling any lawsuit arising out of such incidents.

An expansive view of the administrative power to issue orders on controversial topics turns the police chief into a sort of legislator. Such remedies as the described restrictions on shootings and chases must be employed, with a proper regard for the risks. These administrative fiats ought to be saved for the hot, big issues, lest their effect be weakened by overuse. They will, in any case, engender opposition. Breaches of the policies must be dealt with swiftly and harshly. Since the orders are usually more restrictive than existing law, the chief executive must tread carefully.

The socialization of police recruits in a code of silence starts early and proceeds mercilessly. No cop can escape it. The search for psychological screens that will weed out the brutes will founder on the shoals of the realization that these wrongdoers were shaped by agency forces, not recruited. These factors are challenges to administrators who believe their agencies must engage in a true partnership with the communities they serve.

Training must be extensive, relevant, and continuous. Officers must be sensitized to the issues they will confront. As mentioned earlier the complexity of contemporary American society requires a sophistication hitherto undreamed of. This will require the attraction of suitably educated recruits, drawn into the profession purposefully and early. The Peace Officer Standards and Training process used in Minnesota requires two years of specialized college education, followed by a basic-training curriculum and a licensing test. It holds the promise of providing prepared and motivated recruits. When this process is followed by a rigorous background investigation and thorough training in formal classrooms and by field-training officers during a year's probation, the hope of producing a competent professional police officer is greatly enhanced.

The message must be simple and constant. Serve the people. Perform your job and you'll be supported. Make a good-faith mistake and the organization will try to help. Break the law or make a bad-faith act and we'll go for your throat.

Such values hold the promise of shifting behavior into the desired form. Changing attitudes is a much more difficult process, involving a lot of training and organizational reinforcement.

Reform must start with the entering recruit. The higher the standards, the greater the hope of maintaining integrity and a sense of service. The unprepared, ignorant, or uneducated will be far likelier to succumb to the temptations awaiting them. Even the size of the entering class is important. Cops need to be hired in trainable numbers. Large hirings in haste are repented at leisure. The size of the class must fit comfortably within the agency's training capacity.

Doing It Yourself

The most important element in any reform of a police agency is public awareness and support. The most important tool is the press. The two are closely connected. If the people do not agree that a reform is needed they will withhold their support. That will usually tilt the battle in favor of the entrenched interests anxious to preserve their status.

Educating the public to the urgent need of change is one of the key responsibilities of police chiefs. Their role as educators is a real one. Their tools are the forums available for their use: the press, public meetings, and, not unimportantly but frequently overlooked, the chiefs' own ability to weigh in with an editorial or op-ed piece.

The chief, in order to be effective, must be a skilled communicator, both within and outside the agency. This means not only speaking clearly and effectively, but listening, reading, and writing as well. These are probably the most important skills a police CEO, or any chief executive, can develop.

Issues are best and most clearly illustrated through real cases that embody major questions. It is important that an in-house capability be developed to research, analyze, and develop solutions for the problems that arise. This approach speaks more to a Socratic capability than it does to the routine capability of the research-and-planning unit that so many agencies adopt, but that are frequently unworthy of the name.

Critical events can be turned into opportunities. Crises might be provoked in order to allow the public to understand the issues, such as the decision to switch to one-person patrols or to assign the chief's appointees as precinct commanders. In these cases the debate is triggered by a chief's decision.

If the chief routinely accepts every invitation to speak, to any group, constituencies for reforms will be identified and enlisted. This sort of high-profile effort may make politicians restive, but an anonymous chief whose policies are not widely known will not be able to wield the power necessary to undertake serious reforms; for it is the people's strength, not the chief's, that must be brought to bear on the issues if the reforms are to be achieved.

Police agencies frequently work themselves into such corrupt states as to spark a general and deep demand for reform. The mayor or council may well become the initiators of the needed changes, but even when this is the case the instrument must be the chief, for the chief is the only person with the experience, expertness, ability, and position to follow through with the needed changes.

Everything has its season. While Everett could speak for hours before Lincoln's talk at Gettysburg, today's reality is that each of us, in public life, is afforded seconds to communicate our views. The goal must be the distillation of complex issues and programs into a few sound-bytes that, at once, both convey the message with utter clarity and are gripping enough to be remembered above the din. This goal implies the development of new skills. It requires a lot of thought to first decide the issue, settle on an answer, and then edit and condense the reply into some catchy, sexy image.

Madison Avenue and public relations specialists have taught us the importance of quick, punchy, effective communication. In eradicating a particularly egregious abuse, the most powerful educational weapon to arouse the citizenry to action might well be a slogan. Ideally this should capture the essence of the problem and emblazon the issue indelibly in the public consciousness.

Within the organization, safety values have to be created to allow workers to seek the alternatives of treatment as they accept the realities, or inevitability, of reform. Stress and wellness programs must be provided that encompass a panoply of approaches, from counseling to therapy to Alcoholics or Gamblers Anonymous to physical fitness. Since cops normally confide only in other cops, these programs will probably have to be staffed by cops. Stress and wellness programs constitute a message from the organization: Get help. The other side of the message is that if you're found out, it's too late to claim you were ill and needed assistance. Reforms have to include opportunities for employees to rescue themselves.

Random testing for drugs and alertness to the abuse of alcohol will inhibit the spread of difficulties that sometimes overcome police agencies. The search for abusers transmits a crystal-clear organizational message about tolerated and not tolerated behavior. Holding supervisors accountable for discovering such problems is central to any hope of reform. This is what stewardship is all about.

Again the stick must be employed with the carrot. An open-door policy and total accessibility offer the prospect of contact with decision makers who can offer guidance and deprive those who are engaged in coverups of any excuse that they lacked access or opportunity to complain or report some wrongdoing.

The Mechanics of Reform

There is never a propitious or appropriate time to undertake radical change for the better. The cautious will always raise frightening objections: It is summer, or an election is in the offing, or a contract is being negotiated, or a court decision is awaited—any of a hundred excuses for postponement will be raised. Obviously there can be legitimate impediments to action, but the chief must be alert to the prospects and weigh the circumstances carefully. Real obstacles ought to be clear enough and, even then, determination can be displayed through preparation and the fixing of a timetable for the adoption of reforms. Momentum, expectation, and timing are important elements in the process. Once it is perceived that the glow of action might be dimmed by cautious counsel, the pendulum begins to swing toward those who fight the corrections.

Reform is nothing more than the purging of the police body. It is a way of ensuring that cops will become the servants of the law, not its masters. Reforms may be undertaken with lightning swiftness when circumstances serendipitously deliver a target of opportunity, or they may be tortuous organizational shifts involving months of planning and preparation. It is best to have a rough agenda, which allows shifts in tactics, but which is consistent as to the direction and approximate speed of the changes to be wrought.

Institutionalizing reforms involves weaving organizational change into the body of the agency. As mentioned earlier, this might be done through the creation of inspection or auditing units, the development of a strong internal-affairs unit, the employment of internal spies, or the adoption of aggressive legal techniques. Selection and appointment of key personnel will also be important factors in shaping the future.

The police have much to learn from the strategies of the corporate world, such as polling, independent audits, surprise inspections, and other techniques for verifying what is actually taking place. The police world relies too heavily on self-reporting, its own predictable routine, and up-the-chain-of-command processes. The chief has to develop tools that provide outside verification. Soliciting letters directly to the chief, through, for example, a post office box or calls to a hotline will speed the flow of information. Some will be from cranks or kooks but many will be legitimate and convey a real sense of the true problems. The complaints must not only be acted on, but must be perceived as being followed up as well.

The use of police spies—a terrifically unpopular practice within the ranks—reached an apex following the disclosures of widespread corruption in the New York Police Department by the Knapp Commission in 1972. Public outrage and demand for reform overcame the internal organizational resistance (focused, organized, and led by the union, the Patrolman's Benevolent Association) and strengthened the hand of the determined police chief. In time hundreds of cops were secretly reporting acts of serious wrongdoing to their headquarters controls. They were called, innocently, *police officer associates.* Unremitting resistance and hostility gradually wore down the enthusiasm of subsequent administrators for this unpopular practice. The tipoff would have come when revelations of police crimes stopped appearing in the press. We have not yet developed our analytical skills to the point where we can recognize that the news is the lack of reports, rather than the items making an appearance in our papers or on our screens.

The use of self-initiated integrity tests by the internal affairs unit, where, for example, a "found wallet" containing cash would be turned over to a cop, to see if he or she would turn it in, created a great furor. The sending of hippie-looking people into precincts to inquire how a complaint of police brutality might be lodged against an officer revealed that compliance with regulations was anything but uniform. Commanders lost their posts when the testers were unceremoniously thrown out of the station house. The rest got the message. All of these tactics, and others, were made possible by a climate for reform created by the Knapp Commission and the resultant public demand for action. The strategies are limited only by the confines of the human imagination and the requirements of law.

The problems identified have to be replicated. This may involve "salting" a DOA with jewelry or cash, in order to see if the complained-of thefts really are taking place. A fake drug or gambling operation might be set up to see if the cops pocket the cash they invariably encounter. Traffic laws might be violated, in controlled conditions, to check on how honestly cops enforce them. It is important that the tests pursued match the sort of complaints being received, in order to prevent unfairness or the appearance of a witch hunt.

An ironic twist to the replication theory occurred when a black police sergeant decided to prove racism existed in the country's police departments and invited a camera crew of reporters to accompany him and secretly film his travels.

The nation was horrified at a sequence in which he was stopped by a Long Beach, California, cop, was rousted, searched, and, for no reason other than that he was questioning the officer, had his head thrust through a store's plate-glass window. The sight and sound of the smashing, flying glass, following the whack of his head striking it, proved more eloquent than a hundred protests or a thousand marches. Of course, it was not hard to imagine apologists saying he'd "gotten his" not because he was black, but because he was an "asshole."

Why hadn't the chief in Long Beach tested the waters of racism or brutality in his department?

Any police executive should have been shamed into resigning for having created or tolerated a climate where such behavior was thinkable. Without deep probes, replications, and aggressive investigations the chief will not penetrate the agency's dark, on-the-street doings nor be in any position to control police behavior at 3 A.M.

The objective is to test and verify the true organizational responses through inside and outside probes. The creation of a strong internal-affairs unit and other auditing and investigative units is essential to the development of an effective program of reform. Assignment to the unit should be seen as one of the essentials of progressing in the organization.

Reform is a result, an objective. Many roads can lead to this end. The executive must be aware of the myriad of possible strategies. Some can be wrought through simple administrative fiat—the issuance of an order; others through court orders or litigation. Some require attacking language in the police union's contract. Others necessitate deep and complicated criminal investigations. Flexibility and daring are essential to the process. Determined follow-through, in terms of arrests, discipline, and so on, becomes a more persuasive testimonial of the administration's determination than the most elaborate exhortation.

Reform is a broad term. It connotes correcting flaws. It can range from attacking serious and widespread acts of police brutality or corruption to issues relating to waste, mismanagement, or administrative abuses.

The organizational message must be clear and consistent. The agency is guided by clearly defined legal and moral principles.

In conducting aggressive investigations of wrongdoing, the surest guide is the law. Securing court orders for wiretaps, buggings, or searches invests the process with the protective cloak of the law. Internal processes, however, do not lend themselves that easily to legal directions. In assignments, transfers, promotions, demotions, or other personnel or organizational decisions, the law becomes irrelevant. Here ethics come more clearly into play. Nowhere is the organizational message more clearly transmitted than in these actions.

If such decisions are taken with a decent and obvious regard for honest judgments, then the internal message connects harmoniously with the agency's internal actions. If the administration is seen to accommodate its comfort, whim, or convenience, or if perquisites and privileges are seen to attach to high office, then those on the lower rungs will adapt their behavior accordingly. A shirking of principles at the top will be all the justification the troops will need to do their own thing at the bottom.

Internal Concerns

Chiefs cannot do it all by themselves. Whether one likes it or not, organizations are run by many people, arranged in a pyramidal structure. Thus chiefs must select the best and the brightest as their associates. Why bother enunciating such an obvious bromide? Because too many top executives are insecure and threatened by talented subordinates and, giving in to these feelings, surround themselves with compliant toadies instead.

The importance of bringing the ablest forward cannot be overstressed. Besides communicating the soundest message, it enables the creation of the strongest team, while ensuring the agency's future. Many may well go on to be chiefs in other agencies and this should be seen as a test of whether the quality people are really being chosen. The methods employed in selecting or assigning personnel ought to be objective, relevant, and clear to all. Having them in writing enables everyone to know, and evaluate, the standards employed.

The pressure to perform, so frequently absent in governmental operations, must be there. Obviously mistakes will occur but there must be accountability. It is not enough to say that the purposes of government are high-minded and beyond measuring. Commanders must be held responsible for the state of their commands. Theirs is not an insurer's responsibility, but a steward's. They have to be held accountable for the conditions in their commands that they should or could have known about—and corrected. The commanders set the tone and establish the climate. The distinction between command failures and the occasional and unavoidable mistake is critical if the chief is to avoid the panicky overreactions of the martinet.

General standards can also be elevated through such tactics as the pursuit of accreditation, where an outside agency describes the minimal goals and verifies that they have been adopted. Accreditation policies and goals represent the distilled wisdom and experience of many police agencies. They serve as useful vehicles for the general raising of standards to acceptable minimums, but they should not serve as the one and only path to salvation.

The Union as an Obstacle to Reform

Dealing with powerful, determined, fast-growing police unions has become one of the very complex challenges to contemporary chiefs. Here, as with the press, the chief's attitude must be examined since it will ultimately, although not always in direct or obvious ways, guide actions.

The worker has a right to join others for self-protection against management's power and possible abuse. The two most important factors in the elevation of the American worker in this century have been education and trade unionism. The police executive must see the union as essential to the worker's well-being and must work with it, in a constructive, adversarial relationship that clearly calls for understanding each other's role.

The union is there to secure protections, salaries, and benefits for the worker. The chief is there to manage the enterprise. The accretion of power, such as police unions have experienced in developing the financial and political resources to influence elections and appointments, will lead inevitably to a temptation to use it. Unions have developed powerful allies in all political councils. They frequently control civil service commissions. They take a deep interest in the careers of arbitrators, judges, and referees. They have frozen requirements that impede effective management of the agency by insisting on their inclusion in the labor contract. Many managerial prerogatives have been traded away by city negotiators eager to save dollars. As a result seniority often appears as the arbiter of assignment decisions. Promotions and transfers have also been written into contract language. Unions have become very adept at solidifying power in various repositories, including getting favorable laws passed. They have become increasingly comfortable in the corridors of power.

It cannot be said that unions, anywhere, promote brutality, corruption, or any other act of police wrongdoing. Yet, because of their legal responsibility to represent the accused worker, their identification with the worker, and the need to maximize the worker's protection, unions frequently become the greatest obstacles to reform and battle the disciplinary process even when it is aimed at obvious miscreants in uniform.

In taking on such a powerful body in a battle to control the agency, the strongest ally for the chief, or for the mayor who wants to appoint a reform chief, becomes the public. Securing their support requires that they be informed through the press, public speeches, and so on, and that they see their interests tied, clearly, to the proposed reform.

Thus, in taking on the unions, chiefs must make their support for the institution clear, as they identify the areas of contention and illustrate not only how the abuses harm the people but also how reform will help lead to solutions.

The rhythm and flow of organizational life function on momentum. Stagnation, labor unrest, poor performance, inadequate leadership, and the toleration of wrongs will drag morale to the depths. Reforms, conversely, create an opposite momentum. Their motion generates activism and enlists into battle some who, in other circumstances, might have been content to remain onlookers. These converts will also bring their own agendas, ideas, and targets, thereby spreading the radical effects of reform and greatly increasing the number of problems that can be attacked. A reform mode thus becomes established. It will force interaction with other improvements, thereby providing further momentum. A kind of reform synergy can result.

The morale of an agency is really its spirit, and it is to be judged not by what is said about it but through the surer evidence of actions. An agency in reform, with purposeful, proved workers, will evidence its morale in the élan with which it tackles its challenges. Contradictory organizational messages from above short-circuit the process and sow confusion in the ranks.

Reforms cannot be undertaken with precisely equal zeal. Some wrongs are more serious than others. There has to be a sense of proportion and a clear set of priorities. Each reform will engender resistance. Change threatens the status quo and all who profit from it. Those to be benefited will not risk much for speculative gains. There is a limit to the number of opponents one can take on at one time.

Reform must be like correcting one's children; that is, it must be undertaken with determination and energy and undergirded by love. It must be clearly enunciated that the motivation is to strengthen the organization so that it will serve the people better.

The people are bombarded, daily, with hundreds of messages. Their interests must be made clear to them if the chief's message is to be heard above the clatter. It is not public apathy that stalls reforms but lack of public awareness. The chief's task is to circumvent the overload and get the message in.

The effort must be attended by reasonableness, proportion, objectivity, and integrity.

Alcohol abuse is different from marijuana use, which, in itself, is different from cocaine sniffing. Taking a free cup of coffee is wrong, yet not as wrong as stealing or drug use or dealing. There are gradations of wrong. A sense of proportion is critical. All wrongs are not equal, even if they are all wrongs.

Changing the behavior of tough cops will not occur through exhortations, speeches, or eloquent, threatening orders. Cops respond to actions. They live in a world where the focus is on what one does. The threat of discipline will not faze them. The sequence must include a clear, consistent message—conveyed in every conceivable way, not just in words or memos—followed by swift, decisive actions.

Reforms are necessary because of the great power of the police and the irresistible temptation to abuse it. Brutality and corruption are the great major dangers. The national landscape has been, and continues to be, dotted with examples of the severity of the problem. Reforms are painful, but necessary.

A police agency exists to serve the people. After their appointment, the first and most crucial decision chiefs can make is whether to promote the comfort and convenience of their colleagues, with whom they identify and with whom they grew up in the agency, or serve the interests of the people. While the ideas are, in practice, virtually irreconcilable, choosing the second course will produce a vigorous, healthy, effective police department.

CHAPTER 18

The Future

"In no other branch of government have such remarkable changes been made as those made in the field of police organization and administration during the last quarter of a century." One may well imagine those words in a contemporary text but they appeared in August Vollmer's article in the May–June 1933 issue of the *Journal of Criminal Law and Criminology*.

Vollmer, a practitioner-scholar of great stature in the police profession, went on to extoll the value of a high school diploma requirement, the virtues of civil service, the progress being made in training and education, the use of scientific methods both in investigations and in the administration of the police force, and the growing importance of the radio.

His dewy-eyed excitement about the future was typical of a strangely confident age that produced supermodern architecture and designs, as well as Buck Rogers and Flash Gordon. Somehow the thrill of the future filled his day with an optimism and expectation we'd consider quaint today.

Vollmer remarked that police executives had found "that foot patrol in residential areas is a useless expenditure of the taxpayer's money"; he spoke presciently of crime prevention, sensing the need to get the public involved; he threw in a plug for traffic enforcement; and he predicted a rosy future for the police profession.

Fifty-three years later FBI agent William Tafoya, in *A Delphic Forecast of the Future of Law Enforcement,* foresaw rising computer crime; an increase in terrorism; greater use of technology by criminals; massive urban unrest and civil disorder; greater sophistication in crime, leading to an overwhelming of limited local agencies; growth in the private security sector; greater citizen involvement; movement toward professionalization of the police; more research on crime and criminals; and a closer connection between street crime and economic conditions.

Agent Tafoya's forecasts were based on the assumption that present policies of neglect of the underclass will continue into the future. Radical changes in approach would, of course, alter the outcomes.

In between these studies, in 1985, came one called "The Future of Policing." It found that increasing public fear of violence along with the social and economic forces fueling street crime will force additional tasks onto the police. Cops are the only arm of government permanently present in the ghetto. The concerns expressed in this report centered on the methods of selecting police chiefs, the importance of chiefs' speaking out, and the centrality of the management question in trying to attack the "crisis of policing." The tone of this report contrasts sharply with Vollmer's bully-pulpit confidence in the future. This 1985 study speaks of problems, limitations, and failures. Like Tafoya's work, it takes an essentially gloomy view of the years ahead.

It is becoming ever clearer that underlying social and economic conditions are spawning crime and that society's unwillingness to do anything meaningful about them has really sealed the fate of the police effort to cope with the symptoms. Society wants to fight crime with more cops, tougher judges, and bigger jails, not through such scorned "liberal" schemes as social welfare programs.

Human beings have spent eons figuratively craning their necks in a futile attempt to see what's coming. The future has a long-time claim on our imagination. It has been the subject of numberless fantasies, movies, and novels. Endless speculation and romance surround it. "If only we'd known then" is one of the more fervently repeated human regrets.

Yet there is a way to make good guesses about what the future holds. Futurists attempt to analyze the past, study the present, evaluate all of the forces at work, assess the initiatives and directions pursued, look for trends, and amass data in an attempt to make informed and logical predictions. They will factor in such assumptions as that unattended problems will get worse. It is an inexact art, to be sure, and life has the tendency to shower us with surprises. Yet the whole concept of planning is rooted in the notion that we can, to some degree, see and shape the future. It seems certain that there are inventive souls out there who are sure that if they can only jam enough facts into the computer, it will spew out a pretty accurate photo of what's coming. It's even easier to look into a crystal ball, or to snap out a bunch of cards, but simple methods rarely work, even if they are always temptingly easy to try.

The studies in the police field and the commentaries of police chiefs lead to the inevitable conclusion that any sensible extrapolation of today's factors into tomorrow's likely events will lead to a dark assessment of our prospects.

Police executives believe that today's unattended problems, concentrated in our urban centers, will only get worse, eventually resulting in riots and heightened violence.

What are the factors contributing to this lugubrious assessment?

They can be described in one brief statement: If the problems of the underclass are not addressed, tremendous violence will result.

Street crime is uniquely the province of the poor. With very rare exceptions (such as Ted Bundy, for example) murders, rapes, assaults, robberies, burglaries, thefts, auto thefts, and arsons are committed by males who are poor, ignorant, and involved with drugs. Frequently, they were born to single, often teenage, mothers; were neglected or abused during infancy; are products of the welfare culture; and have otherwise been shaped and brutalized by the conditions of their lives. Racism is a powerful additional ingredient.

The high incidence of drug abuse, whether it be crack, alcohol, or the next fad; the growing plight of the homeless; the powerful effects of that window into the fairy-tale world the poor long to occupy—television; and the psychological attraction of a pleasure principle that finally teaches the abused youth that it is more fun to exercise power over others, and abuse them, than to be abused and exploited themselves—all will work to exacerbate the dangers ahead.

The cycle of violence begins even before birth. Neglect can begin in the womb, with the mother's diet or addictions, prenatal care or neglect, and so on. Birthweight has been found to be an important determinant of a child's future prospects. It has become one of the ironies of our age that our fates may be mostly sealed at the moment of conception, both biologically and deterministically.

The incompetence of the mother in dealing with the baby simply deepens and accelerates the problem. Professionals working with delinquents have moved ever backward in time, with many finally deciding that the answer may begin with the pregnancy itself. By the time many a poor, abused black kid enters kindergarten, his or her path has already been mapped. He or she will have to endure the indignity of school for only a decade or so before escaping into the street.

We have always had the poor, and so have other countries that are far safer than ours. Why is there so much violence now?

The answer may lie in a complex series of factors that probably includes unpopular economic notions about the distribution of wealth, ideas about our morals and values, and racist policies that stubbornly resist even being discussed.

Economic Factors

America is a nation of rapidly shifting forces. Where they were once scorned, fragmented, powerless, and poor, senior citizens have learned how to unite and press for the things they need and want. They've flexed their political muscles at the ballot box, most especially, and through organizations established to promote their interests. Any politician contemplating a reduction in social security benefits, or even an interruption in their rise, will soon feel the seniors' wrath.

The result has been the enrichment of the elderly, as a class, and the impoverishment of the young.

This shift has been one of the prime demographic developments of the age. It helps account for some of the crime and violence concerns relating to fear, victimization, and the growing numbers of perpetrators of crime. Seniors are, statistically, the least victimized, the least victimizing, and the most frightened. Youngsters are the greatest victimizers. The shift of resources has profound implications for the future safety of our citizens.

We now unabashedly speak of an overclass and an underclass. These were once unheard-of, and perhaps unthinkable notions. The economic and taxing policies followed during the 1980s sharpened class divisions by concentrating the wealth in fewer and fewer hands, while leaving the problems of the poor largely unattended.

Capitalism, the most ingenious wealth-producer ever devised, distributes that wealth very inequitably. The result is that a small fraction of Americans annually absorb the overwhelming majority of the created wealth, leaving a large number to divide the remainder. This has always been so, but the process accelerated during the Reagan years, deepening the problems of those excluded.

The number of poor has grown and their plight has worsened. This is especially evident among blacks, whose conditions have deteriorated since the end of the Great Society programs of the late 1960s. Today about three-fourths of black babies are born to single parents, frequently teenage girls. The entrance of blacks into the professions and universities is declining, particularly since there is less financial aid. The welfare experience is increasing. Dropout rates are up. Unemployment has risen. Per capita income has declined *vis-à-vis* that of whites. Every statistic conveys the same dolorous message of increasing failure.

By almost any statistical measure the plight of the poor blacks, so ominously described in the 1968 *Report of the National Advisory Commission on Civil Disorders,* has grown markedly worse since that bleak year. Every report of the National Urban League emphasizes this trend.

As the underclass has grown and its conditions have worsened, the overclass's fate has been increased prosperity, heightened indifference, and induction into the ranks of the neoconservatives. The search for pleasure has characterized the "me generation." Increased mobility, anonymity, alienation, and concern for self have ensured that those in a position to remedy society's flaws are too self-absorbed to bother. The value system represented by the overclass appears decadent and bankrupt. The American family is scattered, isolated, and weakened by dissolution. The rich regularly thread their way around beggars and huddled forms in the cities. It is instructive to note the remarkably coincident pattern of the divorce and crime rates in America. They have both more than tripled since 1960. As the family has fallen into disintegration, no other institution—such as, for example, a commune or some other form of social organization—has arisen to take its place. The overclass sets the tone and establishes the moral climate. It controls the means of communication. Societies thrive or perish depending on the messages sent. A nation full of zest and vigor, growing under values that emphasize "us" rather than "me", altruism over hedonism, sacrifice over pleasure, and service over self, will provide for a much safer society than the one we have today, which is fast sinking into dissolution in the pursuit of happiness. The messages are transmitted subtly and blatantly, in hundreds of different forms. This bombardment ultimately shapes the mores and attitudes of the society. All of it spews out, nightly, in a barrage of shows and commercials that reinforce the values of the "good life." The TV message is not lost on the viewers, middle class or poor.

The Cities

The demographics can be observed in population statistics. Two out of every three white citizens left Detroit for the suburbs over a comparatively brief period in the 1960s and 1970s. Around 1969, thousands of families abandoned the South Bronx, virtually overnight, to escape into the sterile remove of Co-Op City. The results are devastating as dislocations and vacuums create destructive dynamics. Stability disappears and instability reigns.

Every major city is beset by the growing problem of homelessness. The principal problem is housing, but it is exacerbated by mental, drug, alcohol, and personal disorders. Services have to be provided that go far beyond housing, yet there must be accountability from the client, too. In 1989, the horrible abuse of as many as seven children by their parents would have been discovered by housing authorities in New York City if the officials had merely insisted that the rent be paid or the apartment be inspected. Their failure to do so, many months after delinquencies in payment and other irregularities, led to the awful exploitation, and even possibly the murder, of helpless infants, who can themselves be counted upon to be shaped into abusive adults. Thus the cycle continues. Society has the right to demand certain levels of responsible behavior from its citizens and it has an obligation to insist that its bureaucrats monitor the behavior of their charges. Ironically these urban strains take wild swings. Total indifference or neglect is frequently followed by overaggressive corrective measures. A generous, tolerant, liberal people may become so exasperated that they adopt excessive measures of repression. Gradual movements to ameliorate conditions are not the forte of spooked populations. No one today seems to believe that the government has any role to play in this drama, or that, if it has, it could carry it off successfully— even if the effects of contrivances of Reagonomics on the federal budget deficit allowed anyone to think in such terms.

The problems are centered in the cities, where the poverty-stricken abound. The greater the number, the greater the threat of disorder. The warmer the climate, the hotter the prospects. Riots do not thrive in the winters of Frostbelt cities. Police chiefs universally fear the specter of long, hot summers.

When the overclass need to get away they buy tickets to exotic havens. When the underclass need to escape the awfulness of their condition they take the only trip they can afford: drugs or booze. Even abortion, arguably the only effective crime-prevention device adopted in this nation since the late 1960s, becomes an economic question. The overclass can fly its pregnant young women to wherever abortions are legal. The underclass consigns its women to the tender mercies of midwives and butchers who not only are breaking the law (when abortions are illegal) but exact compensation for the risk, or they are forced to produce children they do not want and who they don't know how to raise.

It is something of a contemporary anomaly that antiabortion groups, usually allied to conservative law-and-order causes, have never been attracted by the argument that making abortions freely available to young poor women is an effective method of reducing the number of potential street criminals. Street crime, for example, is affected not by the number of teenaged males, but by the number of "at-risk" fifteen- to nineteen-year-old males in the population. As with the impact of capital punishment on murder rates, it isn't the gross figure that matters, but a statistic within the overall total that may be affected by deterrence programs.

Given the worsening plight of the underclass and the virtually total absence of any programs—or even discussion of programs—that would ameliorate the situation, it seems safe to predict that crime and violence will continue to escalate.

Drug Raids

America is losing its much ballyhooed war on drugs. Yet no professional in the field has embraced legalization, nor should they. The war has been mainly characterized by a lot of motion and very little reflection. Republicans have the same mindless passion for throwing money at defense and crime that Democrats have over welfare, education, and poverty, with the same results. President Reagan signed a 2.5 billion dollar program, in 1988, that would answer every maiden's prayer. There was even money there for "local law enforcement," meaning that cops would be paid time and a half to do drug sweeps and "buy and bust" on-the-street-level operations they normally did at straight time rates. A good way to corrupt the police. There was little or no money for experiments, research, treatment or analysis. Will the crime and defense pimps someday rise to the notoriety of welfare cheats?

We love action and we hate thought. Suggest a study and everybody's eyes glaze over with boredom and hostility. "The thing's been studied to

death. We need action. Stuff the committee," etc. etc. What's wrong with
action that's guided by planning and analysis?

The drug problem in America has been a shifting one, the only
constant being a search for something that makes us feel good all over,
without destroying our lives. Drug companies have conditioned us into
becoming a pretty druggy culture. Just watch the TV commercials. The
drug cycle went, more or less, from marijuana to heroin to cocaine to
crack to whatever comes next. Alcohol overlays all of them.

Drugs are destroying a generation of kids in the ghetto. They tempt
and corrupt both cops and robbers. The public is panicked and demands
action. There is good reason for the fear as the violence produced by drugs
escalates. Minneapolis, New York, and Washington, D.C., among others,
had record numbers of murders in 1988. The pushers are well armed and
their gun battles exact fearful tolls—on the innocent and guilty alike. A lot
of welfare mothers have moved from Gary, Detroit, and Chicago to protect their kids from flying bullets.

The money stakes are huge. The user is in an economic dilemma and
commits crimes to support the habit. People on drugs behave dangerously.
About three-fourths of street crimes are committed by "perps" who have
felony drugs in their bloodstreams at the time.

We're just beginning to learn, by bits and pieces, the facts about
drugs. Treatment works, whether entered voluntarily or not. The key
variable is duration. Polls are showing that education seems to be taking
hold. White America appears to be moving away from hard drugs while
the underclass sinks deeper into the slough of despondency. Among recidivists, studies are showing that the more drugs used, the more crimes
committed. The fewer drugs, the fewer crimes.

Nothing works. New York freezes areas and saturates them with a
blue carpet of cops. It doesn't work. Los Angeles does roundups and
sweeps. They don't work. Minneapolis works with the feds, in task
forces, and targets the bigger dealers (which is why so many local operations feature search warrants and breaking into homes, rather than the
more usual "buy-and bust jump collars," on the street, of lower level
dealers). And it doesn't work.

The tough winters in Minneapolis free up cops for lots of training.
The department runs a very aggressive operation. The pressure to act is
unremitting. The combination produces a lot of arrests and some disasters.
Some of the disasters are so serious that, even when made in good faith,
they prove impossible to tolerate. When they occur, they have to be

acknowledged, investigated, followed up with action, and fully reported to the public. In cases where there is deep suspicion or mistrust it makes sense to have outside bodies, like the FBI or the county attorney, handle the inquiry.

A recent tragedy, the death of two citizens in a raid, looks as if it will prove a costly mistake. It is always hard to imagine how errors might have been prevented, but they must be. An open agency is sometimes going to look pretty sloppy.

The headlines said, "Drug War Claims 2 Innocents." Hardened cops scoff. There are few innocents in that struggle. Still they know that in another city the incident might have sparked a riot.

The clash between press accounts, public expectations, and police reality is accurately demonstrated by the shrinkage occurring in publicized drug arrests. The headlines reads, "Eight Arrested in Drug Raid." The citizens cheer. There are eight persons in a room and one pound of cocaine on the table. They're all going to be taken in, to whirring cameras. As the question of who possessed the contraband gets sorted out six or seven are released without charges. The public is puzzled and angry. Even the one or two held have a very good chance of beating the rap, especially when the drugs are not found on the person. In Minneapolis important drug cases are taken to federal court, where there is still room at the inn and the resources available to devote to the prosecution.

Drug operations are not fixed and stable enterprises. They move about, exploiting opportunities where found. This might involve using grandma's apartment. The raid then focuses on some innocent old lady. Sometimes the cops hit the wrong flat. Operations that use dynamite, "thunderflash stun grenades," and aggressive SWAT teams can experience spectacular failures. There could have been little kids on the other side of that wall collapsed by the front-end loader, despite precautions. And then, on top of everything else, there are the thumpers and Rambos who must be controlled, especially in such popular operations as drug raids, where they like to think they've been granted *carte blanche*.

Mistakes are deplored. Few then remember the screams for action that preceded them. Did the cops do a thorough search? How big and complicated were the premises raided? What advance planning and preparation went into the raid? What does the evidence show? What do witnesses say? If it develops that the cops acted with callous indifference to the consequences they must be held to account.

The overriding and strongest lesson, however, is that nothing is working in this war, despite the casualty lists. We lack a unified vision, a single, coherent national strategy.

A drug czarevitch (*czar* seems too grand a title in the circumstances) has been appointed in Washington. I longed for the chance to hector him on the subject. Finally the chance came. A friend of mine who knows William Bennett called, to see how I was faring in my new life. I begged him to tell the new warrior that we need a national strategy and that the best way to get one is to appoint a Commission on Drug Abuse, to study the problem for eighteen months, and to come up with a report that addresses the issues, from grower to user, from education to interdiction to treatment. Maybe this will offer us the hope of having a road map that law enforcers can follow into what now looks like a very bleak future. The time is passing anyhow, and not very profitably. The cacophony of present efforts can continue, for appearances' sake, although the wisdom of employing the military in law enforcement operations is far from clear in terms of its long-term implications for our society.

Everyone's eyes will glaze over at this unseemly call for reflection and study.

Racism and Exclusion

How does racism come into the equation of crime and social peace?

We are fond of thinking of blacks as another wave of immigrants, whose assimilation appears to have proceeded at a puzzlingly slow pace. We conveniently forget that two groups, blacks and native Americans, have had totally unique experiences in America, which have altered the form of their participation in the life of the nation.

Migrant waves hit our shores not just voluntarily but eagerly—deeply seeking participation in the American Dream—with names, families, religions, traditions, cultures, and visions intact. They have embraced the dream so passionately that we can all still wince at the embarrassment felt over the foreign accents and Old World ways of our forebears. These immigrants shared a number of important secrets: the value of education and the knowledge that the sacrifice of one generation would ensure the success of all those who came later. The strength of the family was crucial to the pursuit of this dream. The adversities and challenges produced a unity that forged the group into a truly dynamic force. Cohesion resulted, and leaders emerged. Such institutions as trade unionism and education adjusted to accommodate the needs and demands of the new arrivals.

Blacks were brought involuntarily, in chains. Their families had been destroyed. They suffered erasure of names, history, religion, and cultural memory. They were forbidden books and an education and were kept in bondage for two hundred years. They were simply property. This was followed by a hundred years of dependence and exclusion. An American apartheid system existed over much of the land.

These three centuries were followed by undeniable legal and political progress. The barriers, so elaborately constructed in tortured legislation, were suddenly demolished. Blacks received legal and political equality with whites. While this was going on, very visibly and attended by high excitement, the cultural, social, and economic barriers were being silently strengthened. The result was slippage, despite blacks' inheriting political power in many of America's cities. Control of the cities proved, increasingly, a Pyrrhic victory as the problems became clearer.

The curious thing is that the dilemma has never even been debated—and America resolves its crises (whether the Vietnam war, the feminist movement, environmental and consumer questions, civil rights, or nuclear war protests) on its streets. The problem of how to elevate members of the underclass into the middle class had never been discussed. The two serious efforts to spark a debate—the Catholic Bishops' Pastoral Letter on Social and Economic Justice and Jesse Jackson's presidential campaign of 1988—both foundered on the gigantic rocks of America's indifference. Spike Lee's important 1989 film *Do the Right Thing* also attempted to start a discussion on the dilemma of blacks in America.

The deracination of peoples struck the native Americans as well. Today we can see this defeated nation staggering through the seedy streets of its neighborhoods or in the pathetic isolation of reservations, shuffling monuments to our dreams of glory.

Both the blacks and the native Americans are groups whose problems must be confronted and discussed, but we prefer to skirt delicately around the subject. The victims have contributed to their own exploitation by labeling open discussions as racist attacks. While there can be no doubt that a full discussion would offer ammunition to racists, it can also be held that they're in no special need of it, managing to dredge up their slime with little difficulty.

A discussion would, at first, undeniably produce painful facts, such as the disproportionate involvement of blacks in crime, as both per-petrators and victims. It is easy to identify some criminals, black or white, as monsters, but that is already taking place in the collective psyche of our national village. Acknowledging the existence of monsters holds out the best hope for questioning where they came from. It may also allow us to differentiate between the criminals and the overwhelming majority of solid black citizens.

What were the conditions that spawned them?

How do we correct them?

To what degree are we responsible for their existence?

The focus should be on devising programs of inclusion, not on the distribution of handouts. These would include educational and em-ployment projects. The programs would flow from discussion and debate, which might hold out the hope that all of us will finally confront the dilemma. The social contract has to offer the promise of participation, as well as the sanctions of prison and punishment for those who respond negatively. Currently we offer only the second half of the deal.

Racism is America's great, guilty crime secret. Such evasion leads to eruptions. Exorcism requires examination, frank acknowledgment, and tough, wide-ranging debates. It is an untidy, risky process, but the hope is to emerge from the crucible freer from the grip of crime and violence that today's racial injustices make inevitable.

Conclusion

The future is headed somewhere and the direction may be discerned in the trends evident today. These are shaped by alterable human deci-sions. There is nothing immutable or inevitable about the choices made. We seem to have opted for a widening of the chasm between the haves and the have-nots. We seem to feel perfectly comfortable with the economic, social, and cultural walls we've erected to keep the underclass out. We seem to have decided to grow ever more unequal. And we seem to have lost our appetite for service or a sense of joy in doing something useful with our lives.

It is easy to see the ever-present bitterness when a spark strikes the kindling of resentments in the ghetto. A white cop shoots a black youth and a riot starts. A black prisoner dies in police custody and chaos breaks loose. The incident is the variable. In the ghetto, anger, resentment, frustration, and defeat are the constants.

Rising levels of technology create walls against the entrance of the uneducated into the work force. The jobs created in recent years are at the ends of the spectrum—either highly skilled or absurdly low-level.

Health and welfare policies are in such wide disrepute that few serious initiatives for reform that would reintegrate the family or assist in getting clients a salary find any significant support. Issues of contraception, sex education, birthweight, maternal care, abortion, treatment programs for adults, or even programs intended to encourage a male's presence get swept aside with derisive comments about foggy liberalism. But today's abused child is tomorrow's rapist.

Educational policies are following the bankrupt notion of educating the overclass, while suffering appalling dropout rates among black male high-schoolers. Urban school systems have been abandoned to the poor, where the blacks and Hispanics compete for the crumbs a failing system provides.

The plight of the homeless adds to the present and future problems of the cities, and the situation is deteriorating rapidly.

The war on drugs is being lost. The oppression of the underclass will continue to produce crime and violence. These will fan the flames of fear licking at the overclass.

The overclass is purchasing its own security and services and abandoning the underclass.

There is a trend toward harsher sentences and greater numbers of people sent to prisons already bursting at the seams. Our jails are our Maginot Line against crime and violence. They will prove just as effective as their namesake.

The street criminal exists against a backdrop of corporate and governmental morality that has in recent years, produced shocking scandals—of the sort that raise troubling questions about the fate of the republic. The overclass mugs with phone, computers, high-tech devices, and fountain pens. Armies of lawyers are enlisted in the fray. The hypocrisy is only too evident to the blacks and Hispanics flooding our prisons.

The irony lies in the fact that civilizations save themselves through altruism, not hedonism.

Addressing the problems reflected in the rising tides of crime and violence in America actually holds out the best hope for reinvigorating the nation, cleansing its soul, and moving forward energetically to the American Dream of equality, justice, and peace.

The future, given our inattention to the urgent problems in our cities, is bleak precisely because the festering sores are not being lanced and cured. They are being papered over and ignored.

Oh for a muse of fire that would touch the public conscience like Rachel Carson's *Silent Spring* and awaken the nation to the danger of neglecting the fateful problems of its cities.

The cops generally, and the chief in particular, might be the muses needed. Like the Vietnam generals, police chiefs are the daily witnesses to the problems of crime and to the social and economic sources fueling the violence. Fighting that war is the chief's principal assignment, but is it the only one? Hasn't the chief a responsibility to report to the people on the complex, underlying forces at work? Police chiefs are uniquely positioned to advise Americans on the sources and causes of urban violence, and they have a moral obligation to inform the nation of what is happening on their battlegrounds and why.

Bibliography

Astor, Gerald. *The New York Cops*. New York: Charles Scribner's Sons, 1971.

Attorney General's Task Force on Family Violence. Washington, D.C.: U.S. Department of Justice, Sept. 1984.

Bailey, William G. (Ed.). *The Encyclopedia of Police Science*. New York: Garland, 1989.

Baker, Mark. *Cops: Their Lives in Their Own Words*. New York: Simon & Schuster, 1985.

Bard, Morton, and Sangrey, Dawn. *The Crime Victim's Book*. New York: Basic Books, 1979.

Bedau, Hugo Adam, and Pierce, Chester M. *Capital Punishment in the United States*. New York: AMS, 1976.

A Better Government for a Better City. New York: Citizen's Budget Commission Report, 1948.

Blumstein, Alfred, *et al. Criminal Careers and Career Criminals*, Vols. 1 and 2. Washington, D.C.: National Academy, 1986.

Bouza, Anthony V. *Police Intelligence*. New York: AMS, 1976.

Bouza, Anthony V. *Police Administration, Organization and Performance*. New York: Pergamon Press, 1978.

Browning, Frank, and Gerassi, John. *The American Way of Crime*. New York: G. P. Putnam's Sons, 1980.

Cahalane, Cornelius F. *The Policeman*. New York: E. P. Dutton, 1923.

Cahalane, Cornelius F. *The Policeman's Guide*. New York: Harper, 1952.

Calling the Police. Washington, D.C.: National Institute of Justice, 1984.

The Challenge of Crime in a Free Society: A Report by the President's Commission on Law Enforcement and Administration of Justice. Washington, D.C.: U.S. Government Printing Office, 1967.

Chevigny, Paul. *Cops and Rebels*. New York: Curtis Books, 1972.

Chevigny, Paul. *Criminal Mischief*. New York: Pantheon, 1977.

Civil Disturbances and Disasters. Washington, D.C.: U.S. Department of the Army Field Manual, March 1968.

Clark, Ramsey. *Crime in America*. New York: Simon & Schuster, 1970.

Cowan, Paul, *et al*. *State Secrets: Police Surveillance in America*. New York: Holt, Rinehart & Winston, 1974.

Crime and Punishment: The Public's View. New York: Edna McConnell Clark Foundation, 1987.

Crime in the United States: Uniform Crime Reports. Washington, D.C.: U.S. Department of Justice, 1987, 1988.

Criminal Justice in Crisis. Washington, D.C.: American Bar Association, 1988.

Crisis at Columbia: The Cox Commission Report. New York: Random House, 1968.

Currie, Elliott. *What Kind of Future?* San Francisco: National Council on Crime and Delinquency, 1987.

Dudycha, George J. *Psychology for Law Enforcement Officers*. Springfield, Ill.: Charles C Thomas, 1955.

Dykstra, Gretchen. *Time to Build? The Realities of Prison Construction*. New York: Edna McConnell Clark Foundation, 1984.

Emergency Situations: Powers and Responsibilities of the Police Forces: Human Rights. Brussels, Tenth International Course of Higher Specialization for Police Forces, 1987.

Essien-Udom, E. U. *Black Nationalism*. New York: Dell, 1962.

Feinberg, Stephen E. *The Evolving Role of Statistical Assessments as Evidence in the Courts*. New York: Springer-Verlag, 1989.

The Figgie Reports. Willoughby, Ohio: A-T-O. 1980, 1981, 1982.

Forer, Louis G. *Criminals and Victims*. New York: W. W. Norton, 1980.

The Future of Policing. Seattle: William O. Douglas Institute, 1984.

Gelb, Barbara. *Varnished Brass*. New York: Putnam's, 1983.

Geller, William A. (Ed.). *Police Leadership in America*. New York: Praeger, 1985.

Goolkasian, Gail. *Confronting Domestic Violence: A Guide for Criminal Justice Agencies*. U.S. Department of Justice, National Institute of Justice, Office of Communication and Research Utilization, May 1986.

Greenwood, Peter, *Selective Incapacitation*. Santa Monica, Calif.: The Rand Corporation, 1982.

Heaphy, John F., and Wolfle, Joan L. *Productivity in Policing*. Washington, D.C.: Police Foundation, 1975.

"Homicide: The Public Health Perspective." *Bulletin of the New York Academy of Medicine*, June 1986,

Iacocca, Lee. *Iacocca*. New York: Bantam, 1984.

Inciardi, James A. *Criminal Justice*. Orlando, Fla.: Harcourt Brace Jovanovich, 1987.

Innovative Programs, Policies, Procedures and Experiments from PERF Members' Agencies. Washington, D.C.: Police Executive Research Forum, 1989.

Irwin, John, and Austin, James. *It's About Time: Solving America's Prison Crowding Crisis*. San Francisco: National Council on Crime and Delinquency, 1987.

Journal of Police Science and Administration. Gaithersburg, MD, 1980–1989.

Konopka, Gisela. *The Adolescent Girl in Conflict*. Englewood Cliffs, N.J.: Prentice-Hall, 1966.

The Law Enforcement Response to Family Violence: The Training Challenge. New York: Victim Services Agency, 1989.

Leonard, V. A. *Police Organization and Management.* Brooklyn, N.Y.: Foundation Press, 1951.

Levin, Jack, and Fox, James Alan. *Mass Murder.* New York: Plenum Press, 1985.

Lincoln, C. Eric. *The Black Muslims in America.* Boston: Beacon Press, 1961.

Machiavelli, Niccolò. *The Prince.* New York: Modern Library, 1940.

Malcolm X Speaks: Selected Speeches and Statements. New York: Merit, 1965.

Marx, Gary T. *Under Cover.* Berkeley, Calif.: Twentieth Century Fund, 1988.

McClure, James. *Cop World.* New York: Pantheon, 1984.

The Meaning of Community in Community Policing. East Lansing: Michigan State University, 1988.

Morris, Norval, and Hawkins, Gordon. *The Honest Politician's Guide to Crime Control.* Chicago: University of Chicago Press, 1970.

Municipal Police Administration. Chicago: International City Managers' Association, 1954.

Niederhoffer, Arthur, and Blumberg, Abraham. *The Ambivalent Force.* Hinsdale, Ill.: Dryden, 1976.

Orfield, Myron W. "The Exclusionary Rule and Deterrence." *University of Chicago Law Review,* Summer 1987.

An Organizational Study of the New York City Police Department. Washington, D.C.: International Association of Chiefs of Police, 1967.

Overcrowded Time: Why Prisons Are So Crowded and What Can Be Done. New York: Edna McConnell Clark Foundation, 1982.

Peters, R. DeV., and McMahon, R. K. (Eds.). *Social Learning and Systems Approaches to Marriage and the Family.* New York: Brunner/Mazel, 1986.

Petersilia, Joan. *The Influence of Criminal Justice Research.* Santa Monica, Calif.: Rand, 1987.

Petersilia, Joan, and Turner, Susan. *Guideline Based Justice.* Santa Monica, Calif.: Rand, 1985.

Philadelphia and Its Police: Toward a New Partnership. Philadelphia: Police Study Task Force Report, 1987.

The Philosophy and Role of Community Policing. East Lansing: Michigan State University, 1988.

Police. Washington, D.C.: National Advisory Commission on Criminal Justice Standards and Goals, 1973.

Police Personnel Administration. Washington, D.C.: Police Foundation, 1974.

Principles of Good Policing: Avoiding Violence between Police and Citizens. Washington, D.C.: Community Relations Service, U.S. Department of Justice, 1987.

Quinney, Richard. *Class, State and Crime.* New York: Longman, 1977.

Reid, Sue Titus. *Crime and Criminology.* New York: Holt, Rinehart & Winston, 1979.

Reiman, Jeffrey. *The Rich Get Richer and the Poor Get Prison.* New York: John Wiley & Sons, 1979.

Reiss, Albert J., Jr. *The Police and the Public*. New Haven, Conn.: Yale University Press, 1971.

Report to the Nation on Crime and Justice. Washington, D.C.: Bureau of Justice Statistics, 1983.

Richardson, James F. *The New York Police*, New York: Oxford University Press, 1970.

Rights in Conflict: The Walker Report. New York: Bantam, 1968.

Rosett, Arthur, and Cressey, Donald R. *Justice by Consent*. New York: J. B. Lippincott, 1976.

Rubenstein, Jonathan. *City Police*. New York: Farrar, Straus & Giroux, 1973.

Sayre, Wallace S., and Kaufman, Herbert. *Governing New York City*. New York: W. W. Norton, 1960.

Schechter, Leonard, with Phillips, William. *On the Pad*. New York: Berkeley, 1973.

Sherman, Lawrence W. (Ed.). *Police Corruption: A Sociological Perspective*. Garden City, N.Y.: Anchor Books, 1976.

Sherman, Lawrence W. *The Quality of Police Education*. San Francisco: Jossey-Bass, 1978.

Sherman, Lawrence W. *Scandal and Reform*. Los Angeles: University of California Press, 1978.

Sherman, Lawrence W., and Berk, Richard A. *The Minneapolis Domestic Violence Experiment*. Washington, D.C.: Police Foundation, April 1984.

Sherman, Lawrence W., and Cohn, Ellen G. "The Impact of Research on Legal Policy: The Minneapolis Domestic Violence Experiment." *Law and Society Review*, 1989, pp. 118–144.

Sherman, Lawrence W., Gartin, Patrick R., and Buerger, Michael E. *Hot Spots of Predatory Crime: Routine Activities and the Criminology of Place*. Washington, D.C.: Criminology, 1989.

Silberman, Charles E. *Crisis in Black and White*. New York: Vintage, 1964.

A Silence Too Loud: Family Violence. Minneapolis: University of Minnesota, 1984.

Skolnick, Jerome H. *The New Blue Line*. New York: Free Press, 1986.

Soderman, Harry, and O'Connell, John J. *Modern Criminal Investigation*. New York: Funk & Wagnalls, 1952.

Stahl, David, *et al*. (Eds.). *The Community and Racial Crises*. New York: Practising Law Institute, 1966.

Stahl, O. Glenn. *Public Personnel Administration*. New York: Harper & Row, 1962.

Staufenberger, Richard A. (Ed.). *Progress in Policing*. Cambridge, Mass.: Ballinger, 1980.

Sutherland, Edwin H., and Cressey, Donald R. *Principles of Criminology*. New York: J. B. Lippincott, 1955.

Sweeney, Thomas J., and Ellingsworth, William. *Issues in Police Patrol*. Washington, D.C.: Police Foundation, 1973.

Sykes, Richard E., and Brent, Edward E. *Policing: A Social Behaviorist Perspective*. New Brunswick, N.J.: Rutgers University Press, 1983.

Task Force Report: The Police. Washington, D.C.: U.S. Government Printing Office, 1967.

Tafoya, William L. *A Delphic Forecast of the Future of Law Enforcement.* Dissertation, University of Maryland, 1986.

Thomas, Piri. *Down These Mean Streets.* New York: Signet, 1967.

Thorwald, Jurgen. *The Century of the Detective.* New York: Harcourt, Brace & World, 1964.

Toch, Hans, *et al. Agents of Change: A Study in Police Reform.* New York: John Wiley & Sons, 1975.

Understanding Police Agency Performance. Washington, D.C.: National Institute of Justice, 1984.

van den Haag, Ernest, and Conrad, John P. *The Death Penalty: A Debate.* New York: Plenum Press, 1986.

Violent Juvenile Crime: What Do We Know about It and What Can We Do about It? Minneapolis: University of Minnesota Press, 1987.

Vollmer, August. "Police Progress in the Past Twenty Five Years." *Journal of Criminal Law and Criminology,* May–June 1933, pp.

Walker, Samuel, *Sense and Nonsense about Crime.* Pacific Grove, Cal.: Brooks-Cole, 1989.

What Kind of Future: Violence and Public Safety in the Year 2000. San Francisco: National Council on Crime and Delinquency, 1987.

What Works: Schools without Drugs. Washington, D.C.: U.S. Department of Education, 1986.

Whisenand, Paul M., and Ferguson, Fred R. *The Managing of Police Organizations.* Englewood Cliffs, N.J.: Prentice-Hall, 1973.

The White House Conference for a Drug Free America: Final Report. Washington, D.C.: Superintendent of Documents, 1988.

Wilson, James Q., and Kelling, George L. "Police and Neighborhood Safety: Broken Windows." *Atlantic Monthly,* March 1982.

Wilson, O. W. *Police Administration.* New York: McGraw-Hill, 1963.

Wise, David, and Ross, Thomas B. *The Invisible Government.* New York: Random House, 1964.

Wolfgang, M. E., Figlio, R. M., and Sellin, T. *Delinquency in a Birth Cohort.* Chicago: University of Chicago Press, 1972.

Index